In

Intimate Exposure

Essays on the Public-Private Divide in British Poetry Since 1950

Edited by
EMILY TAYLOR MERRIMAN *and*
ADRIAN GRAFE

McFarland & Company, Inc., Publishers
Jefferson, North Carolina, and London

LIBRARY OF CONGRESS CATALOGUING-IN-PUBLICATION DATA

Intimate exposure : essays on the public-private divide in British poetry
    since 1950 / edited by Emily Taylor Merriman and Adrian Grafe.
        p.   cm.
    Includes bibliographical references and index.

    ISBN 978-0-7864-4221-8
    softcover : 50# alkaline paper ∞

    1. English poetry — 20th century — History and criticism.
    2. English poetry — 21st century — History and criticism.
    3. Poetics — History — 20th century.   I. Merriman, Emily Taylor.
    II. Grafe, Adrian.
    PR603.I58   2010
    821'.9109 — dc22   2010004222

British Library cataloguing data are available

Cover image ©2010 Shutterstock

Manufactured in the United States of America

McFarland & Company, Inc., Publishers
    Box 611, Jefferson, North Carolina 28640
    www.mcfarlandpub.com

Acknowledgments

Grateful acknowledgment is made for permission to reproduce copyrighted material as follows:

Canongate for excerpts from "Northwestern," "Seeing Red," and "Knew White Speech," *Bloodshot Monochrome* © Patience Agbabi 2008; "Prologue" in *Transformatrix* © Patience Agbabi 2000. Patience Agbabi for excerpts from "R.A.W.," "Rappin it Up," and "Rap Trap" from *R.A.W.* © Patience Agbabi 1995. Gordon Dickerson for permission to quote from Tony Harrison's work and interviews that are copyrighted © by Tony Harrison. Carcanet Press for extracts from "A Transcendental Weekend" and "Les Portes de la Nuit" from *Yellow Studio* © Stephen Romer 2008. Penguin Group for six lines from "September Song" from *Collected Poems* © Geoffrey Hill 1985; four lines from "Pisgah" from *Canaan* © Geoffrey Hill 1996; four lines from "The Mystery of the Charity of Charles Péguy" from *Selected Poems* © Geoffrey Hill 2006; eleven lines from *The Triumph of Love* © Geoffrey Hill 1998; four lines from *Speech! Speech!* © Geoffrey Hill 2001; six lines from *The Orchards of Syon* © Geoffrey Hill 2002; six lines from *Scenes from Comus* © 2005; ten lines from *Without Title* © Geoffrey Hill 2006. Yale University for ten lines from *Without Title* by Geoffrey Hill © Geoffrey Hill 2006 and four lines from "The Mystery of the Charity of Charles Péguy" from *Selected Poems* © Geoffrey Hill 2009. Geoffrey Hill for four lines from *Speech! Speech!* © Geoffrey Hill 2001, and six lines from *The Orchards of Syon* © Geoffrey Hill 2002. Houghton Mifflin Harcourt for six lines from "September Song" from *Collected Poems* © Geoffrey Hill 1985; four lines from "Pisgah" from *Canaan* © Geoffrey Hill 1996; excerpts from *The Triumph of Love* © Geoffrey Hill 1998. The Nobel Foundation for excerpts from Joseph Brodsky, Nobel Lecture © 1987, and Seamus Heaney, Nobel Lecture © 1995. Keston Sutherland, Barque Press for extract from *The Unconditional* by Simon Jarvis © Simon Jarvis 2005; Keston Sutherland's post to the Brit-po mailing list. Tony Lopez for an excerpt from "About Cambridge," copyright © Tony Lopez, reprinted by permission of the author. *Chicago Review* for excerpts from Peter Riley's Letter to the Editor, in *Chicago Review* 53:1 (2007).

The editors acknowledge the backing of: the University of Paris IV-Paris Sorbonne, especially Pierre Iselin, Elisabeth Angel-Perez, heads of the research center *Texte et Critique du Texte,* and Marie-Madeleine Martinet, head of the Doctoral School; Dean Paul Sherwin and the College of Humanities at San Francisco State University.

They also wish to thank Christine Hoff Kraemer (copy editor) and, for their interest and help, Mairead Daugharty, May Whitaker, Sarita Cannon, Stephen Arkin, Camille Dungy, Marc Porée, Stephen Romer, Paul Volsik, René Gallet, and Jean-Marie Fournier.

The editors express their particular gratitude to Catherine Phillips.

Finally, Emily Taylor Merriman and Adrian Grafe thank their respective spouses, Stephen and Natacha, and their families, for their unfailing support during the preparation of this book.

Contents

Introduction

Adrian Grafe and *Emily Taylor Merriman*

The subtitle of this new approach to British poetry takes it for granted that there is a division between public and private — that these two spheres of human life are in some way separate. Even if one considers only Western history, however, this separation has not always existed. In *The Secret History of Domesticity: Public, Private, and the Division of Knowledge* (2005), Michael McKeon argues that over time, "a former tacit whole" has split into "oppositional and self-sufficient parts." McKeon cites concepts such as status, honor, and religion, in all of which the private has gradually been separated from the public: "*status*, sociopolitical rank/economic wealth; *honour*, family lineage/personal virtue; *religion*, institutional and cultural/individual and personal."[1] The five-volume *A History of Private Life* (1987) starts with the Roman Empire, but co-editor Georges Duby recognizes that the study is exploring the "prehistory" of a concept that arose in nineteenth-century Europe.[2] Yet the human desire to shield some aspect of the self from the gaze of the other can be seen in a text as old as Genesis, in which the fig leaf affords the first privacy, a condition necessitated by the Fall.

The boundaries between the categories of public and private are porous and affected by historical circumstance as well as by gender, ethnicity, nationality, and class. Today's private is yesterday's public: in the great houses of the Renaissance, activities we now consider to be private, like taking care of children or relaxing, took place in large rooms in full view. Crying has been privatized — and, in one indication of the significance of gender in the public-private divide, feminized: crying in public has become unworthy, of men especially. This shifting divide between public and private in modern Europe has arisen, some would say, out of the concept of civil society. Theorized by such Scottish thinkers as Adam Ferguson, David Hume, and Adam Smith, civil society takes the form of clubs, associations, and other non-political groupings outside the familial sphere. The separation of the two realms

1

was further established by Victorian English thinkers like J.S. Mill and James Fitzjames Stephen. The latter, for example, writes:

> Legislation and public opinion ought in all cases whatever scrupulously to respect privacy.... To try to regulate the internal affairs of a family, the relations of love or friendship, or many other things of the same sort, by law or by the coercion of public opinion, is like trying to pull an eyelash out of a man's eye with a pair of tongs. They may put out the eye, but they will never get hold of the eyelash.[3]

Private space has traditionally been associated with the household and often linked to femininity, maternity, and the family, in contrast to the supposedly masculine domain of the public world. Even as more women have entered the workforce in the second half of the twentieth century, the family remains central to how we distinguish between public and private: socializing children requires teaching them what can be said and done in public and what should be done in private. Furthermore, in the private space of the household the inhabitant remains supposedly protected from the exterior gaze of society. No one can enter private domestic space without the inhabitant's consent.

Never more so than today has the private space been the subject of easy curiosity. On the American website Intelius it is possible, for a fee, to obtain information about individuals' marriages, divorces, children, lodgings and number of rooms, income, criminal record, and level of education. Social networking sites like Facebook and Twitter enable people to share intimate details of their lives with hundreds of acquaintances (though the potential public role of such websites as Twitter was highlighted by the aftermath of the thwarted election in Iran in June 2009). At the same time, over the past few decades the public realm has become a locus of common mistrust. In Britain, the proportionally small turn-out at elections reveals a disaffection with politics and the public sphere, a disaffection which might hinder a poet's attempts to make his or her voice publicly heard. Princess Diana's canny media manipulation changed the image of the monarchy forever, revealing the intimate, often painful reality behind the all-smiling public individuals heading the state. In Britain, as in America, the private life of a politician is often subjected to moral scrutiny by the media and the public. When a poet is a candidate for a public role, his or her private life can be subjected to the same scrutiny, as witnessed recently in the media's interest in Carol Ann Duffy's sexuality before and after her appointment to the laureateship, as well as the crisis, in the spring of 2009, over the post of Oxford Professor of Poetry. The crisis, which received more public attention than the actual poetry of any of the nominees, included Derek Walcott withdrawing his candidacy and Ruth Padel resigning after her election.

The moveable line between what is private and what is public is determined politically, legally, and even nationally. To focus on the adjective "British" in the volume title, there may be something particularly British in a self-conscious concern with what should be out in the open and what should be kept private. One of the quotations in the *OED* illustrating usage of privacy refers to "all your rusty-fusty British notions about comfort, civility, privacy, and the like"[4]). Yet even if there is a peculiarly British take on the public-private divide, how typical of British citizenry is the modern poet? Poets tend to extremes. The most up-to-date *OED* illustrative quotation indicates, "Browning was a ferocious preserver of his own and his family's privacy."[5] But times change, in ways that the essays presented here set out to show. The volume title suggests, and the essays in the volume confirm, that the consideration of the public-private divide, a subject of interest for many British poets, affects how poetry is both written and read.

While the self-revealing mode that predominated in American poetry after W.D. Snodgrass's *Heart's Needle* and Robert Lowell's *Life Studies* in 1959 never took over British poetry in the same way, it is possible to interpret such confessional elements as poetry's attempt to keep or get the attention of a public who now have many means of stimulation and entertainment other than the arrangement of words and the music of language. The poet's desire to be heard and to maintain a valued public presence is natural — but for so many poets, the yearning for recognition is stymied. Even undergraduates who have chosen to study literature sometimes express reluctance to engage with the challenges of reading poetry. To a poet there are several possible responses to the absence of an audience. In order to seek greater attention, he or she may reveal more of the private or engage more vigorously with the public, even taking on civic roles such as poet laureate or poet in residence. Or, he or she may withdraw into a realm of splendid isolation, writing for a private circle, for self, or for God.

This collection's essays on the public-private divide in poetry reveal how it is connected with questions of personal power and powerlessness. Some texts work with the private as a locus of embarrassment, shame, and weakness (again, as in Genesis after the Fall). Yet in other narratives, privacy paradoxically constitutes the domain of the sacred — in the holy of holies, or in secret rites.

The contemporary public-private divide is indeed implicated in religious changes in the West since the Reformation and the Enlightenment, including the secularization of the public sphere in much of Europe. The Protestant emphasis on the individual conscience has both arisen from and reinforced a sense of personal privacy. In a religious context, that which is kept private or secret can exercise a numinous power in the public sphere, like Moses's face

when he came down from Mt. Sinai. By contrast, even powerful public figures
like Cabinet ministers find themselves subject to all kinds of forces much
greater than themselves. It is little wonder then that the contemporary poet
seeks to harness the sometimes arcane mysteries of verse form and linguistic
experimentation in order to exercise a little dominion upon his or her environment.

One reason, then, that the public-private divide is especially relevant in
relation to the poetry of the period is that poetry has become less visible than
fiction, let alone theatre (despite attempts by poets like Glyn Maxwell to blend
theatre and verse; *Liberty*, performed at the New Globe at the end of 2008,
was advertised as dramatizing "private jealousies and public fears"[6]). The original English version of *Harry Potter and the Philosopher's Stone* sold 790,000
copies in France alone; the print run for a Geoffrey Hill poetry book published
by Penguin is said to be 2,000 copies. Hill himself said in a lecture in Paris
in March 2008, "Poetry is an art of public significance, while at the same time
I recognize that poetry has no public." "Poetry has no public," he repeated,
and declared that it has no prestige in the public domain.[7] Yet if poetry has
no prestige, does that mean that the poet and his or her poem speak with no
authority? Is there no point in the poet's trying to engage the reading public,
the common reader of novels, newspapers, magazines, and blogs? How, then,
if at all, do the poet and the poem inscribe their art in society?

In yoking together an investigation of modern British poetry and of the
public-private divide, the problem, as with everything pertaining to poetry,
is first and foremost not one of prestige but rather of language. "[T]he function of language in much modern poetry, and in much poetry admired by the
moderns," writes Heaney, "is to talk about itself to itself."[8] Perhaps one of
the purposes of the title of Hill's volume *Speech! Speech!* is to allude ironically
to such poetic navel-gazing. Against this approach, we might consider what
Larkin calls "that amazing literary landslide," John Betjeman's best-selling
Collected Poems, published in 1958. "The common reader, and his children after
him," says Larkin, "have lapped it up."[9] Closer to us in time, Ted Hughes's
Birthday Letters became an instant bestseller when published in 1998, though
arguably for reasons not connected to the form itself, but rather to public
prurience about the Hughes-Plath myth. Laurel Peacock quotes one critic as
calling the volume an "open secret," with Hughes as Poet Laureate "presid-
ing over" his suddenly very public negotiation with Plath, their courtship,
marriage, and the disasters that followed.

Yet public and private are not only concepts with specific referents but
also, in some sense, mental spaces, malleable things that poets and artists can
play with. If inwardness is a mental space, so is outwardness. The public, Joe
Public, go public, public relations, public nuisance, public spirit, public enemy,

public opinion, public convenience, public health, public awareness: the list is long, and one could easily construct an equivalent one for "private." Like society, like language and poetry itself, the idea of the public-private divide is in constant evolution, and poetic language has responded to it. Hence the essays that book-end this collection, those by Marc Porée and Catherine Phillips respectively, go back to the nineteenth century or before to highlight new ways in which intimacy is laid bare and human experience made available to "open diagnosis" in more recent poetry (Porée, after the title of a 1994 volume of poetry by Susan Wicks). Porée's opening chapter, "Poetry as 'Open Diagnosis,'" examines some of the risks taken by poets who use their own lives and those of their loved ones as raw material — the risks of laying oneself open, in short. Not without some relish, Porée explores the potentially embarrassed response of the reader to intimate material that may too easily tip over into the mawkish: James Fenton's "In Paris with you" is a case in point.

The group of essays that follows Porée's is broad in scope and tackles the question of poetry and the public-private divide from a number of disparate perspectives, but with a shared focus on excess of publicity either given to, or standing in contrast with, different kinds of privacy and the private sphere. In "Public Faces in Private Places: Messianic Privacy in Cambridge Poetry," the critic and poet Robert Archambeau considers the strange conjunction of forces that has led to the development of the Cambridge School of poetry, which came into being in the shadow of Jeremy Prynne. This school somehow remains private despite its strong public concern because — in some cases voluntarily — it is bereft of appreciable visibility.

Apparently at an opposite extreme from the Cambridge School's hermeticism, Ted Hughes's always flamboyant poetics thrust his poetry into the limelight long before he became Poet Laureate. Following Derrida's analysis in "La bête et le souverain," Laurel Peacock's chapter "Ted Hughes as Poet Laureate: The Beast and the Sovereign" considers similarities between the animals of Hughes's poems, which are outside of human law and responsibility, and the Poet Laureate, whom she sees constructed as sovereign poet, above the laws of poetic convention and civic responsibility. The origin story of laureateship involves the violent wresting of consent from nature (via Apollo's attempted rape of Daphne and her transformation into the authority-granting tree). Likewise, Hughes's poems use animals instrumentally to tell a fable of poetic sovereignty. When Hawk of "Hawk Roosting" proclaims, "My manners are tearing off heads," he proclaims his existence as an animal outside the law of social responsibility. For Peacock, Hughes as Poet Laureate occupies a similar position of sovereignty.

A poet who engaged publicly in the struggle for causes he believed in while staunchly refusing to become, in Andrew Motion's phrase, "public property," was R.S. Thomas. In "R.S. Thomas: Poet of the Threshold," Daniel Szabo examines the ways in which this paradoxical poet — a particularly private man and writer, yet also simultaneously a priest of the Anglican Church in Wales and a Welsh Nationalist — crossed what Szabo calls the "threshold" between public and private. Thomas's poetry, for example, is unorthodox in its approach to God and liturgy, and Szabo explores how this making public of personal doubt relates to, and raises questions about, Thomas's public role as minister and preacher.

In another investigation of how poets mine the established boundaries between public and private for resources, one of the many apparent dichotomies explored by Catherine Murphy in relation to the work of Patience Agbabi is that between the poem as it is read by the private reader and the poem when translated by the poet to the stage. She argues in "Performing, Transforming, and Changing the Question: Patience Agbabi — Poet Enough!" that, for Agbabi, poetry on the page need not be private any more than poetry's presence on the stage need make it public. For Murphy, Agbabi creatively illustrates the limitations of the traditional divide in Caribbean and Black British poetry between the political public performance poet and the private lyric poet.

Before discussing Stephen Romer's poem "Les Portes de la Nuit," Adrian Grafe examines some of the philosophical dimensions of the tension between public and private. Behind this tension lies that between the particular and the universal. According to Aristotle, the human being is not only a political animal (and therefore a public one), but also a conjugal one (conjugality, lying as it does at the heart of the poem, is as much a social as a private phenomenon). Privacy (the particular) is a space on which history (the universal) impacts, and which also affects history. "Les Portes de la Nuit" also implies questions about performance. It involves a "strictly private" mode of expression: the diary, which is nevertheless concerned with exposure, presentation, or performance of the self to the self. The situation is made all the more delicate by the fact that the diary belongs to the poet's late father, who had marked the words "Strictly Private" on the cover.

The third section centers on the poetry of Seamus Heaney. His inclusion in a volume of essays with "British" in the title requires a word of explanation, as he himself protested his inclusion in the *Penguin Book of Contemporary British Poetry* (1982) by announcing in verse "my passport's green."[10] Born in Londonderry, Northern Ireland, in 1939, Heaney here implicitly declares himself Irish by referring to a document that is both personal and public (passports are the legal property of the issuing government). Yet he is a central figure in twentieth- and twenty-first-century British poetry. An *OED* draft revision for September 2008 includes Ireland in the "British Isles," but acknowledges, "The term is generally regarded as a geographical or territorial description, rather than as one which designates a political entity. The term is deprecated by some speakers in the Republic of Ireland." This question about the appropriateness of including particular poets within contested national, geographical, or political groupings suggests that literary critics are themselves not exempt from wrestling with the boundaries between public and private. For the public purposes of this volume, Heaney's significance could not be overlooked, even in the face of his own likely and understandable objections.

In "Joseph Brodsky and Seamus Heaney in the Birch Grove of Art," Daniella Jancsó explores Heaney's approach to Brodsky's Nobel acceptance speech as excerpted by Heaney in "The Birch Grove": the idea that "the human condition is private." She investigates the strategies adopted by Heaney in both poetry and prose to engage with Brodsky's reflections on the public-private dialectic. Despite the poets' friendship, their different national and social experiences lead, as one might expect, to different views of the nature and function of art. Pascale Guibert also pairs Heaney with another poet, Words-worth. She argues in "'We men ... must vanish'—Heaney's Wordsworth: Toward the Configuration of an Event Form" that in a series of writings haunted by the Laker, Heaney has used intertextuality to construct an increasingly public version of the poetic subject. Guibert investigates how Heaney employs Wordsworth to articulate both the private self and the public role of the poet. As with Laurel Peacock's essay, this chapter's appeal to theoretical considerations arises from the writings of Derrida and, in Guibert's case, Badiou. In the final essay in this section, Torsten Caeners's "'Imagined within the gravitational pull of the actual': The Fusion of the Private and the Public in Seamus Heaney's Poetics" shows that, as conceived by Heaney, the highly dynamic poetic process originates in and reacts to the ever-changing boundaries of the private and the public. According to this view of Heaney, poetry can affect its readers in the entire spectrum of their existence, since it constitutes a carefully balanced fusion of the private individual, the public sphere, and contemporary political events.

A common thread in the first three of the essays that make up the fourth section of the volume, "The North, the Nation, and the Public-Private Divide," is the poetry of Tony Harrison, already mentioned in Marc Porée's essay. Cécile Marshall's essay "'Inwardness' and the 'quest for a public poetry' in the Works of Tony Harrison" begins with *The Loiners*, Tony Harrison's first major collection of poems. Marshall shows how the private is understood at its most intimate — sexuality — and how "the privates" are somehow embedded with political questioning. In the "School of Eloquence" sonnets and the long poem "*v.*," the poet's personal dilemmas are harnessed to public discourse, while

Harrison's war poems exemplify his concern with violence and the individual, as well as with public and private memory. In "Private Voice and Public Discourse: A Poetics of Northern Dialect," Claire Hélie explores the encounter of public and private in three autobiographical volumes, Basil Bunting's *Briggflatts* (1965), Ted Hughes's *Remains of Elmet* (1979), and Tony Harrison's *From "The School of Eloquence"* (1978). Northernness as a social construct is internalized and deconstructed through such poetry; hence it engages in constant re-negotiations between private voice and public discourse. The chapter focuses on the idea of voicing the public-private divide in Northern English poetry with special emphasis on the place of dialect.

Carole Birkan-Berz also reads the poetry of Harrison, but this time with that of Geoffrey Hill, the modern poet who has perhaps most consistently engaged with the public-private dialectic. Through her consideration of both poets, she argues that public and private strands of national identity are bound up together. For Birkan-Berz, civic national values come to be embodied in certain poetic forms, so the poet's shaping of form may affect the reader's sense of certain national values. Emily Taylor Merriman considers the way in which Hill's use of the terms "public" and "private" manifests, in the poet's own phrase, a "protean energy"[11] as he chews over how poetry might serve "the people's / greater good"[12] and relates that common good to the individual writer and reader. Hill's voice, or voices, can be at once or alternately public and private. Adducing textual and biographical elements, Merriman's "Geoffrey Hill: 'a public nuisance'" examines how Hill's poetry self-consciously unveils its own awkward but productive sense of speaking both publicly and privately.

Like Marc Porée's opening essay, "The Public Intimacy of the Poetry of Sorrow" by Catherine Phillips closes the collection with an approach that is both synchronic and wide-ranging in its choice of material. As the editors of *Of Poetry and Power*, a collection of poems compiled after the death of President John F. Kennedy, suggest, "traditional elegiac forms" may no longer be available; the role of poetry has changed, and its adequacy as a medium for public grief is a matter of debate.[13] Phillips's essay addresses the question of how the poetry of grieving can be both private (as it by definition must be) and accessible to a reading public. Poets have always sought ways to express sorrow at the death of a loved one and remain true to the dignity of the deceased, while also making public their feelings of loss. The verbal energy the poets' compositions reveal on such occasions and the singular beauty of such compositions serve to offset the private torment the poets themselves may experience.

When grieving poets use traditional forms like the sonnet or other carefully crafted structures — witness the great compression with which Hill enacts his "September Song" elegy, for example — we are reminded that the relationship between poetry and the public-private divide is not merely thematic; rather, it is first and foremost a linguistic and technical matter, fit for consideration from the perspective of poetics.[14] The Platonic-Aristotelian duality that has always dominated discussion of poetics in the West is relevant here.[15] If we propose an analogy between this duality and poetry in its relationship with the public-private divide, the private side of the dialectic is Platonic, inward, psychological, the inspiration lying behind the poem, the beauty of ideal poetic form or forms; the public side is Aristotelian, the technical or linguistic realization in the form of inspiration in the poet's mind, the utterance of the idea. In short, intimacy is Platonic, exposure Aristotelian. Given the importance of form in this dialectic, it will come as no surprise to the reader that in the essays that make up this volume, attention is paid to song, sonnet and elegy, stanza shape and enjambment, voice, register, and tone; dialect; syllable and meter; chant, rhythm, rhyme, and counterpoint. A poem can be private without being autobiographical, or at least factually autobiographical; a poem may be both inward and public.

Yet ultimately a poem's defining feature is its form. While the first aim of this collection of peer-reviewed essays, then, is to analyze how British poetry has interacted with the public-private divide since the middle of the twentieth century, we hope that it will also suggest new ways not only of approaching a poem, but of thinking about what gives a poem its linguistic, textual and performative singularity.

NOTES

1. Michael McKeon, *The Secret History of Domesticity: Public, Private, and the Division of Knowledge* (Baltimore: The Johns Hopkins University Press, 2005), xx.

2. George Duby, "Foreword," *A History of Private Life*, ed. Phillipe Ariès and Georges Duby, trans. Arthur Goldhammer, vol. I ed. Paul Veyne (Cambridge: Harvard University Press, 1987), viii. First published as *Histoire de la vie privée* (Editions du Seuil, 1985).

3. James Fitzjames Stephen, *Liberty, Equality, Fraternity*, ed. Stuart D. Warner (Indianapolis: Liberty Fund, 1993), 106, 107–8.

4. *Daily Telegraph*, 13 Oct. 1864, 5/1. The quotation can be found in context in George Augustus Sala's *My Diary in America in the Midst of War*, parts of which were published in the *Daily Telegraph* (*Diary in America*, vol. II [London: Tinsley Brothers, 1865], 264).

5. *Times Literary Supplement*, 2 Apr. 2004, 5/1.

6. Globelink. 2008 Season. <http://www.globe link.org/2008season/newwriting/>.

7. 18 Mar. 2008. Audio version: <http://www. college-de-france.fr/default/EN/all/etu_cre/con ferenciers.htm.>

8. Seamus Heaney, *Preoccupations. Selected Prose 1968–1978* (London: Faber & Faber, 1984), 81.

9. Philip Larkin, "Brief for Betjeman," *Further Requirements: Interviews, Broadcasts, Statements and Book Reviews*, ed. Anthony Thwaite. (London: Faber and Faber, 2001), 34–37 (34).

10. Seamus Heaney, *An Open Letter* (Dublin: Field Day Publications, 1983), 9.

11. Geoffrey Hill, "Common Weal, Common Woe," *Collected Critical Writings* (Oxford: Oxford United Press, 2008, 265–279), 274.

12. Geoffrey Hill, section XXVI, *The Triumph of Love* (Boston: Houghton Mifflin, 1998), 14.

13. Erwin A. Glikes and Paul Schwaber (eds.), *Of Poetry and Power: Poems Occasioned by the Presidency and Death of John F. Kennedy* (New York: Basic Books, 1964), 2.

14. Witness Hill, as quoted by Carole Birkan-Berz: "Each sequence [of poems] has its own set of

problems, which, as always in my case, are predominantly technical questions" (Blake Morrison, "Under Judgment," *The New Statesman*, 8 Feb. 1980 [212–214], 212.) It is also worth citing in this context the opening of Charles Olson's 1950 essay, "Projective Verse," whose call for the energetic breaking open of poetic composition has influenced writing on both sides of the Atlantic. Olson indicates that in its formal development poetry must evolve beyond the sound of what he calls the "private-soul-at-any-public-wall" ("Projective Verse," *Twentieth-Century American Poetics: Poets on the Art of Poetry*, ed. Dana Gioa, David Mason, and Meg Schoerke [Boston: McGraw Hill, 2004], 174). Originally published in pamphlet form, *Poetry New York* (New York, 1950). Collected in *Selected Writings*, ed. Robert Creeley (New York: New Directions, 1966).

15. Especially since being updated in *Inspiration and Technique: Ancient and Modern Views on Beauty and Art*, ed. John Roe and Michael Stanco (Bern: Peter Lang, 2007).

PART I

Stating the Case

1. Poetry as "Open Diagnosis"

Marc Porée

Is poetry really as far "off the radar of both the general population and the power elite" as Sam Ladkin and Robin Purves claim in a recent issue of the *Chicago Review*?[1] Never less so than when poetry *is* the radar — both emitting and transmitting, beaming and detecting, penetrating and searching, reaching, in short, those places other genres cannot or will not reach. Poetry conducts "soundings" (Seamus Heaney's potent word), supplants the "sourcier" (also a sorcerer) of yore, and offers anatomies of the body politic as well as insights into the lovers' "most secret heart" — for whose "common wages" poets will vie for attention, no matter how little attention the lovers pay to their more or less histrionic tricks.[2] One phrase lifted from Dylan Thomas's programmatic "In my craft or sullen art" is "ivory stages," a most felicitous compound that encapsulates two seemingly opposite yearnings: the privacy of the Yeatsian ivory tower, standing proudly apart from the madding crowd, and the publicity of poetry practiced as a performing art by such bard-like figures as Thomas himself: the private and the public, to put it succinctly.

One of the last occasions when poetry struck a chord with the (British) nation was when the then–Poet Laureate published his 1998 collection *Birthday Letters*. Shortly before he was to die of cancer, Ted Hughes decided to go public with his own version of his controversial relationship with Sylvia Plath — his own invaluable insight into the "most secret heart" of the star-crossed lovers they had been. Whereas everyone thought that their affair had ended tragically on that cold February night of 1963, the poems revealed the length and breadth of the relationship, its "Duration" to utilize a Hughesian word.[3] Suddenly, it was as if long-suppressed feelings, in the form of powerfully crafted and resurgent poems, were brought to the fore by a poet who had always insisted that his approach to poetry was anthropological, mythopoetic, archetypal, epic, shamanic — anything but personal. There was of course a whiff of scandal in the air, and part of the resounding success encountered by the collection had to do with the fact that readers felt they were being

13

treated to something extraordinarily personal. Some strictly confidential matter, totally off limits, was being aired after years of silence; what one had thought to be retention had allegedly more to do with subterranean elaboration — nay, with a virtually posthumous collaboration or conspiracy between the dead and the living poet.

An added frisson presumably derived from the bitterly ironic awareness that Hughes was aligning himself at long last with a self-confessed confessional poetics. For such a poetics, *diagnosis* (in the form of pathology and therapy, auscultation and self-torture dramatically stylized and rolled into one) had always been conducted in public, in full awareness of the dangers involved in such searing self-examination. But let us leave aside for now the myth-making faculties characteristically displayed by Hughes in the collection, which might be construed either as a not-totally-sincere piece of self-justification or as a moving testimony to the vitality of Plath's "Real Presence" in and beyond death, as well as to her shaping influence on the work of her ex-husband. In either case, there is no gainsaying that the collection mattered to the nation at large. If sales are anything to go by, the collection struck a raw nerve in the nation — the reading nation at any rate — and it was a rawer nerve than struck by the poems of (pomp and) circumstance penned by the poet in his official capacity as Laureate. Even a piece like "Rain Charm for the Duchy," which obligingly purported to conflate pell-mell great private, public, civic, and halieutic events (the christening of Prince Harry, the end of a five-month drought, and the salmon beginning to move in the rivers of South West England), failed to stir the nation so deeply.[4]

Having said that, poetry need not be consensual to be picked up by the radar; dissent and dissension are indispensable components of the public-private divide. Likewise, the sought-for resonance need not be loud and booming, provided the writing is fully attuned to the "lower frequencies" emanating from not just the individual psyche, but also from its collective representation, the imagined community. Here are three instances in which, who knows, the poet as diagnostician might be speaking "for you."[5]

Uniting public and private: v.

It might be said of *v.* by Tony Harrison (a poet committed, in his own words, to giving back to poetry its public voice) that it is a poem of two nations, of those who have and those who do not have speech at their disposal or command. Its auscultation of the ills of the country — of the North of the country, to be more precise — is "revealed" by crude words reminiscent of W.H. Auden's "paysages moralisés," concerned with the condition of England during the Great Depression when geographic features were used as existential metaphors and conspiratorial imagery was brought to bear on an industry "already comatose."[6] Yet the piece takes more willingly after the radical vein of Shelley's "England in 1819," when the madness of the king, easy to diagnose even from abroad, was made to dovetail with more widespread symptoms of a nation-wide corruption. Published in 1985, *v.* really hit the radar two years later, when it transpired that Channel 4 intended to broadcast a film made after the poem. The announcement caused a furore among the tabloid press and Tory politicians, outraged by the prospect of so many four-letter words being aired. On the occasion, the radar was nearly smashed to smithereens, together with all the tellies, boxes, and television screens of the United Kingdom.

The poem opens in a graveyard as in Thomas Gray's "Elegy," but an urban and contemporary one. The space is half public — it is open on all sides and football fans take a short cut through the tombs on their way back from the Leeds home ground — and half private: the speaker stands on the family plot, witnesses the graves desecrated by graffiti tags, and bemoans the deeply divisive state of the nation. All the social "versuses" listed by the verses should not blind the reader to the one divide that does not attract much attention in the journalistic discussions of the poem: namely the division between public and private that the poem is committed to papering over, whatever the cost. Rhythmically, structurally, thematically, dramatically, *v.* is a deeply dialogic, even contrapuntal poem. By way of a tightly woven network of echoes and analogies, it connects the prose and the passion, the punk's profanity and the poet's urbanity, the tags of the former and the words of the latter, litter and letters, aerosol and ink, "Harp" and *furor poeticus*, chanting and rhyming. Last but not least, it calls upon the two fundamental voices of poetry, public and private, to blend and contract a "*working* marriage,"[7] to *unite*— to cease *versusing* one another: "*Here Comes the Bride!*"[8] The point made about the skin "underwriting" the poet, about the measures of the one carved "below" those of the other, should indeed apply, ideally and practically, to the two poetic veins.[9]

The poem is deeply concerned about the subsidence of the pit underneath the graves and the obelisks, as well as about the eons that elapsed before coal emerged from the rotting debris underneath, first as fossil energy, second as fuel for the industrial revolution, and third as a bone of contention between the Coal Board and Arthur Scargill. Accordingly, the word "vein" cannot be quite fortuitous. The private vein is home-oriented, and possibly self-oriented (though never self-centered); the public vein is nation-conscious, even world-conscious. The former speaks of home — Leeds's polar opposite — as the site of love, sex, and high culture (Alban Berg), but also of home as family, as the site of a beleaguered and virtually "out of place" Englishness[10];

the latter speaks to the nation, invokes shared responsibility ("Much is ours"[11]), wails and rages, talks tall and down to the yobs ("aspirations"[12]). Gradually, however, the hectoring public vein is undermined (from above and from below), undergoes a process of recession (one of the key words of the poem, along with subsidence), and is ultimately eclipsed by the private voice, "the voice talking to itself—or to nobody."[13]

T.S. Eliot refused to assimilate the private voice to what is loosely called lyrical poetry, preferring to call it "meditative verse."[14] In Eliot's construction of this voice, the poet is not concerned with other people at all, only with finding the least wrong words. His evocation of the poet obsessed by a "burden which he must bring to birth in order to obtain relief"[15] corresponds to the impression experienced when reading *v.*, that Tony Harrison is haunted by a private demon of his own, "a demon against which he feels powerless because in its first manifestation it has no face, no name, nothing."[16] In *v.*, the existential and metaphysical meditation among the industrial ruins becomes quasi-Hamletian, as the interiority of the speaker's self is made to rise from under the graves at dusk and to gain substance (and a face) as it pierces through the gaps in the poem.

One such gap occurs two-thirds into the text, when the poet discovers that he shares with a punk — his imaginary alter ego, his daemonic "autre" — four letters and a name. Such a moment of truth, treated by the once-President of the Classical Association of Britain as a perfect instance of *anagnorisis*, triggers a train of agonized thoughts on the subjects of identity and appropriation. The blazoning of the poet's name on book covers and on Broadway[17] is thus implicitly equated to that of Prince Charles's name above West Yorkshire mines[18] and to that of the punk's aerosoled and neoned signature. At this stage, consciously or not, the poem may lend itself to an anthropological reading, which a recent essay by the French philosopher Michel Serres helps bring into focus. In the punningly titled *Mal propre*, Serres argues that men take after tigers and dogs that beshit and bepiss their territory in order to seal it off from their enemies, thus making it their own. What Serres calls the "propre" (which might be translated as "what belongs to one in particular") is thus the result of the "sale" (the unclean, the dirty) as induced by various pollutions, excremental and other. In a sweeping gesture, Serres goes back to the origins of property as stealth (as retraced, among others, by Jean-Jacques Rousseau in the *Discours sur l'origine et les fondements de l'inégalité parmi les hommes* of 1755). He contends that the major impropriety of befouling and marking the private space of others to deprive them of their property rights further increases the unashamed privacy of the polluter and savages the notion of public space. Serres even goes so far as to suggest that, bent on blackening page after page and securing their names on book covers printed by prestigious publishing houses, writers would be in danger of acting more or less like tigers and dogs, if, deep down, they were not drawn instead to another type of ownership, altogether more peaceful and less selfishly hide-bound in its approach.

Harrison's poem confirms Serres's insight with a twist by granting the punk's four-letter words (SHIT, CUNT, FUCK) the force of a symbolic profanation/desecration, which is tantamount to the kind of appropriation/pollution by way of urine and feces. Looked at in that new/old scatological light, the poem only confirms its intensely Swiftian political agenda: *v.* hints obliquely at the (hidden, because buried) foundations of violated privacy, diagnosed as resulting from the corruption of the proper at the hands of the improper — the corruption and division of language following necessarily suit. Via the provocative inclusion of expletives within its quatrains, made possible by the would-not-be-Poet Laureate's consummate poetic and prosodic skills, *v.* stands up to and beats aggro, whether nihilistic or genteel, proves that poetry can "grow from SHIT,"[19] and affirms the true subversion of (re)public(an) art: *"then look behind."*[20]

Publicizing the private:
Open Diagnosis; The Clever Daughter

In the early 1990s, Susan Wicks was allegedly diagnosed with multiple sclerosis, a disease that causes alterations of the nervous system including changes in sensations, difficulties with coordination and balance, visual problems, and bladder and bowel difficulties. The central section of *Open Diagnosis* attempts to chart this disease, and the cover features a magnetic resonance image of the author's head. The odds of such a cliché ending up on the front page of a volume published by Faber and Faber were, the reader will agree, pretty slim. Such a bold move intersects, however, with many contemporary interrogations in the field of art (and body art in particular) about the nature of one's imago. *Interior Scroll* (1975) is the title of a filmed performance by Carolee Schneeman. In the film, the naked artist removes a long sheet of written paper from the inside of her vagina. The interior of the feminine body is included within its external image, producing a fully visible image of femininity. *Corps étranger* (1994) is an installation by the Anglo-Palestinian artist Mona Hatoum in which she projects images of her own endoscopies/colonoscopies on a screen — knowing full well that there is "Rien à voir" (nothing to be seen), to paraphrase Daniel Arasse. In her case, the *corps étranger* of the title is both the camera's inquisitive eye penetrating deep inside her viscera and this other image of herself. Hitherto unseen and hard to reconcile with one's own narcissistic image, this second image has the dirty, hidden aspect of that perfect stranger, that Doppelganger — anything but her *corps propre*. From the installation, one can draw the provisional conclusion that medical imagery (as boosted by recent technological breakthroughs, be it applied to the field of art or not[21]) is contributing to massive changes in the perception of the inside/outside divide.[22] Granted, the latter does not totally coincide with the public-private separation, but it prompts all kinds of fascinating overlaps when inside becomes outside and vice versa, whether becomingly or not. Wicks's "Coming Out" — a term stolen from the gay and lesbian community — is one such overlap.[23]

As foregrounded in the title's mind-boggling ambiguity, *Open Diagnosis* is uncertain about the evolution and outcome of the disease, but adamant about laying one's brain bare. On the front page, not a poet's face, but a drab plate stares at us as an unprecedented and potentially embarrassing substitute for her portrait. Seen from above, the head is neither a cranium, nor a skull, nor a death mask; not quite a *memento mori*, it is nevertheless likely to serve as a *vanitas*. No bones are presented, but instead, the soft, perishable matter — the software — of a head is brought to the fore, exhibited and displayed for all to see: the recesses, intricacies, ins and outs of the brain are flattened, ironed out, if one will, to facilitate the diagnosis, incidentally making of Susan Wicks a *res cogitans* rather than a *cogito*. Having nothing to hide, and seemingly indifferent to the perils of the society of surveillance,[24] Wicks makes no bones about citing her apparently damaged, dysfunctional brain as the *corpus delicti*. The move is a calculated one, despite its apparently indiscreet and virtually obscene nature, for two reasons at least. First, no matter how strictly personal or confidential, the image of one's brain cannot be recognized or identified as such. All the data processed and digitalized in the computer can only be interpreted by a specialist, therefore guaranteeing a certain measure of anonymity and impenetrability. Second, obvious differences between image and word, digit and letter, make for interesting variations on the theme of openness (in the relative rather than the absolute meaning of the word).

Mapping is the most appropriate metaphor to help the poet account for and convey the symptoms of her illness to the readers. One remembers Susan Sontag's influential essay *Illness as Metaphor* (1978), in which the essayist protested against the reduction of cancer and AIDS to a single overriding metaphor, preventing patients from coming to terms with the reality of their ailment. Susan Wicks, it seems, reverses the move and proposes metaphors for illness based on the fantastically bright and motley colors of the plates alluded to in the poems (but never shown). After the black and white drabness of X-ray, the sudden outburst of Technicolor-illuminated plates ("the gift of so much colour"[25]), visually exciting and causing a cinematic sense of wonder at the visibility of the living brain, very nearly outweighs the distressing nature of the diagnosis: her brain makes "rainbows."[26] Indeed, a characteristic gesture inside the collection consists in holding such plates up to the window and seeing the world through them — either because the world on the other side of the transparent pane shines through or because the shapes, involutions, and convolutions of the cerebral matter suggest, or look like, real rivers, twigs, etc. in the world on the other side. Interposed halfway between the public and private worlds, a glassy membrane thus posits a zero-degree transparency that both reader and writer know to be a mere illusion, advantageously replaced by rapturously extravagant stylization.

On a less spectacular plane, the collection also enrolls the resources of coenaesthesia so as to convey from inside the slightest sensations, the smallest alterations in the balance of the speaker's inner and outer being, together with the hardly perceptible distortions in her altered *Weltanschauung* ("Motion-Sickness"[27]) as well as in that of complete strangers ("Blind Skiers"[28]). This is as intimate as it can get, and turns the slightest erratic twitchings into disturbingly confident poetic matter ("Ticking Hands"[29]). As was noted by critics, however, this is risky territory, as anticipated in the opening "Bear Country."[30] A shadow of danger hangs over this otherwise charmingly innocuous poem, the possibility of forthcoming perils in the guise of threatening animality (confer "Carpenter Ant," "On Being Eaten by a Snake"[31]).

Susan Wicks is frequently nicknamed the Indoor Laureate because of the domestic, filial nature of much of what she has written since *Singing Underwater* (1992). In her work, privacy is treasured in view of its extreme vulnerability and affective dimension. Family matter, potentially parochial and strictly private, is material to be handled with care: an aging and bereaved father; photographs; drawings (of bubbles); fragile family relics folded in a blue envelope ("My Father's Caul"[32]); letters sought for under stairs, in dark passages, recesses, nooks, and crannies ("Caves"[33]) or in the attic ("Protected Species"[34]). The second stage in the saga of those "vies minuscules"[35] is when their privacy is dispersed, cleared out, prised open.

"Open" is the open sesame of Wicks's poetry. The tropism is present in both collections, being conspicuously enacted by an insistent gesture of unfurling, unfolding, and unraveling. However minute, "intimate things" find themselves exposed to an environment that is no longer close and protective ("Grandmother"[36]). In the process, privacy is put to the test of the open sea, as in "Airborne,"[37] and the open air, as in "Propaganda,"[38] to name two of the poems revisiting World War II, in which Susan Wicks's father served. Hence the see-saw rhythm of the collections, alternating in emphasis now on the private (praying for it to remain private), now on the publicizing of apparently highly personal material for the sake of breaking free from domesticity's stifling comfort. The alternation is even between almost anecdotal poems ("Bear Country") and deliberately non-personal ones. At the closure of *Open Diagnosis*, "The Ark speaks" reads as a self-conscious prosopopeia in which a personified Noah's ark, modeling an open-house policy that is not so much biblical as programmatic, lays itself open to the coming and going of animals.[39]

Several of Wicks's poems are about the porosity of walls, partitions between hotel rooms or houses that separate private from private and private from public. Wicks is always on the lookout for those critical moments when somebody's privacy ceases to be purely private and begins to intrude or obtrude, more or less obnoxiously, upon one's own private space or upon the public. Eavesdropping, voyeurism, peeping underneath the door and the seat of a Toilet "for the disabled"[40] — such are the eccentric experiences that appeal to the poet's quirky taste for the potentially indecent point of view. Not only is Wicks's staring eye oddly curious, it is cold, clinical, detached, and unsparing. It is unembarrassed too, even when the situations evoked are objectively embarrassing, calling for a compassion that is manifestly not on the agenda. While not particularly charitable, her point of view is not openly callous either. A case in point is "Communion," when the spittle of a "cripple" eating his meal in what one takes to be an old people's home is made to shine and glisten in the poem's last line.[41] The image forms an unusual epiphany of the act of *"spinning,"* i.e., of bridging the gap between the private and the public. In that respect, "My father's handkerchiefs"[42] is also characteristic of her highly idiosyncratic approach. The speaker stands in the laundry, the traditional unemphatic private space of suburban femininity, despised by public men and recently exalted by women poets and feminists like Vicki Feaver or Penelope Shuttle, thanks to an ingenious process of retrieval. Shown ironing her aging and bereaved father's muslin handkerchiefs, she sounds perfectly unabashed about the reappropriation of domesticity as a locus for poetry. The poem strikes the right (albeit frail) balance between gross exposure and moving disclosure, as the hardened stuff of nasal secretions, initially discharged into handkerchiefs and prised open to the tearing tunes of detonations and explosions, is made to match some minor act of writing and reading, some artistic work or "creation" in progress that lies open to the anxious interpretation of a daughter. Ironed over with an eye to diagnosing the progress of her father's disease, the changing but ultimately ominous shapes of snot are indeed construed as the equivalent of a Rorschach test, to be diagnosed as ancient soothsayers did while poring over the innards of sacrificed chickens.

Intertextuality is summoned by "Germinal," a poem in which the perils of the mining industry, never meant to be literal, nevertheless correlate with the forthcoming collapse of synapses and the lethal catastrophe masterminded by Souvarine inside the pits of Montsou in Zola's nineteenth-century masterpiece.[43] A lecturer in French literature, Susan Wicks must know that the disaster in Zola's novel is not only a private one, but a collective one too — and a reversible one into the bargain, since the hammerings rising from the depths of the mine where Etienne Lantier's comrades are trapped are hailed as pointers to promising new crops in the work's last pages. Clearly, the cultural reference serves a purpose, which is to de-privatize the disease and turn it into a form of trans-national mode of ownership — the ownership of acknowledged literariness, not necessarily accessible beyond the happy few, and pointing possibly to the limitations of such an otherwise poetically apposite analogy. With all due respect to Susan Wicks, the telling absence of the political dimension from her version of *Germinal* is potentially damaging, in view of the reduction to mere pathology that it operates. Likewise, "Hitler and His Mother," while being the sole poem in the collection to refer at least nominally to History (following Patrick Modiano's lead), hastens to revert — to regress? — to the private history of Hitler, when he was a mere suckling and probably lacking maternal love.[44] The result is a confusion of genres that over-sentimentalizes as well as personalizes History with its "grande hache."[45] In that respect, the poem "Hitler and His Mother" compares most unfavorably with practically any poem in the collection *The World's Wife* by Carol Ann Duffy, in which the return of the private sphere to the public stage with a vengeance (as in the Freudian phrase "the return of the repressed") makes for all kinds of well-deserved ironies.[46]

But Wicks's originality lies elsewhere. Her dryly eccentric fondness for incorrection, aberration, and dysfunctionality are welcomed more than they are resented (that Walter de la Mare's poems were an influence here is a distinct possibility). Knowing the extent to which privacy and secrecy are essential components in the historical and epistemological formation of subjectivity,[47] her presumably impish self is over-eager to test the limits thereof. Her apparent lack of shame, together with the cold-blooded scrutiny of her dysfunctional brain — examined as if it were someone else's — denote undeniable fondness for the taking of risks. Granted, the risks incurred will never even remotely match those taken by the matador, as postulated by Michel Leiris in his seminal essay, "De la littérature considérée comme une tauromachie."[48] However, for Susan Wicks and such writers as work in the autobiographical tradition, the fear that a bull's horn, however imaginary, should gore them to death due to a failure to abide by their public art's rigorous rules keeps their writing alive.

De-privatizing the private: Out of Danger; Rapture

One does not diagnose the heart as one diagnoses the nation (Harrison) or the brain (Wicks), and the former task may well prove by far the most perilous. The career of James Fenton (b. 1949) is a case in point. Hailed as the major British poet of his generation, he offers in the words of Sean O'Brien a unique combination of "plainness of utterance with a strong sense of poetry as a public and political art."[49] His career speaks for itself, ranging from his essays on all the *Wrong Places* that he covered as a war correspondent, to the lyrics composed for a commemorative piece of contemporary music in the wake of the Tsunami disaster (premiered in May 2008), and including a four-year stint at the Chair of Poetry at Oxford (1994–1999). *Out of Danger*, his eclectic 1993 collection, gathers some of the tensions underlying the public-private divide. The first poem, "Beauty, Danger and Dismay,"[50] speaks of encountering one's poetic subjects on the road — trivial matters, literally, albeit matters of war and peace, life and death, Famine in the South and Strife in the North, "Blood and Lead."[51] The title of the first section, "Out of Danger," would seem to point to the dangers of the Far East where Fenton served as a war correspondent, but where he proved unable to write poetry — unlike W.H. Auden, the poet to whom he is most frequently compared, and unlike Tony Harrison, whose Bosnian poems were faxed from the front and appeared in the *Guardian* barely six hours after the battle. *Out of Danger*, then, should be construed as a Wordsworthian title, smacking of "emotion recollected in tranquillity": only when the dangers of the war zone were behind him and at a remove was Fenton able to write about them in verse. Poetry about what is met on the road cannot be written on the theatre of war, on the open field of operations. It takes removal from the public stage, private decantation, for the poems to come about. But deception sets in, since *Out of Danger*, together with the eponymous poem in the collection, proves to be about far more hazardous waters: the perils of falling in and out of love, feelings and situations that are much more dangerous than the minefields of Cambodia. The deliberate juxtaposition of "Jerusalem," one of Fenton's strongest political poems; of "Tiananmen" (delivered to the tunes of a Brechtian musical comedy); and of a sleazy hotel room shared with his male lover, with cracks in the ceiling and peeling walls, leads us to reconsider the meaning of the title. Out of danger, as in the phrase out of fear or out of hope, means therefore not the removal of danger, but the promptings of danger, the choice of danger as an inspiration, private and public. Fenton, himself a powerful public reader on the "ivory stages" where prominent poets like to strut, delivers the same home truths, be they truths "for the dark and a pillow"[52] or for the stones of Jerusalem. But does he do so with the same amount of brazen confidence as displayed in the more theoretical section of "The Manilla Manifesto"?[53] The answer is bound to be negative, as evidenced by the involuntarily comic Freudian denial whereby the speaker affirms that he is not in the least embarrassed to affront the public gaze: to expose himself to the dangers of going public with private matters like a Paris love affair, however embarrassing to himself, his lover, and possibly the reader. Even the editor of *The New Faber Book of Love Poems*, it seems, cannot steer clear from the cliché of the romance in dirty Paris ("In Paris with You"[54])!

How can such perils be courted without incurring disaster? A consideration of *Rapture*, a 2005 collection by Carol Ann Duffy, might be of some help. At first sight, *Rapture* may strike one as objectionable for all kinds of reasons, bad and good. Coming under an embarrassingly cloying title, the volume seems to mark a sad and unexpected regression in the career of the uncompromising author of *Feminine Gospels* (2002) and of the forthcoming and long overdue *The World's Second Wife*. What has happened to the witty dramatic monologues, to the chameleon voice of *The World's Wife*? Where have all the wry and cuttingly detached anachronisms gone? How could a wittily hard-boiled feminist have gone all soft and mellow, stooping so low as to fall in line with the stereotypically gendered appropriation by women of romance and sentimentality? The question is indeed a moot one. *Rapture* is the relation of a love affair with a fellow woman poet that took them from love at first sight to "Unloving,"[55] from rapture to rupture, in just under one year, and it gives the impression that Duffy has indeed caved in to what Roland Barthes calls the "grand Autre narratif" (the great Narrative other):

> to the general opinion that disparages every excessive force and demands that the subject should reduce of itself the great imaginary stream without order or end by which he is shot through, to a painful, morbid crisis, from which one just has to be cured (just like any Hippocratic disease): romance is the tribute to be paid by the lover to the world if he or she wants to be reconciled with it.[56]

On a second look, however, the collection appears extraordinarily inventive, bringing a very sophisticated *dispositif* (to use Giorgio Agamben's word) to bear on the stuff of an inevitably banal story. The "dispositif" is at one remove from psychology, which "yields a space or site of speech: the space or site of someone who talks to himself/herself, lovingly, in front of the other (the beloved) who does not talk."[57] It is one in which the private lover, and lover of privacy, effaces herself in the act of writing for the public and in public — while virtually effacing the object of her love, too. Indeed, although the secret surrounding the identity of the author's lover, most certainly another woman poet, is a fairly open secret, all too telling gender marks are neutralized (the appeal of the Barthesian "Neutre" immediately springs to mind). Most of the minute particulars of the loved one's identity are carefully phased out, beginning with the name, in a poem ironically called "Name" that repeatedly omits or overlooks it by making it rhyme with "everything."[58] With painstaking care, anything susceptible of being construed as (too) personal has been studiously avoided (as in a lipogrammatic piece of writing by Perec). Instead, one is left with a set of different enunciative postures, a whole range of *figures* (not so much along the lines of rhetoric as along those of calisthenics) forming part and parcel of what Barthes called *Fragments d'un discours amoureux*. The figure, as Barthes puts it, is bound to be "cernée" (like a sign surrounded on all sides) and "memorable" (like an image or a tale); it is fully substantiated provided one can exclaim: "How true! I recognize this scene of language" by way of its having already passed the test of public recognition or acknowledgment.[59]

A case in point is "The Love Poem," made up of numerous excerpts from famous love poems that nearly everyone recognizes, the lines in question having become virtually proverbial.[60] Further compounding this well-wrought "exercice de style," aposiopesis, suspension, dismemberment, and truncation are brought to bear on the textual and discursive fabric so that the articulation becomes pure disarticulation. These techniques produce the ultimate synthetic poem, generated by accumulation (never reaching the desired consummation, however, in view of its exclusively inchoative nature) and always on the brink of degenerating into mere fabrication. It is a poem with many blanks, a fill-in-the-lines-by-yourself work, in which famous beginnings and equally notable endings are allowed to trail off into the void — a poem immediately acknowledged as being no longer protected by copyright laws (being part and parcel of the "domaine public," as the French would say). The composition, composite despite being discontinuous, sounds supremely impersonal, purposefully generic, almost archetypal and very nearly anonymous — de-privatized, as it were. The text is no one's in particular, making it a cooperative venture along the lines of "Aux Auteurs-aux Lecteurs-Réunis,"[61] defeating such a thing as literary property.

Virginia Woolf once famously declared that Anon. must have been a woman poet, and one also recalls her inveighing against the urge to appropriate and turn everything into something privately owned, which she considered to be characteristically masculine/male/patriarchal:

> Women will pass a tombstone or a signpost without feeling an irresistible desire to cut their names on it, as Alf, Bert, or Chas must do in obedience to their instinct, which murmurs if it sees a fine woman go by, or even a dog, *Ce Chien est à moi*.[62]

This might help reclaim Duffy's gesture as feminist, notwithstanding the fact that the bits and snippets of poetry cited here were written mostly by men (and what men!— Shakespeare, Sidney, Marlowe, Donne, Shelley, Meredith, MacNeice, etc.— Elizabeth Barrett Browning being the exception that proves the rule). Needless to say, the contrivance reflects on the exhaustion of love as a feeling — we are inexorably drawing to the end of the relationship — but more essentially, it brings grist to the slow-grinding mills of fragmentation, incompleteness, and ruin, all part and parcel of a topos that once had a historical foundation in Romantic poetry and has now found a posthistorical posterity in the recyclings of postmodernism.

"The Love Poem" in particular, and the poems of *Rapture* in general, foreground the anonymity of authorship in the postmodern world, which tends to reduce literature (or literariness) to a free-wheeling intertextuality that is up for grabs. The private, solitary poet's voice intersects with the innumerable echoes of poetic formulations and citations floating in the air; wistfully, it reflects on the diminishing or even vanishing aura of the original, induced and caused by the glibly technical reproducibility of the citation in the age of technical reproducibility, to paraphrase Walter Benjamin. This happens whenever the bottomless "pool of verse" is tapped.[63]

Indeed, it seems as if Duffy were availing herself of the technique of sampling, as initiated by "musique concrète" and later perfected by jungle, house music, and hip hop culture — urban culture, in other words, as made manifest in the public space or sphere. Sampling, the act of taking a sample — a looped portion of a sound recording — and re-using it as an element of a new recording may be construed as a transposition of the cutting and pasting that software technology has enabled (without really authorizing it) in the field of writing. In the process, the samples are decontextualized, and so are the famous literary quotations: they are eventually treated as if they were mere soundbites. "The Love Poem" (definite article) is a poem unauthored (indefinite article), or better, co-authored. Neither private nor public, if one will, it reads both as the very negation of creation and as the epitome of art, posited as "croaking" by Carol Ann Duffy, hence hoarse and exhausted.[64] By way of consequence this would tend to be "art pauvre." Indeed, what with its deliberate poverty of language and the willful choice of time-worn and threadbare clichés — "small words, / and few," rubbed at till they gleam "as though" they were new[65] — *Rapture* is forced to rely on its own artifice, its own artefactuality. For that reason alone, it commands respect and impresses more than it moves with its superb command of the codes, tropes, and commonplaces of the amorous discourse. If, as evidenced most particularly in "Art," experience came first — of a clearly private nature — poetry writes "over" it so that the moment when the love affair comes to an end coincides with its going public as "art": "Only art now" — albeit fragmented, pigmented, chiseled, printed, "fizzled into poems."[66]

The exit line of "Over," the last poem in the collection, delivers a parting gift, conveyed by means of a piercing "blush of memory" that emanates from a bird about to begin a song on that early Christmas dawn, marking at once the first anniversary of the love affair and its demise.[67] To commemorate the "death of love," the poet enrolls a seriously sensual utterance, paradoxically lush and crisp, taut and mellow, terminal and inaugural — one that ends and is born anew on what is, after all, Christmas Eve. Sounding some-what neo-Keatsian, despite the explicit reference to Robert Browning at the outset of the poem, its subtly rosy echoes remind one of the importance of embarrassment in life and art. One of the reasons why art is to be valued, as argued by Christopher Ricks, is that it helps us deal with embarrassment, not by abolishing or ignoring it, but by refining it. In the words of the author of *Keats and Embarrassment*, raising embarrassability to the level of art is an art, is the art of arts:

> Art, in its unique combination of the private and the public, offers us a unique kind of human relationship freed from the possibility, which is incident to other human relationships, of an embarrassment that clogs, paralyses, or coarsens.[68]

All things considered, the liberating force that through the red fuse drives public poetry also drives the poet's personal emotions and refines them in the process — from the unembarrassability of brazen-faced Susan Wicks to Harrison's hot flush of indignation, via the latest display of passionate self-consciousness on the part of Carol Ann Duffy. The force is the same, for it is the force of poetry. Likewise, as evidenced by Peter Ackroyd in his biography of T.S. Eliot, the insight into the blight of Western civilization exemplified in *The Waste Land* owed a great deal to the dry months spent at Margate, at a time when both Eliot and Vivienne were undergoing mental therapy and both could connect "Nothing with nothing."[69] The force that blasted the Zeitgeist was their destroyer, turning the couple's psyche to sand. Further back, the force in "Dover Beach" that drove the global waters of the sea of faith, once full and now "like the folds of a bright girdle furl'd," drove the two lovers of Matthew Arnold's poem into each other's arms, deprived as they were of any other certitude on the darkling plain, "Swept with confused alarms of struggle and flight."[70] Both the sea and love would have receded with the outgoing tide, sooner or later; in the meantime the poem encompasses, even embraces the public and the private, rolling them into one disenchanted stronghold of all-enchanting melancholy.

Granted, the sameness postulated at the end of the day is not the sameness of identity, but that of likeness and analogy; the modalities are bound to differ, but barring formal disparities, there can be no true disjunction or dissociation of sensibility between public and private poetry. To paraphrase Dylan Thomas for the last time, at the sheet (of paper) goes the "same crooked worm" — the same pen.[71]

NOTES

1. S. Ladkin & R. Purves, "An Introduction," *Chicago Review* 53:1 (2007, 6–13), 12.

2. Dylan Thomas, *Collected Poems 1934–1953* (London: Everyman, 1993; first edition 1955), 106.

3. Ted Hughes, *New Selected Poems 1957–1994* (London: Faber and Faber, 1995), 273.
4. Ibid., 285.
5. Ralph Ellison, *Invisible Man* (London: Penguin Books, 1952), 469.
6. W.H. Auden, *The Collected Poems of W.H. Auden* (London: Faber and Faber, 1974), 163.
7. Tony Harrison, *v.* (Highgreen: Bloodaxe Books, 1989; first edition 1985), 21.
8. Ibid., 23.
9. Ibid., 31.
10. Ian Baucom, *Out of Place, Englishness, Empire and the Locations of Identity* (Princeton: Princeton University Press, 1999), 3–40.
11. Harrison, *v.*, 13.
12. Ibid., 17.
13. T.S. Eliot, *On Poetry and Poets* (London: Faber and Faber, 1957), 101.
14. Ibid., 97.
15. Ibid., 98.
16. Ibid.
17. Harrison, *v.*, 16.
18. Ibid., 15.
19. Ibid., 33.
20. Ibid.
21. Cf. Philip K. Dick, *A Scanner Darkly* (New York: Vintage Books, 1991; first edition 1977).
22. Philippe Comar, *Les images du corps* (Paris: Découvertes Gallimard, 1993), 88–91.
23. Susan Wicks, *Open Diagnosis* (London: Faber and Faber, 1994), 42.
24. Cf. George Banu, *La scène surveillée* (Arles: Actes Sud, 2006).
25. Wicks, *Open Diagnosis*, 29.
26. Ibid., 35.
27. Ibid., 21.
28. Ibid., 40.
29. Ibid., 20.
30. Ibid., 3.
31. Ibid., 46, 48.
32. Ibid., 33.
33. Susan Wicks, *The Clever Daughter* (London: Faber and Faber, 1996), 13.
34. Ibid., 35.
35. Pierre Michon, *Vies minuscules* (Paris: Gallimard, 1984).
36. Wicks, *The Clever Daughter*, 15.
37. Ibid., 31.
38. Wicks, *Open Diagnosis*, 32.
39. Ibid., 62.
40. Ibid., 39.
41. Ibid., 23.
42. Wicks, *The Clever Daughter*, 30.
43. Wicks, *Open Diagnosis*, 30.
44. Ibid., 55.
45. George Perec, *W ou le souvenir d'enfance* (Paris: Denoël, 1975), 37.
46. Wicks, *Open Diagnosis*, 55.
47. Michael McKeon, *The Secret History of Domesticity: Public, Private, and the Division of Knowledge* (Baltimore: The Johns Hopkins University Press, 2005), 11.
48. Michel Leiris, "De la littérature considérée comme une tauromachie," preface to *L'Age d'homme* (Paris: Gallimard, 1946; first edition 1939).
49. Sean O'Brien, ed., *The Firebox, Poetry in Britain and Ireland after 1945* (London: Picador, 1998), 95.
50. James Fenton, *Out of Danger* (London: Penguin Books, 1993), 3.
51. Ibid., 34.
52. Ibid., 11.
53. Ibid., 79–103.
54. Ibid., 12–13.
55. Carol Ann Duffy, *Rapture* (London: Picador, 2005), 31.
56. Roland Barthes, *Fragments d'un discours amoureux* (Paris: Seuil, 1977), 11 (my translation).
57. Ibid., 2.
58. Duffy, *Rapture*, 3.
59. Barthes, *Fragments d'un discours amoureux*, 6.
60. Duffy, *Rapture*, 58.
61. Barthes, *Fragments d'un discours amoureux*, 9.
62. Virginia Woolf, *A Room of One's Own* (Cambridge: Cambridge University Press, 1999; first edition 1929), 57.
63. Duffy, *Rapture*, 58.
64. Ibid., 32.
65. Ibid., 31.
66. Ibid., 60.
67. Ibid., 62.
68. Christopher Ricks, *Keats and Embarrassment* (Oxford: Oxford University Press, 1976), 1.
69. T.S. Eliot, *The Waste Land* (London: Faber and Faber, 1963; first edition 1922), 74.
70. Matthew Arnold, "Dover Beach" (1867), *Victorian Poetry and Poetic Theory* (Toronto: Broadview Press, 1999), 732.
71. Dylan Thomas, "The force that through the green fuse," *Collected Poems 1934–1953* (London: Everyman, 1993; first edition 1955), 13.

Works Cited

Ackroyd, Peter (1984). *T.S. Eliot.* London: Penguin Books.

Agamben, Giorgio (2007). *Qu'est-ce qu'un dispositif?* Paris: Rivages Poche.

Arasse, Daniel (2000). *On n'y voit rien: Descriptions.* Paris: Folio/ Essais Gallimard.

Arnold, Matthew (1867). "Dover Beach." *Victorian Poetry and Poetic Theory* (1999). Ed. Thomas J. Collins and Vivienne J. Rundle. Toronto: Broadview Press.

Auden, W.H. (1974). *The Collected Poems of W.H. Auden.* London: Faber and Faber.

Banu, George (2006). *La scène surveillée.* Arles: Actes Sud.

Barthes, Roland (1977). *Fragments d'un discours amoureux.* Paris: Seuil.

Baucom, Ian (1999). *Out of Place, Englishness, Empire and the Locations of Identity.* Princeton: Princeton University Press.

Benjamin, Walter (1936, 2008). *The Work of Art in the Age of its Technological Reproducibility, and Other Writings on Media.* Harvard: The Belknap Press.

Chicago Review (2007). "Four Poets." Ed. Sam Ladkin & Robin Purves, 53:1 (Spring). Chicago: University of Chicago.

Comar, Philippe (1993). *Les images du corps.* Paris: Découvertes Gallimard.

Duffy, Carol Ann (1999). *The World's Wife.* London: Picador.

_____ (2005). *Rapture.* London: Picador.

Eco, Umberto (1985). *Apostille au Nom de la Rose.* Paris: Grasset.

Eliot, T.S. (1922, 1963). *The Waste Land.* London: Faber and Faber.

_____ (1957). *On Poets and Poetry.* London: Faber and Faber.

Ellison, Ralph (1952). *Invisible Man.* London: Penguin Books.

Fenton, James (1993). *Out of Danger.* London: Penguin Books.

_____ ed. (2006). *The New Faber Book of Love Poems.* London: Faber and Faber.

Harrison, Tony (1985). *v.* Highgreen: Bloodaxe Books.

Hughes, Ted (1995). *New Selected Poems 1957– 1994.* London: Faber and Faber.

_____ (1998). *Birthday Letters.* London: Faber and Faber.

Leiris, Michel (1939, 1946). "De la littérature considérée comme une tauromachie." Preface to *L'Age d'homme.* Paris: Gallimard.

McKeon, Michael (2005). *The Secret History of Domesticity: Public, Private, and the Division of Knowledge.* Baltimore: The Johns Hopkins University Press.

Michon, Pierre (1984). *Vies minuscules.* Paris: Gallimard.

O'Brien, Sean (ed.) (1998). *The Firebox, Poetry in Britain and Ireland after 1945.* London: Picador.

Perec, George (1975). *W ou le souvenir d'enfance.* Paris: Denoël.

Ricks, Christopher (1976). *Keats and Embarrassment.* Oxford: Oxford University Press.

Rousseau, Jean-Jacques (1755, 2005). *Discours sur l'origine et les fondements de l'inégalité parmi les hommes.* Paris: Folio essais Gallimard.

Serres, Michel (2008). *Le Mal propre: Polluer pour s'approprier?* Paris: Le Pommier.

Shelley, Percy Bysshe (2003). *The Major Works.* Ed. Zachary Leader and Michael O'Neill. Oxford: Oxford University Press.

Sontag, Susan (1978, 2001). *Illness as Metaphor and Aids and Its Metaphors.* London: Picador.

Thomas, Dylan (1993). *Collected Poems 1934– 1953.* London: J.M. Dent.

Wicks, Susan (1994). *Open Diagnosis.* London: Faber and Faber.

_____ (1996). *The Clever Daughter.* London: Faber and Faber.

Woolf, Virginia (1929, 1995). *A Room of One's Own.* Ed. Jenifer Smith. Cambridge: Cambridge University Press.

PART II

Strictly Public?

2. Public Faces in Private Places: Messianic Privacy in Cambridge Poetry

Robert Archambeau

My title comes from some proverbial lines of W.H. Auden's in *The Orators*: "Private faces in public places / Are wiser and nicer / Than public faces in private places."[1] Often, modern poets have presented their work as a matter of private faces in public places — that is, as the voice of private, authentic individual conscience entering the public sphere. Such a vision of poetry is, no doubt, fraught with its own problems and contradictions, but none of those concern me here. When we look at what has come to be known in some circles as Cambridge School poetry — the experimental poetry of Tom Raworth, John Wilkinson, and Jeremy Prynne, as well as Keston Sutherland, Andrea Brady, and Simon Jarvis, to name a few poets of the younger generation — we're faced with a very different conception of poetry. We find ourselves asking a question something like this: what ought we to make of a school of poetry that has a strong public concern, but no appreciable public presence? In Auden's terms, it is a poetry of public faces in private places.

Characteristically, poets of the Cambridge School create a hermetic poetry, circulated outside the regular system of publication among a small group of cognoscenti. In some sense, this is a very private poetry, both in its formal qualities and in its support-culture. On the other hand, the claims for this poetry represent it as anything but private: it is often justified and explained as a poetry with a specific and far-reaching political goal and effect. In this sense, it is profoundly public poetry, at least in theory. The position is inherently contradictory, and is deeply complicated by the refusal on the part of some of the Cambridge School's leading figures to allow their work to be published (that is, to become public) by commercial presses and prominent journals, even when it is sought out by editors. The choice of private publication — quite literally, since some of the most important work of the school has appeared in self-published pamphlets — defies the idea of a poetry of public, political significance.

This is the point for disclaimers, and I will not fail to provide one. I admit there is some debate about how much one can generalize about the Cambridge School of poetry. Not all of the poets are of a uniform view about the relationship of hermetic poetry and political efficacy. In fact, a good place to begin may be with a recent controversy between two poets associated with the Cambridge School, John Wilkinson and Peter Riley. In their debate, conducted over three issues of the *Chicago Review* in 2007, Wilkinson took what I understand to be the more orthodox Cambridge School position about the relationship of poetry and politics, while Riley took the apostate's position, a questioning of the norms of the group from within the group itself.

Although Wilkinson's initial salvo in this exchange took the form of a long review of Simon Jarvis' book-length poem *The Unconditional,* the publication of Jarvis' book was really just the occasion for a more significant project. The real intent of the piece was to introduce the Cambridge School to an American readership heretofore largely unfamiliar with it. Wilkinson begins with a brief description of Jarvis' book, in which he claims (not unreasonably) that *The Unconditional* is one of the most unusual books of poetry ever published. "Imagine if you can," Wilkinson continues, "a continuous poem of 237 pages, mainly in iambic pentameter, in which whole pages pass without a full stop." Jarvis' *The Unconditional,* says Wilkinson, is deeply challenging even to habitual poetry readers, as it is a poem "dedicated to a high level of discourse on prosody, critical theory, and phenomenology; all this conducted in a philosophical language drawing on Adorno's negative dialectics" and "a narrative language that is the unnatural offspring of Wyndham Lewis and P.B. Shelley." Moreover, Wilkinson tells us, the book is filled with a particularly unusual cast of characters. Resembling nothing so much as "refugees from an Iain Sinclair novel finally fed up with walking" and with names like "=x," "Agramant," "Qnuxmuxkyl" and "Jobless," the group starts out on a *Canterbury Tales*–like trip, but winds up in a dingy pub displaying unlikely degrees of alienation and erudition.[2] After this description, however, much of what Wilkinson has to say is really a more general statement of what he takes to be the program of Cambridge poetics.

As described by Wilkinson, one of the most significant elements of this program is the idea of poetry as "a special kind of cognition wherein knowledge and information cannot be distinguished from formal attributes."[3] The language of Jarvis and associated poets is anti-instrumental, and even anti-communicative, refusing to be at the service of communication or conceptual clarity. In a somewhat uncharacteristic passage within *The Unconditional*—a passage as close to authoritative statement as we'll find in a poetry that eschews authoritative statement — Jarvis gives us something close to his poetics, saying that he is

> willing a meaning to the edge of birth
> renewing thought in beating down all dearth
> as when apparently from scraps of noise
> apparently not placed but simply thrown
> or simply falling through the atmosphere
> a non-contingent pressure or a sense
> patterns a ripple....[4]

Poetry, it seems, should avoid giving a clear and paraphrasable meaning, by keeping meaning on "the edge of birth." The "noise" of the poem, with all of its etymological and syntactic disturbances, keeps the patterns of meaning from becoming entirely clear. The goal of a poetry like this, says Wilkinson, is to avoid totalization or transferable meaning, lest it be appropriated into what he (echoing Adorno and the thinkers of the Frankfurt School) calls "administrative reason." All of this argument against utility or total comprehensibility leads to Wilkinson's statement that "aesthetic objects," in their anti-instrumentality, "constitute a special class" of things.

This is a surprising statement, though it wouldn't be surprising coming from the pen of a formalist or an aesthete. If, for example, you're hearing echoes of the American New Criticism, I think you are hearing aright: the contention that we can't separate the cognitive statement of the poem "from formal attributes" sounds a great deal like Cleanth Brooks' argument in "The Heresy of Paraphrase" that it is not possible "to frame a proposition, a statement, which will adequately represent the total meaning of the poem."[5] Moreover, in Wilkinson's words you may hear echoes of an even more venerable tradition — the anti-utilitarian tradition of aestheticism. But there's a big difference between a Wilkinson and a Brooks, or any of a host of other writers who set themselves against paraphrasability and utility one could mention (one thinks of Mallarmé's essay condemning newspapers, or of Oscar Wilde and his "Preface" to *The Picture of Dorian Gray* or his "Decay of Lying"). Unlike those resolutely apolitical writers, Wilkinson insists on describing the work he advocates as a political poetry.

For Wilkinson, a poem can be political by insisting on the inseparability of its significance from its form. By so insisting, the poem embodies a resistance to the idea of being treated as a means to any end beyond itself. It can remain private in circulation and resistant to interpretation because its political role is not to enter the public sphere and persuade readers. Rather, its role is to challenge the kinds of language that are used in public persuasion by providing a counter-example in the form of a very different kind of language. It is, in a sense, an implicit critique of all forms of linguistic instrumentalization. Ideally, it will resist incorporation into any part of the political or economic system (as product, as ideology, as entertainment property).

Of course, ideas such as this are by no means original, nor are they exclusive to Wilkinson or the Cambridge poets he studies and advocates. Behind Wilkinson's insistence on the political relevance of the difficult and elusive work he describes lie sentiments like those of Adorno's famous footnote to *Philosophy of Modern Music*, where he claims that "the closed work of art belongs to the bourgeois ... and the fragmentary work, in its state of complete negativity, belongs to utopia."[6] Indeed, Wilkinson sees Jarvis as upholding an Adorno-inflected "negative utopianism" as "the necessary horizon for art."[7] The insistence on the non-communicative, the non-paraphrasable, and the non-instrumental lies behind a host of techniques associated with the Cambridge School, and is invoked to justify the refusal of mainstream publication and the cultivation of private networks of distribution. We see such an insistence on non-communication in the works of all of the major figures of the Cambridge School, not just in the works of Jarvis, who serves as Wilkinson's representative figure. One common technique is the disruption of traditional sentence structure, in which (to cite the words of the critic Peter Middleton) "syntax retains a haunting awareness of what authoritative statement and authorial sincerity sound like, yet the fragmentation of sense compels this communicative bond to question itself repeatedly."[8] Another common technique (also described by Middleton) involves the creation of complex discursive contexts for individual words, in which it becomes difficult for the reader to know in just what sense a word is meant, since these words come to "carry the full weight of variant meanings and etymological connections" rather than settling into a single, primary denotation.[9] If there is a single dominant technique of the school, however, it involves what we might call a kind of striation of discourses, a mixing of poetic verbal registers with resolutely un-poetic kinds of language — scientific discourse, technocratic forms of language, and the like. We see this technique throughout the work of Jeremy Prynne, which the critic David Shepard has characterized as an attempt to "recombine a language fragmented into technical jargons," incorporating the vocabulary of specialized discourses into his poetry and thereby "return[ing] this knowledge to the public sphere from its sequestration in the ivory tower."[10]

"L'Extase de M. Poher," a poem from the 1971 collection *Brass*, is perhaps the best example of a poem that both displays Prynne's most characteristic techniques and foregrounds his sense of poetry being properly concerned with public, rather than private, matters. The poem begins by invoking private experience, and juxtaposing it with a disorderly public world. In language that eschews syntactic coherence and clear reference to a specific scene, Prynne calls upon images of theatres and gardens — both of which are spaces traditionally reserved for private pleasures. Gardens, of course, are either private preserves or public spaces designed for private recreation, and the French context of the poem invites one to think of Rousseau's take on theatre in the famous *Letter to M. D'Alembert*, in which Rousseau argues that theatre turns the public into a group of passive, atomized individuals privately consuming a spectacle. These spaces are set against disorderly public space: the gardens are surrounded by rubbish-strewn streets with roughly hung telegraph wires. As N.H. Reeve and Richard Kerridge put it in their reading of the poem,

> Gardens are contained pastoral spaces, in which artistic or natural freedoms apparently prevail, but they are decorative spaces in the midst of urban environments less successful in suppressing unwanted residues. Gardens are maintained by the larger social economy as recreation grounds, small worlds of contrived harmony whose connection with the larger economy is concealed.... [T]he "free hand to refuse everything" enjoys an ideal freedom incompatible with any social or political existence. The "alpha rhythm" is an effect which occurs when the brain is idling...."[11]

Prynne's gardens are associated with a kind of pastoral experience: they are places from which one can dismiss larger concerns and the disorderly world of rubbish with a wave of the hand.

Prynne has, however, invoked the world of private, aesthetic, pastoralized experience only to dismiss it. No poetry of private experience will do, for him: he calls such poetry "gabble," and claims it avoids our responsibility to seek out the historical and political conditions of pastoral pleasures.[12]

Against pastoralism, Prynne turns in the remaining parts of the poem to what can best be described as a smashed pile of verbal excerpts from the scientific and technological discourses, and represents a turn to language from outside the sphere of private experience. Rather than embracing any particular scientific or technocratic language, however, Prynne makes a collage of fragments, rendering such language useless and subverting it from its usual instrumental function. Pastoralism of the garden and private life is a false resistance to such discourses of power. For Prynne, the *détournement* and decontextualization of such languages is a more positive engagement of them: he acknowledges them, but refuses to allow them to function in the service of power.

This is, unquestionably, very odd stuff. The poem charges us to leave our gardens of private experience and to engage with and subvert the languages through which the larger world is run (that opening image of telegraph wires foreshadows the poem's later concern with communication). One wonders, though, just what the nature of the poem's politics could be. One might think of this as a kind of Bakhtinian poetry of dialogism and polyvocality (although generally the different kinds of language are collaged together, not associated with different speakers, as in the novels Bakhtin so admired). But critical advocates of this kind of poetry tend to take things further. N.H. Reeve and Richard Kerridge's claim for work of this kind is grandiose, but far from atypical: for them, Cambridge poetry "collide[s] with the powerful instrumental discourses of the culture" with the effect of "smashing them into pieces."[13]

The same critics have also claimed that, in bringing together different kinds of language and placing them in contexts not normally their own, Prynne's work "break[s] out of the institutional space allotted to poetry and literature in late-capitalist culture." This claim is important, and has entered into the most institutionally authoritative accounts of Cambridge School poetry — *The Cambridge History of Twentieth Century Literature*, for example, claims that such poetry "is capable of challenging the public sphere."[14] The claim should give one pause, though, because here we see a certain messianic role claimed for the poetry: it will escape the confines of mere aesthetic entertainment and change the world. This gives rise, or ought to give rise, to a number of questions, such as: *how?* and *for whom?* and *with what demonstrable consequence?*

The messianic role assigned to Cambridge School poetry by its advocates is all the more puzzling when one considers the publication venues and distribution networks that the poets tended to choose for their work. Prynne's publishing career is indicative of the general tendency among these poets to avoid prominent publishing (most poets of the school, argues Peter Barry, "learned their clinically modest stance from Prynne").[15] While the career trajectory of many more mainstream poets involves beginning with modest private printings or fugitive small-press publications, then moving on to larger academic and commercial presses, Prynne's career follows the opposite trajectory. His first collection *Force of Circumstance and Other Poems* appeared in 1962 under the Routledge and Kegan Paul imprint. Rather than celebrating what another kind of poet might see as an auspicious beginning, though, Prynne (who came to see the poems of the collection as too formally conservative) ordered all unsold copies destroyed.[16] Prynne's second book, *Kitchen Poems* (published by Cape Goliard in 1968), was the last work of his to appear from a conventional press until Bloodaxe published *Poems* in 2005. In the interim, nearly 30 small collections appeared from tiny presses such as Equipage, Barque, and Blacksuede Boot Press. Such presses lacked commercial distribution and their books were rarely reviewed by the popular press. Some of Prynne's most important collections, such as 1975's *High Pink on Chrome* and 1983's *The Oval Window* lacked even this degree of public presence and were privately printed and distributed.

It is important to note that this wasn't a matter of a forced exile from the world of larger presses and prominent literary journals, but a deliberate choice on Prynne's part. When Eric Mottram, the head of the prestigious Poetry Society, wrote to Prynne in 1976 asking for work to print in the Society's journal *Poetry Review*, Prynne demurred, writing:

> At the moment I do not have anything suitable, so that I cannot respond very positively; and I must admit that there are times when I do not feel altogether enthusiastic about publishing work in magazines.[17]

Prynne's reticence here is remarkable, especially given the political ambitions of his work, and the reticence isn't merely passing: Prynne refused to let his work be included in the *Oxford Anthology of British and Irish Poetry* edited by Keith Tuma in 2001.

Can poets who choose such marginal venues and who eschew the pursuit of a more popular distribution really "challenge the public sphere"? Can they liberate knowledge from the ivory tower and "return it to the public sphere"? Can they, with such a small reach, smash "the powerful instrumental discourses of the culture" into pieces? For much of its history, Cambridge School poetry seems not so much to have challenged the public sphere, as to have withdrawn from it.

In more recent years, though, the obscurity of the Cambridge School has been mitigated, and it has obtained a rather modest public presence. Peter Barry dates the change from the 1990s, when, he says,

> ... the avant-garde began to establish an above-ground presence, which is to say, one which was visible beyond the parallel infrastructure of low-tech, small-press publication and distribution networks and regionally-based reading circuits. The result is that the "parallel tradition" of poetry now has more of a public identity (see, for instance, the reputation of J.H. Prynne, the success of Salt Publishing, the prominence of online journals like *Jacket*, and the interest in this work from British academics, as evidenced by the British Electronic Poetry Centre at Southampton).[18]

Even these small steps onto the public stage have been greeted with ambivalence from all sides. Representatives of the mainstream press and the Cambridge School alike have expressed skepticism about the development. In 2004, for example, *The Sunday Times* printed an article on Prynne by Maurice Chittenden with the headline "Oxbridge Split by the Baffling Bard." Chittenden's article, occasioned by strong praise for Prynne in a new volume of *The Oxford English Literary History*, began with an image of Prynne as a very private poet, publishing in pamphlets with tiny print runs, before contrasting his work with that of one of the most popular and public figures in modern British poetry, Philip Larkin.[19] The question animating Chittenden's

article is whether one can be a great poet without cultivating a broad readership. Significantly, there is no discussion of the public themes or political
implications of Prynne's work in Chittenden's article. Rather, he chooses to
focus on Prynne's deliberate privacy: "Prynne," writes Chittenden, "shuns
interviews," nor will he allow himself to be photographed for the jackets of
his books. As far as the mainstream press is concerned, it is not Prynne's politics so much as it is his medium of publication and his eschewal of publicity that constitutes Prynne's message.

Ambivalence about the modest public presence of Cambridge School
poetry since the 1990s comes from within the movement, too. One Cambridge
poet, Tony Lopez, takes on the issue of growing publicity in his 2002 poem
"About Cambridge." The poem exhibits one of the signature stylistic features
of Cambridge poetry — the dialogic cross-cutting of different forms of discourse — in this case combining the language of commercial real-estate with
stereotypical images of pastoralized academic privilege. Certainly there's a
political point about the economic basis of such privilege in the poem, but
there's more at work here. From the opening couplet ("About Cambridge they
were never wrong / the old masters...") onwards, much of the Lopez's poem
alludes to Auden's famous "Musée des Beaux Arts," a poem about the private
nature of suffering in a busy and uncaring world. The concern with private
versus public experience comes to the fore in the second half of the poem,
most of which consists of an anaphoric incantation invoking a lost community of Cambridge poets. The idyllic community of poet-radicals seems to
Lopez to have come to an end for a variety of reasons, including death, personal animosity, and significantly, the migration of some of the poets from
the world of privately printed and circulated pamphlets to the larger world
of more prominent, mainstream publishers. The community existed, says
Lopez, "before Kelvin Corcoran left Reality" — that is, before the poet Kelvin
Corcoran left the micro-press Reality Street Editions. It existed before other
poets moved on, too:

> before Jeremy Prynne became a BLOODAXE poet
> before John James was collected by SALT
> before Peter Riley signed a transfer deal to CARCANET[20]

and it existed before Tom Raworth and Rod Mengham went on to their modest public successes, "before the Raworth.com flotation/before Mengham was
re-issued in PENGUIN."[21] For Lopez, the movement toward a public presence by some poets associated with Cambridge is a fall from grace.

A similar ambivalence about the public presence of Cambridge poetry
comes across in a statement by Keston Sutherland, a younger poet of the
Cambridge School with a particular affinity for Prynne (Sutherland received

a doctorate at Cambridge after completing his thesis, *J.H. Prynne and Philology*). In a 2008 discussion on a British Poetry email list devoted to discussion of experimental poetry, Sutherland engaged in an exchange with Chris Hamilton-Emery, the head of Salt Publishing, regarding Prynne's public image. Replying to Hamilton-Emery's claim that Prynne has developed a mystique even among those poetry readers ill-acquainted with his poetry, Sutherland says:

> I suppose that's probably true, but before I went along with it I'd want to distinguish between readers and consumers. It must assuredly be true that lots of people have bought Prynne's books because they think he's a weird or fascinating figure, and I'm sure the great majority of those consumers do take a look inside and maybe get to the end once or even twice. I don't think I'm disparaging that use of the object if I say that for Prynne at least it wouldn't amount to "reading" the book, just as it wouldn't amount to knowing, or looking closely at, a painting if I just lingered in front of it at the National Gallery for a minute or two. On Prynne's terms, at least, and perhaps they are not uncommon among members of this list, being a reader of poetry means engaging closely and carefully with it, staking an intimacy on the work of interpretation, in some way perhaps even needing that intimacy or submitting to it as a sort of definition of oneself, or the component of a definition.[22]

There's a very real resentment here of the kind of reader who reads poetry casually. The only true reader of Prynne, Sutherland implies, is one who devotes his life to Prynne's poetry, letting that devotion become a central part of one's identity.

It is significant that Sutherland doesn't see this kind of intense devotion as something relevant to all kinds of poetry. "Some poetry demands and makes possible that sort of intimacy more than other poetry," he writes. While Sutherland tells us that he imagines many poets "are more interested in readers, even to the no doubt partly pathological extent that they'd prefer three readers to a hundred consumers," he draws a clear line between the poets who merit these true readers and those who'd prefer consumers. "I leave out," he says, "the Andrew Motions and other ditzy glamour models of Oxford." There's a powerful sense of Prynne's work not belonging in the public sphere with that of Andrew Motion and his kind. Like Lopez, Sutherland looks longingly back on a time when Prynne's work (and that of many other Cambridge School poets) was privately published and circulated only among the truly devoted.

Clearly, the Cambridge move toward publicity doesn't sit easily with either the mainstream press or the poets themselves (no matter how public-spirited and political the concerns of those poets may be). As to the messianic role claimed for the poetry, it seems to bear relevance and consequence only for the tiniest of readerships. Such a limited reach isn't in itself of any particular importance — it is, after all, the condition of much poetry. The small size of its audience does present a powerful contradiction, however, if one of the main claims made for the kind of poetry in question is its ability to enter the public sphere and challenge the prevailing ideologies.

This contradiction is, in fact, one of Peter Riley's main concerns in his response to John Wilkinson. Riley challenges Wilkinson's claims for Cambridge School poetry:

> For Wilkinson as for most other commentators on the forward side of things, to speak of poetical virtue is to speak of political virtue, there is no distinction. Poems and poetical thinking are politically good or they have no good in them.... The one big claim left to the poem, that it (rather "somehow") holds the answer or counter to political harm by occulted inference.... It is not just that the poet "knows better" than the working politician ... but that only the poet has the spirit to inhabit the sphere of total oppositional negation which is the only political register to be tolerated. Doesn't this mean that in a sense there is actually a withdrawal from politics, from the politics that happens and can happen, into one that can't possibly? An understanding of how politics works and how amelioration can be wrought through the science of it, of what the mechanisms are and so of what could be done — all this would be beneath us? To assume that you can go straight from aesthetics to ethics is worrying enough, but aren't the two here fused into one substance?[23]

The contradictions of a publicly-concerned poetry that works only by negation and obscurity come to a head here. It isn't just the idea that such poetry doesn't so much engage politics as it withdraws from politics that bothers Riley, either: he's haunted by the sense that poets of this kind have become elitists, unwilling to sully their hands with the practicalities of political struggle. After the passage quoted above comes Riley's *cri de coeur,* directed toward the avant-garde community in which he himself has much standing: "How did we get to be so *haughty?*"[24]

In a reply to Riley in a subsequent issue of *Chicago Review,* Wilkinson's faith in the messianic political power of Cambridge School appears to remain unshaken. He still maintains that the Cambridge mode of combining lyrical language with language from economic, scientific, and technological discourses — a poetry of "lyric writing tied to other modes of writing" — is "more likely to exert a political influence" than more traditional kinds of poetry.[25] While Wilkinson doesn't directly address the question of whether there has been any actual political effect, he does seem to have been sensitized to the issue, and claims that the moment of truth is yet to come. Cambridge poetry, specifically the poetry of younger poets like Keston Sutherland and Andrea Brady, still has the possibility of bringing about real change, says Wilkinson, because "their poetry is being written at a point of historical convergence where it might exercise an incidental political potency."[26]

Wilkinson's view, though, seems more and more beleaguered. Among poets of the Cambridge School, Riley is not alone in his disaffection with the idea that obscure and formally difficult poetry has a significant political role to play. As Andrew Duncan, a poet and former student of Prynne affiliated with the Cambridge School, recently put it, "form as politics" is a "mirage."[27] Such criticism comes, increasingly, from beyond the Cambridge School itself. In the very same issue of *Chicago Review* in which Wilkinson defends himself against Riley, for example, we find a review of Prynne's *To Pollen* in which the author, the American poet Kent Johnson, addresses himself directly to Prynne. After comparing Prynne's project to that of American Language Poetry, Johnson says: "The political impulses of such writing are well rehearsed, and I believe you have done a bit of that yourself. But is it enough? Is it possible avant poetry has begun to hit its head against an increasingly comfortable and welcoming wall?"[28] It's an odd image, that comforting wall against which one hits one's head, but it is an apt one, giving us both the apparent futility of Cambridge School poetry's political ambitions and a sense of the comforting private confinement in which it has so often circulated.

NOTES

1. W.H. Auden, *The Orators: An English Study* (London: Faber and Faber, 1932), 5.

2. John Wilkinson, review of Simon Jarvis' *The Unconditional, Chicago Review* 52: 2/3/4 (2007, 369–375), 370.

3. Ibid.

4. Ibid., 375.

5. Cleanth Brooks, *The Well-Wrought Urn: Studies in the Structure of Poetry* (New York: Harcourt, 1956), 205.

6. Theodor Adorno, *Philosophy of Modern Music*, trans. Anne G. Mitchell and Wesley V. Blomster (London: Continuum, 2003), 126 n55.

7. Wilkinson, review, 371.

8. Peter Middleton, "Poetry After 1970," *The Cambridge History of Twentieth Century Literature*, ed. Laura Marcus and Peter Nicholls (Cambridge: Cambridge University Press, 2004, 768–86), 782–3.

9. Ibid., 783.

10. David Shepard, review of J.H. Prynne's *The Furtherance, Verse* online supplement, 20 October 2004 *http://versemag.blogspot.com/2004/10/new-review-of-jh-prynne.html*.

11. N.H. Reeve and Richard Kerridge, *Nearly Too Much: The Poetry of J.H. Prynne*, (Liverpool: Liverpool University Press, 1995), 8.

12. Jeremy Prynne, *Poems* (Highgreen: Bloodaxe, 2005), 161.

13. Reeve and Kerridge, *Nearly Too Much*, 9.

14. Middleton, "Poetry After 1970," 770.

15. Peter Barry, *Poetry Wars: British Poetry of the 1970s and the Battle of Earls Court* (Cambridge: Salt, 2006), 158.

16. Paul March-Russell, "J.H. Prynne," *The Literary Encyclopedia*, 21 January 2005 <http://www.litencyc.com/php/speople.php?rec=true&UID=5881>.

17. Letter from J.H. Prynne to Eric Mottram, June 22, 1976. The Eric Mottram Collection, King's College, London (Archive Reading Room, Room 302, Strand). Document: Mottram 4/2/52.

18. Barry, *Poetry Wars*, 179.

19. Maurice Chittenden, "Oxbridge Split by the Baffling Bard," *The Sunday Times*, Feb. 22, 2004 <http://www.timesonline.co.uk/tol/news/uk/article1026513.ece>.

20. Tony Lopez, "About Cambridge," *Jacket* 20, December 2002 <http://jacketmagazine.com/20/lopez-about.html>.

21. Ibid.

22. Quoted in Robert Archambeau, "Fit Audience Though Few: Cambridge Poetry and its Readers," *Samizdat Blog*, July 2, 2008 <http://samizdatblog.blogspot.com/2008_07_02_archive.html>.

23. Peter Riley, Letter to the Editor, *Chicago Review* 53: 1 (2007, 221–227), 222.

24. Ibid.

25. John Wilkinson, Letter to the Editor, *Chicago Review* 53: 2/3 (2007, 231–238), 231.

26. Ibid., 232.

27. Andrew Duncan, *The Failure of Conservatism in Modern British Poetry* (Cambridge: Salt, 2003), 244.

28. Kent Johnson, review of Jeremy Prynne's *To Pollen, Chicago Review* 53: 2/3 (2007, 218–225), 223.

WORKS CITED

Adorno, Theodor (2003). *Philosophy of Modern Music.* Trans. Anne G. Mitchell and Wesley V. Blomster. London: Continuum.

Archambeau, Robert (2008). "Fit Audience Though Few: Cambridge Poetry and its Readers." *Samizdat Blog* (2 July). <http://www.samizdat blog.blogspot.com/2008_07_02_archive.html>.

Auden, W.H. (1932). *The Orators: An English Study.* London: Faber and Faber.

Barry, Peter (2006). *Poetry Wars: British Poetry of the 1970s and the Battle of Earls Court.* Cambridge: Salt.

Brooks, Cleanth (1956). *The Well-Wrought Urn: Studies in the Structure of Poetry.* New York: Harcourt.

Chittenden, Maurice (2004). "Oxbridge Split by the Baffling Bard." *The Sunday Times* (22 Feb). <http://www.timesonline.co.uk/tol/news/uk/article1026513.ece>.

Duncan, Andrew (2003). *The Failure of Conservatism in Modern British Poetry.* Cambridge: Salt.

Johnson, Kent (2007). Review of Jeremy Prynne's *To Pollen. Chicago Review* 53: 2/3, 218–225.

Lopez, Tony (2002). "About Cambridge." *Jacket* 20 (1 Dec.). <http://jacketmagazine.com/20/lopez-about.html>.

Mallarmé, Stéphane (1992). "The Book: A Spiritual Instrument." *Critical Theory Since Plato.* Ed. Hazard Adams. New York: Harcourt, 674–676.

March-Russell, Paul (2005). "J.H. Prynne." *The Literary Encyclopedia* (21 Jan.). <http://www.litencyc.com/php/speople.php?rec=true&UID=5881>.

Middleton, Peter (2004). "Poetry After 1970." *The*

Cambridge History of Twentieth Century Literature. Ed. Laura Marcus and Peter Nicholls. Cambridge: Cambridge University Press, 768–86.

Prynne, Jeremy (1976). Unpublished letter to Eric Mottram, June 22, 1976. The Eric Mottram Collection, King's College, London (Archive Reading Room, Room 302, Strand). Document: Mottram 4/2/52.

———— (2005). *Poems.* Highgreen: Bloodaxe.

Reeve, N.H., and Richard Kerridge (1995), *Nearly Too Much: The Poetry of J.H. Prynne.* Liverpool: Liverpool University Press.

Riley, Peter (2007). Letter to the Editor. *Chicago Review,* 53:1, 221–227.

Rousseau, Jean-Jacques (1960). *Letter to M. D'Alembert on the Theater.* Trans. Allan Bloom. Ithaca: Cornell University Press.

Shepard, David (2004). Review of J.H. Prynne's *The Furtherance. Verse* (20 Oct.). <http://versemag.blogspot.com/2004/10/new-review-of-jh-prynne.html>.

Sutherland, Keston (2004). *J.H. Prynne and Philology.* Unpublished PhD thesis, Cambridge University.

Wilde, Oscar (1992). "The Decay of Lying." *Critical Theory Since Plato.* Ed. Hazard Adams. New York: Harcourt, 658–670.

———— (2003). "Preface." *The Picture of Dorian Gray.* Ed. Isobel Murray. New York: Barnes and Noble, xxiii–xxv.

Wilkinson, John (2007). Review of Simon Jarvis' *The Unconditional. Chicago Review,* 52: 2/3/4, 369–375.

———— (2007). Letter to the Editor. *Chicago Review,* 53:2/3, 231–238.

3. Ted Hughes as Poet Laureate: The Beast and the Sovereign

Laurel Peacock

I kill where I please because it is all mine—Ted Hughes, "Hawk Roosting," 1960[1]

Like kingly sovereignty, poetic sovereignty is paradoxically both public and unaccountable to public taste; it is even expected to transgress and remap those boundaries. A Poet Laureate must perform poetic interiority publicly, if it is to be performed. As such, when considering the dynamics of the public-private divide, the Laureateship troubles any easy division. In this essay, I intend to develop a figural reading of the Poet Laureate as constructed out of the raw materials of the nonhuman and explore theories of sovereignty, particularly in relation to Ted Hughes' body of work.

The above line from "Hawk Roosting" articulates the pure sovereignty of a predator at the top of the food chain, soaring above the field of lesser beings; all beneath the hawk are subject to his will in choosing who will become his next meal. It also allegorizes the poetic sovereignty of the public post of Poet Laureate. As part of Hughes' oeuvre, this line occupied the Laureateship — the humanist public role *par excellence*— and advanced the perspective of a sovereign subject above the law, and it is "spoken" by an animal. Animals are hierarchically constructed in humanist thought as being lower on the food chain — indeed beneath and subject to — the human sovereign, and yet Hughes uses animals both to voice and to trouble such sovereignty. The importance of the animal in the poetry and figure of Hughes situates the humanist public post of Post Laureate in the context of posthumanism. As a consequence, the role comes to occupy a peculiar position that is both eminently public and entirely beyond the public-private divide.

In 1984, Ted Hughes was crowned Poet Laureate. On this occasion, Hughes was lauded by Seamus Heaney as "beyond, and other than, the usual literary animal."[2] Provoked by this claim, I want to examine Hughes' Laureateship through critical questions of animal studies, a field informed by feminist science studies (Haraway) and posthumanism (Wolfe) that brings philosophy face-to-face with animal others. I will begin by examining the historical figuration of the role of Poet Laureate in the Daphne myth, as this is a foundational myth for a public role that claims aesthetic supremacy through its use of nature. Then I will consider the implications of Hughes occupying such a position of sovereignty in relation to poetry, and characterize him as an agent of poetic change rather than a follower of convention (all according to certain critical paradigms). Here I bring in Derrida's analysis of sovereignty in "La bête et le souverain" ("The Beast and the Sovereign") relating his analysis specifically to poetic authority. Finally, I consider Hughes' appropriations of the animals of his poems; following Derrida, I argue that the animals, in being depicted as "beneath" social law and incapable of response and public responsibility, uncannily resemble Hughes himself, who in the eminently public role of Poet Laureate is above the laws of poetry and according to critical paradigm, unaccountable to the ordinary poetic responsibility often ascribed to the post. While Hughes wrote animal poems well before becoming Poet Laureate, his occupation of this role placed the poems in a new position. This unaccountability, in the case of Hughes, comes not from a claim to privacy, but more radically from the use of the figure of the animal, which confounds any one division between the public and the private.

In speaking of the Poet Laureate as sovereign poet, I mean to refer not only to his appointed sovereignty over nature (royal license to use it as "material" for signification), but also to refer to the history of the post in its granting by and connection to the Sovereign of England. Although Seamus Heaney comments that the post "seemed to imply a civic function for the poet," I argue that, rather than a civic function (responsible to and serving the public), the role has its own kind of symbolic sovereignty.[3] For Hughes, according to the estimation of his critics, that poetic sovereignty took the form of a certain modernist view of poetic invention as a breaking of the rules, an individualistic refusal of convention (especially conventional morality). As one critic writes of Hughes, "He prefers to go beneath and beyond society."[4]

The categories of public and private are fraught territory for feminist theory, and some of the insights from this area of inquiry apply here. Is it a coincidence that poetry's most public face has been masculine, that its paradigmatic public role for poetry, that of Poet Laureate, was occupied in Britain solely by men throughout its 400-year history until 2009? In asking such a question I want to do more than simply point out an unfortunate exclusion that can be remedied by including women in the institution, as has been done in the U.S. and now in Great Britain with the appointment of Carol Ann Duffy. Instead, I seek to examine the deep structure of carnophallogocentrism

(Derrida's term for the symbolic primacy of carnivorous virility) in this public role, a structure that implicates and makes use of not only the feminine, but the nonhuman, as raw material for the construction of public masculine poetic sovereignty.

Many feminists have troubled the self-evidence of the public-private divide by pointing out that the private sphere is far from a solace for women, who are often both restricted to representing the merely private and at the same time heavily monitored and restricted in how their lives in the private realm are performed. Yet at the same time, the public realm is off limits to all but the most virile and aggressive performances from women, suggesting that the public realm, like the private, is gendered — and moreover, that it is not really accessible other than through assumptions of symbolic power. Further, we can consider to what degree the feminine is constituted as an outside to *both* the realms of public and private. Just as in Derrida, the beast is beneath the law and the sovereign is above it, so too the feminine resists easy inclusion in the realms of either the public or the private, which are both domains of the symbolic law.

Hannah Arendt initiated the consideration of the public-private divide that would be taken up by poststructuralist feminists. Judith Butler offers a deep critique of the supposed neutrality of the construction of the public sphere, writing of Arendt's definition:

> Arendt, of course, problematically distinguished the public and the private, arguing that in classical Greece the former alone was the sphere of the political, that the latter was mute, violent, and based on the despotic power of the patriarch. Of course, she did not explain how there might be a prepolitical despotism, or how the "political" must be expanded to describe the status of a population of the less than human, those who were not permitted into the interlocutory scene of the public sphere where the human is constituted through words and deeds and most forcefully constituted when its word becomes its deed. What she failed to read in *The Human Condition* was precisely the way in which the boundaries of the public and political sphere were secured through the production of a constitutive outside.[5]

Butler here asks how, according to any feminist critique of patriarchal despotism in the private realm, the private realm could possibly be understood as nonpolitical, and therefore according to Arendt's terms, public. Conversely, the public realm depends on a limit to give it meaning, and this limit is often gendered through images of feminine domesticity, as correlative to private interiority. The feminine, then, along with the animal, is not just a human subject inhabiting the private realm, but rather is made up of what is abjected from the public realm altogether: paradoxically, it is not constituted as an entirely human subject. Butler is speaking in a philosophical tradition distinct from

rights or legal discourse (e.g., Catharine A. MacKinnon's *Are Women Human?*),
in which exclusion from the order of the human is both chronicled and fought;
her discussion of ways in which the rights-bearing humanist subject is constructed instead calls attention to the exclusions inherent in the human public realm.

Since Aristotle, the human has been constructed as the "political animal."
As Derrida points out, such a construction ironically relies on the animal, on
the materiality of all that is abjected from full human subjectivity, for its very
being. Humanist institutions like the Laureateship can be theorized in this
way as well: as mythically constructed from the raw materials of laurel leaves,
lovely goddesses, and frolicking animals, and yet excluding these others from
the proper subjectivity of the role. While women and animals are othered in
different ways at different times, poetry often links the feminine with the realm
of nature and animals. Neither private nor public, the animals of Hughes'
poems speak a human sovereignty that is not their own; neither, then, is it
fully human. If this is true of the Poet Laureateship, traditionally the highest
humanist artistic honor, then even here, as Donna Haraway writes, "we have
never been human."[6]

These issues of the exclusion of the feminine from constructions of the
human subject are at play in the different constructions of poetic authorship
in Ted Hughes's and Sylvia Plath's reception histories. Hughes, as Poet Laureate, is constructed as having a public role in rhetorical contrast to a woman
poet who is considered too private for such a role and labeled "confessional."
Hughes has been figured repeatedly in opposition to Plath's supposedly minor
or confessional poetry. In his introduction to Plath's collected works, for
example, Harold Bloom minimizes Plath's contribution to poetry in order to
celebrate, in pointed juxtaposition, the voice of Hughes as one that can properly speak for a public, a nation.

Sarah Churchwell examines the construction of public-private around
these two poets to document how it unfolded in criticism and the academy.
Churchwell argues that Hughes, in *Birthday Letters*, constructs a "private"
correspondence with Plath through rhetorical techniques to produce an "'open
secret,' a volume hesitating uneasily between disclosure and encryption, unset-
tled by its inability to fix the boundaries between public and private."[7] All of
this, of course, happens in the public realm of publication and publicity, the
realm eminently available to, indeed presided over, by the Poet Laureate. In
contrast, any revelation about Plath is preconditioned to be "private" by her
critical reception history. Plath has been accused of drawing inordinately from
her "private" life, and of being both more famous and more artistically sus-
pect for it. Churchwell writes, "Plath's authority — both authorship and
power — hovers uncertainly between public and private, as many public

accounts seek to undermine her iconic status by locating it in the private, feminine, trivialized realm of 'glamour'"[8]— or madness, one might add. Such authority, by contrast, is never challenged in Hughes, despite (as Churchwell outlines) his occasional use of similar constructions of interiority and privacy, and despite Plath's mythological and dramatic registers.

It is clearly more than these two poets' deployment of tropes of the public and the private that determines their different reception histories; rather, they are both subject to a gendered division of public from private that grants male poets a public role while consistently determining women's poetry to be private. Critics such as Harold Bloom are not acting in isolation, but are reflecting a poetic order in which women's writing can never completely escape suspicion as being addressed to a more private audience, in a more limited capacity, and by a less universal subject. Keeping in mind the domestic role forced on Plath by some critics, I will examine the laureateship of Hughes in the context of this phallogocentric order.

The Laureateship is a system for the production of poetic sovereignty, and it has tended (till 2009) to exclude subjects who are never fully sovereign, such as women. This sovereignty does not mean, of course, that a Poet Laureate ever has much real political power, or even that women will always be excluded from the role; it only begins to explain how this has been the case for 400 years of the post's history in Great Britain. The Poet Laureate is only sovereign in relation to the rules of poetry, crowned by the state and by critics as the one licensed to break rules and change them. Such sovereignty represents a use of the symbolic that has been figured as a masculine form of power.

Hughes' poetic virility, in this critical parlance, is said to place him outside of social convention. For Heaney, "Hughes's appointment breaks the mould,"[9] and his role is compared to that of sovereign: "The England he physically inhabits and the one he imaginatively embraces is old, the land of King Harold and King Alfred and King Arthur."[10] Here his only responsibility is considered to be to sovereignty itself (not even to living kings, let alone the queen, but to ancient kingship), and Hughes is celebrated for being above social or political concerns, "without a word to say on contemporary politics but with a strong trust in the pre-industrial realities of the natural world."[11] Now, rather than contest these ideological accounts of Hughes' sovereignty by showing how he is actually indebted to social convention (which could be done), I think it more interesting to consider the investments that cast Hughes in this sovereign role. The animal speakers of Hughes' poetry are indispensable to his figuration as sovereign; they are used to say something about the human, and yet in doing so they mock the human as reliant on them.

This figuration of the Poet Laureate as sovereign poet goes back to the

earliest articulations of the role. The perhaps socially vestigial and yet powerfully ideological public role of Poet Laureate invokes the tradition of honoring a poet with a laurel crown, symbolizing the successful "immortalization"
of his verse (we might now prefer to call it the inclusion of his verse in the
nation's public archive). Resisting this symbolic use of the laurel crown for a
moment, however, let us remember the Daphne story that makes the laurel
crown available as such a symbol. Ovid's treatment of Daphne's transformation dramatizes the way Apollo wrested "consent" from nature. Apollo's pursuit of Daphne is compared to the chase of prey by predator in nature; however,
the attempted rape is used later in a distinctly cultural narrative of conquest
and sovereignty over nature. While she is "saved" by her father from being
raped, Daphne's agency in resisting Apollo is cancelled by her transformation.
Nevertheless, Apollo reads the movements of the laurel tree as signifying consent to his violation and to his symbolic use of her new form. He addresses
the tree:

> "Since you cannot be my bride, surely you will at least be my tree. My hair, my
> lyre, my quivers will always display the laurel. You will accompany the generals
> of Rome, when the Capitol beholds their long triumphal processions, when joy-
> ful voices raise the song of victory. You will stand by Augustus' gateposts too
> [...]. Further, as my head is ever young, my tresses never shorn, so do you also,
> at all times, wear the crowning glory of never-fading foliage." Paen, the healer,
> had done: the laurel tree inclined her new made branches, and seemed to nod
> her leafy head, as if it were a head, in consent.[12]

Ever after, the tree's leaves are displayed to symbolize nature's forced consent,
not only to rulers and soldiers, but also to the poet's vision of land and nation
at his moment of victory. The laurel leaves are appropriated from nature to
symbolize sovereign power in certain fields of human culture. This gendered
origin story of public authority in poetic accomplishment (among other things)
uses a violated, feminized nature to confer authority and power on a virile,
masculine poet in a display of sovereignty.

Petrarch, crowned the first poet laureate by some accounts (in an early,
non-official instance of the role in 1341), made extensive use of the symbolism
of the laurel crown in his poetry, as if to cement the connection between the
symbol and his poetic sovereignty — one that would later be exploited in the
official use of the title in Britain beginning in 1670. He further establishes this
connection by calling his beloved Laura. In the following lines from poem 23
of the *Canzoniere*, Petrarch makes a claim for poetic power, figuring his poetic
immortality through his own transformation into the laurel tree. He alters the
story to cast himself in the role of Daphne, pursued and threatened by Eros
and by Laura, who are said to have "transformed me into what I am, making
me of a living man a green laurel that loses no leaf for all the cold season."[13]

The point I want to make here involves a shift in interpretive practice that comes from the emergent field of posthumanism or animal studies. Uses of violated nature like Petrarch's above, central to humanism in its placement of the bounded human subject at the center of the universe, are no longer so easily subsumed into their symbolic function. Until recently, the use of the living in fables could be accepted as unproblematic if quaint; however, fables have come to seem more like a form of appropriation. Derrida cautions that fables are a "*mettre en scène des vivants*"[14] — a staging of the living — for use by progressive humanist narratives, to make known ideologies of the powerful. While in humanist interpretation, there was a tendency to read symbolically or metaphorically to bolster humanist values (in this case the celebration of the power of poetry to "immortalize" human culture), in posthumanist interpretation there is a return to the scene of the originary appropriation that makes this kind of message possible, and a consideration of the living there appropriated. Rather than stopping at this rather bleak scene in the woods, however, posthumanist interpretation may ask to what degree the living resist being subsumed into the humanist project, or even make humanism strange to itself by inhabiting its center. In this case, the strangely transformed prey of Apollo's / Petrarch's pursuit, Laura/Daphne, morphs into pursuer, and the poet himself morphs into tree form. He is transformed by this otherness, no longer human, at the very moment he makes a claim of immortality, central to humanism. The Daphne fable is both used by and changes Petrarch. The poet's appropriation of nature is most marked when he exercises his sovereign right as poet, as supreme maker of human culture, but it is then that his dependence on the living is most keenly felt. All of this is to say that the public post of Poet Laureate is figured through the appropriation of the nonhuman, casting doubt on the possibility of response or responsibility at the center of the role.

Once this appropriation of nature has happened, once he is crowned, the Poet Laureate has the sovereign power to stand above and outside of poetic convention. Analogously to what Derrida calls, echoing a La Fontaine fable, "la droit du plus fort" (the right of the strongest, or might is right), the poet's use of poetic power means that he decides what is right or just, rather than complying with public opinion on such decisions. But in being outside of the laws of poetry, the Poet Laureate mirrors uncannily the other being outside of the law, the beast who inhabits his poetry. Derrida explains in "La bête et le souverain" that the sovereign has the power to suspend the law as well as to make and change the law, and that the sovereign's exceptional right is to place himself above the law or to risk becoming the worst, most brutal beast in disrespecting it. Derrida writes, "*le souverain et la bête semblent avoir en commun leur être-hors-la-loi*"[15] (the sovereign and the beast seem to have in common their being-outside-the-law),[16] both failing to respect the law, either from above or beneath its purview, and ultimately remaining outside the law. In this regard, the beast and the sovereign are troublingly similar; they are uncannily familiar, and there is complicity between them as well. The sovereign, like the beast, is outside the law in his right not to respond, and in this he seems a bit beastly.

There are other ways than the Daphne myth to use a *mettre en scène des vivants*. Sovereign power sometimes masquerades in the guise of the animals of fables and evades the responsibility to the social that may otherwise accompany stories so treated. Writing of the fable of the wolf and the lamb, Derrida argues that when animals are used in fables, "*La force du loup est d'autant plus forte, voire souveraine, elle a d'autant plus raison de tout que le loup n'est pas là, qu'il n'y a pas le loup lui-même*"[17] (The force of the wolf is that much stronger, even sovereign, it is that much more right for the fact that the wolf is not there, that it is not the wolf himself). The animals of Hughes' poems are not the naturalistically described animals themselves, but masks for the sovereign, who is masquerading in animal form. As a consequence, Hughes and his poems are often described as animals or in animalistic terms: Stan Smith, for example, writes, "Hughes' own poems are wolf-masks."[18] Hughes, the sovereign poet, gazes out from behind the wolf masks of his poems, from behind the fables.

"Hawk Roosting" (1960), written well before Hughes' appointment as Poet Laureate, illustrates his use of animals as a way of existing outside of response and responsibility to tell a fable of his own sovereignty. The poem is widely anthologized, and it contains one of Hughes' most overt constructions of sovereignty through animal mythology. In this poem, the hawk boasts, "I kill where I please because it is all mine."[19] As sovereign being, this animal has no need to justify himself, arguing that he needs no justification to assert his right to kill, to choose his prey. Manners, argument, and sophistry are all literally beneath him. Uncannily mirroring a king exerting *la droit du plus fort*, this hawk's bloodthirstiness serves as a mocking cry. Kinglike, hunterlike, but issuing from an "animal" consciousness, the poem challenges the primacy of the human by underlining how the human is constructed, after all, of an amalgam of "animal" traits and behaviors, no one of which can provide the definitive dividing line between two realms. Human sovereignty, this poem implies, is no more than the belief of the right of a top predator to act without deliberation or justification — as a dictator, in fact.

In the collection *Crow* (1970), Hughes establishes a relationship of fraught complicity between Crow, the speaker of the poems, and God, the collection's other major figure. Crow represents a being outside of the law and is mirrored in the poet as sovereign. One might expect that God would figure as the sovereign of the poems, but God actually figures more as an Oedipal father figure for the crow to mock and disappoint. In "Crow's First Lesson," God and Crow conspire to try to create humans and take on the roles of impotent do-gooder (God) and nihilist trickster (Crow). "God tried to teach crow how to talk,"[20] but instead, Crow resists, producing a scene of a botched creation in which a man is strangled in a rebirth, causing despair. Crow here plays a trick by ignoring the Law of the Father and creating a fable that produces a certain view of the human, in this case a male subject strangled and limited by a woman's body. This scene echoes the biblical account of original sin, and although it acts here in the service of Hughes' anti-theology, it is accomplished at the expense of women.

Pascal Aquien's analysis of "Crow and the Birds" similarly argues for the Crow's function as an outside to the ordinary rules of the symbolic law. Crow's cries constitute "*le refus de ce qui, au nom de la loi symbolique, celle en particulier du langage qui implique que la relation du sujet à l'objet ne soit pas immédiate, vient interdire l'absolu de la jouissance*"[21] (the refusal of that which, in the name of the symbolic law, that in particular of language that implies that the relation of subject to object will not be immediate, comes to forbid the absolute of jouissance). Crow is in a position outside the law, able to refuse the interdictions and repressive power of the symbolic order. His cry represents "*la crudité et la pulsion contre l'ordre symbolique*"[22] (the rawness and the drive against the symbolic order) that is contrasted with the socialized roles of other birds described in strangely banal human terms, as in the line, "the peewit tumbled clear of the Laundromat."[23] Aquien explains Hughes' crudeness of diction "*comme critique des constructions — esthétiques et éthiques — ordinaires*"[24] (as critique of ordinary constructions — esthetic and ethical); again, the ordinary rules of social expression are depicted as merely an obstacle for Hughes to sail above, like the Hawk, or to mock, like the Crow.

In another poem from the collection, "Crow Goes Hunting," however, Crow exercises a sovereign poetic power with words, using words like weapons. Taking aim at a series of targets, Crow "turned the words into shotguns, they shot down the starlings."[25] Each new target that transforms to escape Crow's blast requires a new weapon, in the end commanding Crow's respect and admiration. Here the power of the symbolic, the power of words spoken by the Crow, is granted by the sovereign poet. As in "Crow and the Birds," references to discordant discourses appear in this poem. The "bombs," the "concrete bunker," and the "reservoir" could be cited as evidence of postmodern play; however, as well as being jarring and playful, these terms are distinctly human, making it clear that Crow is not *a crow*, but a symbol used to naturalize human destructiveness.

Is there a way to read against the grain of a Crow poem and instead of arriving at another *telos*, another "message" about humanity, to return to the appropriation that makes the poem's "message" possible? What is the problem with mobilizing the living symbolically? Aquien demonstrates a way in which Crow can be thought of simultaneously as the animal disguise for the human sovereign (as I have argued), *and* as the radical outside to the human subject, as a drive against the symbolic that inhabits his core. The playfulness and the chaotic, antisocial impulses of Crow can be thought of as representing the incursion of the semiotic realm into the symbolic — as happens, paradoxically, when the poems' God (the Law of the Father) tries to make use of the living to play out scenes of human sovereignty. The living resist, miss the point, exceed symbolic roles. An incursion of such beastliness into scenes of human creation is closely accompanied by the monstrous feminine in the Crow poems, underscoring the connection between the animal and the feminine in that they are both radical outsides to the human order, public or private.

This essay has tried to suggest that animals, rather than functioning as pure symbol with no remainder, exceed the uses to which they are put in expressions of human mastery of nature. They do more than allegorize; they mimic and mock. The poetry of Ted Hughes, Poet Laureate and animal poet, exemplifies such a dynamic; animals are used to express sovereignty in a humanist public role, and yet they escape such a use, pacing uneasily around the clearing in the woods that delineates both the public and the private realms of the human.

NOTES

1. Ted Hughes, "Hawk Roosting," *Collected Poems*, ed. Paul Keegan (New York: Faber and Faber, 2004), 69.

2. Seamus Heaney, "The New Poet Laureate," *Critical Essays on Ted Hughes*, ed. Leonard M. Scigaj (New York: Hall, 1992), 45–6.

3. Ibid., 45.

4. Frederick Grubb in *Critical Essays on Ted Hughes*, ed. Leonard M. Scigaj (New York: Hall, 1992), 131.

5. Judith Butler, *Antigone's Claim: Kinship Between Life and Death* (New York: Columbia University Press, 2000), 81–2.

6. Donna Haraway, *When Species Meet* (Minneapolis: University of Minnesota Press, 2008), 1.

7. Sarah Churchwell, "Secrets and Lies: Privacy, Publication and Ted Hughes' 'Birthday Letters,'" *Contemporary Literature* 42.1 (2001), 102–148.

8. Ibid., 108.

9. Seamus Heaney, "The New Poet Laureate," *Critical Essays on Ted Hughes*, ed. Leonard M. Scigaj (New York: Hall, 1992), 45.

10. Ibid., 46.

11. Ibid.

12. Ovid, *Metamorphoses*, trans. Mary M. Innes (New York: Penguin, 1995), 43–4.

13. Ibid., 60.

14. Jacques Derrida, "La bête et le souverain," *La démocratie a venir: Autour de Jacques Derrida*, ed. Marie-Louise Mallet (Paris: Galilee, 2004), 458.

15. Ibid., 445.

16. This and subsequent translations are my own.

17. Derrida, "La bête et le souverain," 437.

18. Stan Smith, in *Critical Essays on Ted Hughes*, ed. Leonard M. Scigaj (New York: Hall, 1992), 81.

19. Ted Hughes in *Collected Poems*, ed. Paul Keegan (New York: Faber and Faber, 2004), 69.

20. Ibid., 211.

21. Pascal Aquien, "Le cru et le cri: 'Crow and the Birds' (*Crow*, 1970), de Ted Hughes," *Etudes britanniques contemporaines* 24 (2003), 31–43, 41.

22. Ibid., 41.

23. Ted Hughes in *Collected Poems*, ed. Paul Keegan (New York: Faber and Faber, 2004), 210.
24. Aquien, "Le cru et le cri," 32.

25. Ted Hughes, *Collected Poems*, ed. Paul Keegan (New York: Faber and Faber, 2004), 236.

WORKS CITED

Aquien, Pascal (2003). "Le cru et le cri: 'Crow and the Birds' (*Crow*, 1970), de Ted Hughes." *Etudes britanniques contemporaines* 24, 31–43.

Bloom, Harold (ed.) (1989). *Sylvia Plath*. New York: Chelsea House.

Butler, Judith (2000). *Antigone's Claim: Kinship Between Life and Death*. New York: Columbia University Press.

Churchwell, Sarah (2001). "Secrets and Lies: Privacy, Publication and Ted Hughes' 'Birthday Letters.'" *Contemporary Literature*, 42.1, 102–148.

Derrida, Jacques (2004). "La bête et le souverain." *La démocratie a venir: Autour de Jacques Derrida*. Ed. Marie-Louise Mallet. Paris: Galilee.

Durling, Robert M., trans. (2006). *Petrarch's Lyric Poems: The* Rime sparse *and Other Lyrics*. Cambridge: Harvard University Press.

Haraway, Donna (2008). *When Species Meet*. Minneapolis: University of Minnesota Press.

Heaney, Seamus (1992). "The New Poet Laureate." *Critical Essays on Ted Hughes*. Ed. Leonard M. Scigaj. New York: Hall.

Hughes, Ted (2004). *Collected Poems*. Ed. Paul Keegan. New York: Faber and Faber.

Jed, Stephanie H. (1989). *Chaste Thinking: The Rape of Lucrece and the Birth of Humanism*. Indianapolis: Indiana University Press.

MacKinnon, Catharine A. (2006). *Are Women Human? And Other International Dialogues*. London: Harvard University Press.

Ovid (1995). *Metamorphoses*. Trans. Mary M. Innes. New York: Penguin.

Smith, Stan (1992). "Wolf Masks: The Early Poetry of Ted Hughes." *Critical Essays on Ted Hughes*. Ed. Leonard M. Scigaj. New York: Hall.

Walcott, Derek. (1992). "Medusa Face." *Critical Essays on Ted Hughes*. Ed. Leonard M. Scigaj. New York: Hall.

Wolfe, Cary (2003). *Animal Rites: American Culture, the Discourse of Species, and Posthumanist Theory*. Chicago: University of Chicago Press.

4. R.S. Thomas: Poet of the Threshold

Daniel Szabo

Not many photographs of R.S. Thomas have survived his desire for — or even what some might term his public obsession with — privacy. One of them, however, is emblematic of his character and symbolizes most adequately the public-private divide in his works. It shows an elderly Thomas leaning out of the half-door of his cottage at Sarn, resolutely inside, frowning, puzzled or startled as if reluctant to come out to meet the intruder and yet resting on one elbow as if in the middle of an informal chat.[1] This photograph represents many of Thomas's contradictions as well as the mystery surrounding him. Christopher Morgan, in his comprehensive study *R.S. Thomas: Identity, Environment, and Deity*, underlines the contradictions and paradoxes that characterize the divide between the public and the private in both Thomas the man and in his poetry:

> In answer to the questions one discovers the life of the man, rife with tensions, straddling paradox: a priest grappling with despair, a pacifist-nationalist, an activist-poet ardent for his second tongue. Thomas has been the quiet man embroiled in public controversy, the private man of outspoken causes, the shy man feared for the heat of his convictions.[2]

Despite or, more likely, because of these paradoxes, R.S. Thomas was undoubtedly Wales's most prominent poet of the second half of the twentieth century. He was the first member of the clergy to receive the Queen's Gold Medal for poetry in 1964 and was nominated for the Nobel Prize in 1996. In 1986 — the year he was on the English literature A-level syllabus — at a time when poetry books did not sell well, he sold twenty thousand copies of a paperback edition of his *Selected Poems* and over nine thousand of each of his last four books of poetry.[3] He was known for his elegies for Welsh nature and his depiction of the hardships endured by the Welsh peasant, as well as for his constant struggle with an absent God, materialized in his struggle with words. Thomas was a priest in the Anglican Church in Wales, a nationalist-yet-pacifist who once notoriously said after the bombing of English-owned holiday houses in rural Wales in 1998: "What is one death against the death of the whole Welsh nation?"[4] He was a Welsh nationalist who spoke with an exaggerated English accent and sent his son to a public school in England, an Anglo-Welsh poet who hated the term "Anglo-Welsh" and despised the English language almost as much as he despised the English invader. As his first biographer Justin Wintle puts it: "Anyone who is a poet *and* an Anglican priest *and* a Welsh nationalist must, to the casual contemporary English or anglicized Welsh onlooker at least, seem definably odd."[5]

R.S. Thomas was a private man who avoided photographers, journalists, and literary salons and preferred to go bird watching in north Wales or in Sweden, Norway and Spain. Yet he had a public role as one of the foremost poets of his time and as a minister of the Church. He was forced to speak regularly in public however uncomfortable it made him feel, as he confessed in his third-person autobiography: "He couldn't deal with a bishop, let alone a committee. He was unable to argue, he was much less formidable than people thought, and very nervous in public, even preaching."[6]

When Justin Wintle approached Thomas about writing his biography, his response was both aggressive and amusing: he did not wish for a biography, especially if its author was not a Welsh speaker. His response was published in a newspaper: "I don't want fingers poked into my life. I don't know what they can unearth. I've never murdered anybody or robbed a bank."[7] Wintle nevertheless went ahead with his biography and argued in the preface that it is "hardly the case that R.S. Thomas is a blushing violet hidden away from the world [...]. If Thomas finds himself in the public eye, it is because he has put himself there."[8] This paradoxical position is the fate of many poets, especially one whose work is as strongly autobiographical and as popular as Thomas's. What could biographers and scholars unearth since, as his second biographer Byron Rogers puts it, "for over half a century he had been poking fingers into his own life"?[9]

Some remember him as rugged, straightforward, and almost frightening — his daughter-in-law, for example, compared him to Heathcliff when he took her to the edge of a cliff to deliver her a sermon on morals and his position as a priest — while others saw him as kind and sensitive.[10] "Despite the enigmatic personal details lyric poetry compelled him to provide," Rogers considered that "he remained an intensely private figure. In twenty years of cuttings in the *Daily Telegraph* library files there was just one interview."[11] As if the emergence of his already complex character was not enough, his son and literary executor confessed that this was not just a question of character: "My father had this public persona at which he worked long and hard all his life [...]. My father was an actor."[12]

The public-private divide and his need for privacy also emerge in his paradoxical desire to write several autobiographies (four in total) in Welsh, the language he would have loved to master, the one he felt a real affinity with, but learned only in his thirties while resenting his mother for not teaching him his true "mother tongue." As Jason W. Davies points out in his introduction to *Autobiographies*, Thomas's collection of autobiographies is "complex, balancing reticence and immodesty"[13] and seems to contradict Larkin's provoking thought that "beneath it all, desire of oblivion runs."[14] Why write an autobiography if you want to preserve your privacy and why write it in Welsh if you want to go public? Thomas also gives his autobiography the equivocal name of *Neb,* which literally means "no one" but can also mean "someone." To Davies, this choice of title underlines Thomas's particular position in the literary canon as an Anglo-Welsh writer: "It emphasises the sheer Welsh *otherness* of this major English-language poet. It prompts us to wonder just how visible Wales *is* from centralising London or distant New York, to ask whether the culture of Wales is important, or just importable."[15]

The tension that Thomas felt between his mother tongue and his desired tongue enhanced the paradox of having to write in English about the preservation and survival of the Welsh language. Thomas' friend, the poet Raymond Garlick recalled how in his forties, Thomas tried to get one of his poems published in Welsh:

> The editor, Euros Bowen, told me he had found himself in a dilemma when it was submitted. There were some linguistic mistakes, so what was he to do, tell R.S. or correct them? He quietly corrected them, and Ronald would have seen that and he would have known what it meant. I don't think there were many poems in Welsh after.[16]

In 1946, when asked by the magazine *Wales* as part of a questionnaire sent to various writers if he considered himself an Anglo-Welsh writer, he answered vehemently: "No! A Welsh writer. An Indian journal recently described me as a young Welsh writer, and that pleased me as being essentially correct. The question of a writer's language is a mere matter of historical accident, and will seem to have little significance."[17] As Christopher Morgan rightly argues, however, Thomas's Anglo-Welshness and his provincialism are central to the public-private divide in his poetics as well as in his subject matter. What Morgan calls "Thomas's inbetweenness" paradoxically broadens his horizon and his influence. If he is confessional at times, he also becomes universal and therefore more public through the very provincialism that Robert Frost deemed essential to being universal:

> I want to suggest that R.S. Thomas's "provincialism" — that is his close, intimate, even at times microscopic attention to and scrutiny of his own immediate

localities, both exterior and interior — ultimately branches into a broader relevance, the reason for this being not only the depth of his poetic or philosophical probings, the pressing even farther and deeper in a quest for understanding and meaning but, equally and in conjunction with this drive, the relentless demand by Thomas for the real, the actual, for poetic renderings which reflect the truths of physical and spiritual experience. Together these compulsions discover a shared human ground which ultimately transcends the personal. These requirements often confront and even explode Thomas's own romantic penchant for ideal states of being. But my point here is that such demands, for meaning and for truth, according to their urgency for Thomas, effectively broaden his most private explorations into wider representations. Thomas becomes not only a Welsh poet writing in English from the edge of Western Europe, but a poet who, by way of pursuing and exploring these "fated particulars," has, paradoxically, broadened or even mythologised them into a wider human context and connection.[18]

Morgan is convinced that Thomas's confessional tone, his personal philosophical probings, and his "provincialism" are transcended by a "shared human ground" that is present in his poetry. In other words, the depth of Thomas's religious and metaphysical questionings transforms and broadens private concerns into universal and "wider representations." His struggle with the language and his despised Anglo-Welshness are thus entirely reconfigured.

In the same issue of that 1946 *Wales* magazine, Thomas curses this "historical accident" in a poem entitled "The Old Language,"[19] in which he wonders despairingly why England has turned his beloved, fantasized language into "An offence to the ear, a shackle on the tongue." The Welsh language is compared to an exile, a prisoner enslaved to the ruler England. Thomas's political themes start to emerge here as he laments the quandary, or worse, the disaster that awaits future generations. Thomas reminds his reader of the long tradition of Welsh bards going back to Taliesin, Aneirin, and Dafydd ap Gwilym, whose role was to transmit the traditions and the history of the nation, a role of reminiscence as well as glorification.

According to John Jenkins, the bard performed important functions: "In peace he delighted his lord with songs of chivalry, love and courtship. In war he accompanied his prince to battle, and recited the might and prowess of his leader and the martial virtue of his hosts."[20] Jenkins considered that the poetry of the Welsh bards could be divided into six parts: the sublime, the beautiful, the patriotic, the humorous, the sentimental, and the religious. Alternating between those categories at various times in his poetry, unlike Blake, Thomas appears more like a bard than a prophet despite his religious themes. "The Old Language" thus expresses in a poem what he pondered in Welsh in his autobiography:

> How would things have turned out if he had been able to speak Welsh from the beginning? A futile question. But what he became more conscious of in Aber-

daron was the fact that he had to write poetry in English. The conflict was more acute, although it was too late to do much about it. Many people asked him during his career in the Church whether there was a conflict between his role as priest and his role as poet, but he did not see one. But it was different in the case of the languages involved: living in a traditionally Welsh area such as the Llŷn Peninsula, speaking the language every day, and yet expressing himself in a foreign language. For that was how he viewed the language on the lips of the visitors. Silently, he cursed their language.[21]

His mother tongue being that of the invader, he feels he must curse it, but this curse, although performed in silence, is printed on the page of the poem that steps over the threshold from the private into the public sphere. Yet it is in his autobiography that he crosses the gap, cursing the English language "silently" but in Welsh, as though to keep some privacy. The poem "It Hurts Him to Think,"[22] which concludes his book devoted entirely to Wales, *What is a Welshman?*, summarizes his bitterness towards English — his mother tongue — as well as his conflict with his over-protective and possessive mother. In the poem, the persona is not allowed to use the Welsh word "cariad," but is forced to use the English word "love." The ironic choice of the word "love" is symptomatic of the absence of the poet's love for the compulsory language that is English; it also underlines the tense relationship with his mother as exemplified by the expression "nursing future." This phrase prepares the reader for the violence of the expression "my mother's / infected milk" as well as the final words: "so that whatever / I throw up now is still theirs." In this poem, Thomas not only crosses the threshold between public (his vindictive accusation of the oppressor) and private (his resentment and bitterness towards his mother), he crosses the boundaries to the point of making his reader uneasy. His reader moves from an almost political role to an unwanted voyeuristic position. If it is uncommon for a poet to attack his mother tongue with such aggressiveness, to include his mother so explicitly in his hatred of the English invader is even more striking.

In an autobiographical essay entitled "The Creative Writer's Suicide," Thomas takes up his public role again as a Welsh nationalist, protector of the language and the culture that are in danger of decrepitude. He explains his hatred for the term Anglo-Welsh and what it means to him: "When we come to the Anglo-Welsh, as they are called — for the sake of convenience only, remember — the situation is a hundred times worse. An Anglo-Welsh writer is neither one thing nor the other. He subsists in no-man's-land between two cultures."[23] The Welsh writer thus contributes to English culture and deserves the rebuke of his fellow Welshmen, but if he endeavors to make his work more Welsh, he incurs the hostility or lack of interest of his English reader — the prototypical example of a double-bind situation.

In the 1960s at the height of political tensions in Wales, when some Welsh activists took it upon themselves to right the wrongs inflicted on them by the British government, Thomas chose not to take part in these actions for reasons he gave in *Neb*:

> This was the period of some of his most bitter poems against the English. But he did not act directly, remembering Saunders Lewis's advice when he said that one should not expect too many actions from a writer, because it is through his work that he is able to influence others.[24]

Though he never betrayed the Welsh nationalism of his early career, he decided to move onto apparently less public themes in his poetry, following Lewis's recommendation: "R.S. felt that he had said what he had to say about the political situation of Wales. He had tried to write as a Welshman, even though it was in English that he did so."[25]

More tension was to come from the fact that Thomas was not only a public figure — being a famous poet — but also a priest in the Anglican Church, a priest whose quality of doubt was at least as good as the quality of his faith. His poems register and develop his doubts and constant struggle with his *Deus absconditus*. He could always hide behind a poetic voice or a persona, but in his autobiography he does not shirk from revealing his private questioning: "What was nature to him? Did he seriously believe in God and in eternal life? He gave sermon after sermon to his congregation, trying in his immature, idealistic way to get them to see things as he did."[26] Despite these questionings on fundamental theological issues, Thomas claimed that he did not find any "conflict between his role as priest and his role as poet." Perhaps this absence of conflict or contradiction emanated from the fact that he considered his poems to be neither an incursion nor an excursion into his private life. Yet it would be difficult to argue that his poems are not strongly autobiographical — which he tried to deny about "The Minister" for example.[27] His religious poems can hardly be more intimate, as he repeatedly describes his problematic relationship with an almost always absent God and confesses doubts that he could not confess in his sermons. The border between private and public is constantly crossed or even erased in his religious poems, where he uses the first person pronoun more and more frequently. "Mass For Hard Times" is an interesting poem in this respect, for the poet follows the order of the mass in order to subvert its message and question his personal faith.[28] It is composed of the six sections of the Communion Service of the Anglican Church; the first three belong to the liturgy of the Word and the last three to the Eucharist.

Thomas's poem starts with the *Kyrie*, a song or a prayer of penitence situated at the beginning of the Mass, just after the penitential ceremony. The

four tercets that compose this *Kyrie* all start with the anaphora "Because" and
end with the litany "Lord have mercy," which translates the Greek *Kyrie Elei-
son*. However, what the priest and (supposedly) his congregation ask mercy
for are not the usual sins. In the incipit, Thomas regrets that one cannot be
both "clever and honest" at the same time; one cannot be quick to understand
and be sincere; one always needs to "complexify" things and thus reject the
simplicity required by Christ. The *Kyrie* as an act of repentance is the most
private part of the Mass, and yet it is performed in public, which underlines
one of the many paradoxes Thomas finds in his faith and duty as a priest.
Crossing once more the border between private and public, Thomas dedicates
"Mass for Hard Times" to his wife M. E. Eldridge, who died the year before
its publication.

    The second tercet deals with pride, which is considered the primal sin
committed by Adam and Eve, who wanted to be like God. But here it is the
sin of false modesty or pride in being humble that Thomas denounces. Paradox ("full of pride / in our humility") is one of Thomas's favorite devices: he
uses the *via negativa* repeatedly to describe his relationship with God. The
belief in one's disbelief is the other paradox of that tercet and seems to have
been one of the poet's main temptations. The last two tercets contain two
more paradoxes: destroying oneself out of a sense of self-protection and being
halfway down instead of halfway up on the "slope to perfection." Thomas,
who so often criticizes his fellow Welshmen for their numerous weaknesses
and shortcomings, seems to be sincerely repentant in that *Kyrie*, and he points
the finger towards himself despite the use of the first person plural pronoun.
In this poem, he uses the form of the Mass to repent publicly of some of his
sins.

    In the second section of the poem, the *Gloria*, where praise is usually
given to God for the birth of Christ (following the praise of the angels in
Luke 2: 13–14), Thomas praises God in a highly unconventional way. In the
first four couplets, he describes the universe that surrounds him in the *hic et
nunc* ("the body at its meal's end"). Words such as "mushroom" and "viruses"
suggest the presence of Evil. The next six couplets all start with "because" as
in the first stanza, but the conjunctions here introduce a reason to praise
God instead of a reason to ask for forgiveness, and each couplet ends with
"Gloria." Once again, the reasons are more private than public, as the poet-
priest gives glory to God for the paradoxes that press him towards a more
intimate relationship with God. This stanza is the most moving, as Thomas
reveals himself in his humanity, his weakness, his doubt — also in his enduring faith, despite and because of all these paradoxes. The first of these couplets is both a confession of doubt and an affirmation of faith, as he knows
God is there when he does not see Him ("not there / When I turn"). The turn

reminds one of T. S. Eliot's "Ash Wednesday" ("Because I do not hope to turn again"), which starts with the same conjunction "Because" and is a poem of penitence as well as a confession of enduring doubt. The verb "turn" can be understood in numerous ways, whether as turning away from God, turning back to God, or just a swift movement to try and catch a glimpse of God who has already disappeared, as in Thomas's analogy of God and a bird.

The next couplet describes God's ability to go past appearances and see directly through the soul. Thomas attempts to show that God is the first to act and is not a passive God that is sought, talked to and found, but on the contrary is a God who seeks man, listens, talks and eventually finds him. The third couplet plays on the Pauline paradox of finding true freedom as a servant of God: not enslaved by sin but set free by Christ the truth, no longer subject to the law, but only to the grace of God. The last three couplets are emblematic of the *via negativa* and are slightly more rhetorical than the first three: the poet is comforted by the fact that there "must be something" since "nothing is nothing." The last couplet describes the joy of being "overcome" — not necessarily overcome by God, but perhaps by "nothing," as if to prove the point once more of the *Deus absconditus* that seems to be the only God Thomas truly knows.

The *Deus absconditus* had been "omnipresent" in Thomas's poetry since early poems such as "In a Country Church" and "In Church." In *Poetry and Theology*, William V. Davis wonders whether God's absence in the poem "In Church" can be explained by the fact that the service is ended — which would suggest that this God is only a public figure:

> Are we to assume that the hour during which the light held was the hour of a service recently ended? That the God who is now "hiding" *was* there then? That this God is primarily a public, not a private God — one who appears as if on cue or call for ceremonies but eludes all private searches and entreaties?[29]

Davis's suggestion is attractive, but of course, one has to account for Thomas's irony in this poem. It would be quite unlike Thomas actually to claim that God is exclusively a public God that only ritual can conjure up. "In Church" is perhaps more likely to be one more variation on Thomas's despair at God's elusiveness.

The paradoxes in Thomas's *Credo* would probably be a source of anguish and despair for most of his parishioners and for believers in general, but for Thomas they are a source of, and a reason for, praise and glory. He could not easily share his true vision of God in his public sermons, and therefore had to do it in private poems that were paradoxically much more public than his sermons since they eventually reached a much larger audience. He was "vicar of large things / in a small parish,"[30] and very little trace remains of his sermons as opposed to his 1500 published poems.

The *Credo* seems to work almost as a sort of comic relief after such intimate and revealing confessions. Although it starts with the same words as the
Nicene Creed, parentheses come to debunk each affirmation of faith. The
poet asks whether God the Father is married or not, and more seriously he
wonders whether it is worth repeating the same prayers if God is listening.
Thomas mixes serious concerns and humorous comments as though to dilute
the agony of theological questions and doubts he carried with him all his life.
His *Credo* turns into a series of dramatic questions that his parentheses attempt
to lighten or enlighten. When Thomas asks if he is "too late, then" with his
language, it is to introduce the idea that silence is the only solution, since
"words are the kiss of Judas." He ends what is supposed to be a universal
affirmation of faith with a request to be able to remain silent in front of God's
silence. Silence, which is a way of keeping privacy, becomes Thomas's public response to God's private silence.

Thomas's *Sanctus* starts with the regret that this earth has been made
unholy partly by scientists and financiers. Poetry, however, can be a sanctified
and sanctifying response to God's holiness as, despite humanity's unholiness,
"poetry / sings on," trying to celebrate the "holiness of its affections." The
references to Keats in this tercet and in the last tercet seem to denounce the
transfer of holiness operated by poetry in general and by Keats and Romanticism in particular.

Through absurdity and a fable-like tone, the *Benedictus* that originated
in Christ's triumphant entrance into Jerusalem describes the cruelty of this
world as well as its apparent lack of meaning. As priest and poet with a relatively large readership, Thomas takes up his public role when he warns his
readers, especially those who wish to follow God, with his "cross warning:
No through road." If everybody seems to be blessed in this *Benedictus*, maybe
no one is truly blessed. Thomas is certainly criticizing the vacuity of certain
rituals and prayers, which are repeated so many times that they are perhaps
no longer listened to by God, nor by those pronouncing them.

Finally, the *Agnus Dei* that celebrates Christ the Lamb of God sacrificed
for the sins of the world (John 1: 29) becomes a mock celebration, as this
long-awaited moment in the Mass has become, for Thomas, a ritual bereft of
all meaning. It is not the Lamb that is celebrated anymore, but what Thomas
calls "the idea of it"; as he suggests, an idea cannot bleed and cannot give "its
life / for the world." If everything becomes a meaningless symbol, even the
central tenet of the New Testament and of Christianity becomes a lie. Thomas
ends his poem with an almost blasphemous suggestion: "Where / there is no
love, no God?" Since there is no visible love in this world, perhaps God is
absent from this earth. Yet what appears to be blasphemy is a perfectly arguable
doctrine, as he reverses 1 John 4: 12, one of the fundamental verses on which

Christian doctrine is based: "No man hath seen God at any time. If we love one another, God dwelleth in us, and his love is perfected in us." If the last three verses of the poem appear cynical, they summarize Thomas's defiance towards ritual. Here the idea, the concept, is the symbol of the *Agnus Dei*, but it is also the symbol of what lies between action and words — the gap Thomas tries to fill. Symbols are sometimes words, sometimes actions; rituals are made of words, actions, and what lies in between: silence. Rituals present in the Mass should help fill in the gaps, the emptiness found between word and action, but Thomas, paradoxically, uses rituals to signify the absence of meaning. "Mass For Hard Times" is characterized by an absence of ritual, an absence of solemnity, and a kind of comic relief, all of which enable the poet to cross over the threshold dividing private from public while escaping from his "serious" role as a priest.

"Mass for Hard Times" is a poem; it is not intended to be used in a religious ceremony, despite its title and despite its form that respects the order of the ceremony. If as a priest who speaks in public, Thomas cannot express his doubts without the risk of shocking his parishioners and provoking the ire of his ecclesiastical hierarchy, as a poet who writes in the privacy of his room, he can, by contrast, put into words and onto paper all his wavering and questioning. The paradox of the public-private threshold for Thomas is that his public role as a priest is much less public than his supposedly more private role as a poet because of his surprising popularity. Yet as a poet he addresses one reader at a time as opposed to the collective audience present at church. If interest in poetry has dwindled through the years, interest in the Church has perhaps dwindled even more.

Thomas's relationship with the Church was at least as paradoxical and ambiguous as his relationship with God. At the beginning of his career as a priest, he even tried to preach Welsh nationalism from the pulpit, but was rebuked by the rector of the church. Once again he was on the threshold, as he expressed in *Neb*:

> It is so easy to believe in God when you are on your knees with your eyes closed, just as it is easy to be a Christian far away from the clamour and the trials of the world of people. But the memory would come of him on his knees in the church porch as far back as Manafon. He was neither inside nor outside, but on the border between the two, a ready symbol of contemporary man.[31]

Similar words appear in "The Porch,"[32] which exemplifies perfectly this idea of threshold as a symbol of the public-private divide in his works. In this emblematic poem of the threshold, the persona does not seem to have the strength to pray; the poem starts with a question, and the reader does not know whether the poet is evoking the name of a man or that of the Incarnate God: "Do you want to know his name?" The question of the name is central for the God of the Bible — Jehovah's "I am that I am" (Exodus 3: 14). Similarly, the Psalms focus on three things: the different names of God, his attributes, and his blessings. But here the name is forgotten; language stays on the threshold of memory. Then the poem reproduces a situation that is repeated numerous times in Thomas's poems: "in a church porch [...] he was driven to his knees." As if exhausted and vanquished, the man seems propelled to his knees by an invisible force "for no reason / he knew." The enjambment — typical of Thomas's poetics — represents another threshold between reason and knowledge, between habit and instinct. The man is numbed by the coldness of the outside world that comes "at him" like a revelation; what comes out of him, his "breath [...] carved angularly / as the tombstones," is synonymous with death. The second stanza starts with a sentence that summarizes the bare coldness and spiritual aridity of the first stanza and introduces the extremely uncomfortable position of the priest who is at home neither in, nor outside of the church: "He had no power to pray."

In his prose works, Thomas often elaborates on the hardships and the solitude of being a priest, as well as on the essential flexibility and time it gives him to write his poetry. For a priest, even when it is a constant struggle, prayer is unavoidable, as he writes in his autobiography: "As a priest in the Church R.S. knew that he should pray regularly."[33] But in "The Porch," the man remains on the threshold of prayer, unable to utter a word in the same way as he remains, symptomatically, on the church doorstep, awaiting an answer that does not come "on that lean threshold, neither outside nor in." The only punctuation mark in the last stanza, apart from the full stop after "pray" and the final full stop, is the comma that follows the word "threshold," as though to intimate the loneliness of the man who remains there. This isolation of the word "threshold" is emphasized by a look at the skeleton of the poem where, as opposed to Thomas's habit, all the central thematic words are at the end of the line except for "threshold," which is the only noun at the beginning of a line. The man turns his back to the church, and his physical position is characteristic of his psychological position towards the Church of England. But when he looks out "on the universe," he looks at a world that does not know, recognize, or understand him. He lingers on that uncomfortable threshold, "neither outside nor in."

This threshold between word and silence, prayer and inertia, between the internal world and the external one, between nature and the church, parallels and almost symbolizes the threshold between the private and the public in Thomas's poetry, in his autobiographies, and in his life in general — a threshold made of paradox and ambiguity, faith and doubt, love and hatred and, of course, presence and absence. It appears that this threshold was often a blurry frontier for Thomas, as his public role as a priest regularly encroached on his privacy, and his reluctance to unveil much of his private life was endangered by the strongly autobiographical dimension of his poetry. As a priest in the Anglican Church in Wales in typically non-conformist country, a position full of paradoxes, Thomas constantly avoided revealing too much of his metaphysical doubt. As a poet, however, he recorded over his entire career a struggle with God similar to that of Jacob wrestling with the angel.[34] God's silence, which affected him deeply in the privacy and intimacy of his inner life and in his prayers, was answered by a large quantity of poems on the subject: sometimes underlining his suffering, sometimes his hope of communicating with God through ritual, through nature, and finally through his own silence. The silence developed in his later poetry, in a reconciliation of paradoxes, is perhaps what enabled him, somehow, to bridge the public-private divide.

NOTES

1. Photograph by Howard Barlow for the *Telegraph* reproduced as the cover page for Justin Wintle's *Furious Interiors*.

2. Christopher Morgan, *R.S. Thomas: Identity, Environment, and Deity* (Manchester: Manchester University Press, 2004), vii.

3. Byron Rogers, *The Man Who Went Into The West* (London: Aurum Press, 2006), 299–300.

4. John Ezard and Geoff Gibbs, "Wales Loses Its Most Sustained Lyric Voice" (http://www.guardian.co.uk/uk/2000/sep/27/books.booksnews), March 2009.

5. Justin Wintle, *Furious Interiors* (London: Flamingo, 1996), xiv.

6. Rogers, *The Man Who Went Into The West*, 43.

7. Wintle, *Furious Interiors*, xvi.

8. Ibid., xvii.

9. Rogers, *The Man Who Went Into The West*, 22.

10. Ibid., 158.

11. Ibid., 7.

12. Ibid., 23.

13. R.S. Thomas, *Autobiographies* (London: Orion, 1998), ix.

14. Ibid.

15. Ibid., xi.

16. Rogers, *The Man Who Went Into The West*, 170.

17. Ibid., 158.

18. Morgan, *R.S. Thomas*, 8.

19. Thomas, *Collected Poems*, 25.

20. John Jenkins, *The Poetry of Wales* (London: Houlston and Sons, 1873), 11.

21. Thomas, *Autobiographies*, 77.

22. Thomas, *Collected Poems*, 262.

23. Thomas, *Autobiographies*, 22.

24. Ibid., 67.

25. Ibid., 77.

26. Ibid., 59.

27. Thomas, *Collected Poems*, 42.

28. Ibid., 135.

29. William V. Davis, *R.S. Thomas: Poetry and Theology* (Waco: Baylor University Press, 2007), 47.

30. Thomas, *Collected Poems*, 23.

31. Thomas, *Autobiographies*, 78.

32. Thomas, *Collected Poems*, 326.

33. Thomas, *Autobiographies*, 106.

34. In "The Combat" (*Collected Poems*, 291), Thomas compares his struggle with words to address God and to write poetry with Jacob's wrestle with the angel.

WORKS CITED

Davies, Jason W. (1998). Introduction to *Autobiographies*. London: Orion.

Davis, William V. (2007). *R.S. Thomas: Poetry and Theology*. Waco: Baylor University Press.

Jenkins, John (1873). *The Poetry of Wales*. London: Houlston and Sons.

Morgan, Christopher (2004). *R.S. Thomas: Identity, Environment, and Deity*. Manchester: Manchester University Press.

Rogers, Byron (2006). *The Man Who Went Into The West*. London: Aurum Press.

Thomas, R.S. (1993). *Collected Poems: 1945–1990*. London: Phoenix.

_____. (1998). *Autobiographies*. London: Orion.

_____. (2004). *Collected Later Poems: 1988–2000*. Highgreen: Bloodaxe.

Wintle, Justin (1996). *Furious Interiors*. London: Flamingo.

5. Performing, Transforming, and Changing the Question: Patience Agbabi — Poet Enough!

Catherine Murphy

A twenty-first century sonneteer, Patience Agbabi takes her poetics back to the future. Her work proclaims that poetry's significance, achieved by crafting a form that reflects both its oral and its literary inheritance, depends on its public relevance and its private resonance. She riffs on tradition, raps without apology, and refuses to be a "black" or "white" poet, demanding instead that poetry question its relationship with the categorical costumes of the past and present in order to explore what is politically and poetically possible in its future. Underneath her explicit refutation of the notion that erudition and entertainment are mutually incompatible lies Agbabi's more subtle subversion of the public-private divide. Implicit in her work is the claim that the production and consumption of poetry is a communal activity; neither stage in the creation of the poem can be designated as a purely public or private event. Shunning labels, her interrogation of the ownership of ideas reveals a poetics grounded in shared experience; public and private boundaries do not disappear, but become increasingly fraught with valuable questions.

Agbabi's British Council website profile traces her poetic line of inheritance directly to dub poetry, a late twentieth-century export from the Caribbean to Britain.[1] Born out of cultural upheaval and social protest, dub has been considered an inherently political form by detractors and adherents alike. Feeling that a black poetry that ignored its immediate public context was not simply a luxury, but a collaboration with the racist hegemony, adherents wore the castigation as a badge of honor. Detractors, in contrast, considered the label an indictment; political poetry sacrificed the integrity of the creative process to a pre-determined agenda that compromised artistic ends. While her work as a performance poet certainly bears the imprint of dub, Agbabi's reformulation of what "performance" means reflects a significantly more expansive scope.

Competing claims about the public and private dimensions of poetry and the concomitant obligations of the poet have presented themselves most clearly in the Afro-Caribbean context by way of the Derek Walcott/Kamau Brathwaite debate, a crude summation of which posits the latter as the "voice of the people" and the former as a more introspective, private speaker.[2] Although neither poet is fairly represented by these reductive, polarized positions, the discourse around their opposition influenced the evolution of performance poetry in Britain. While never specifically referencing this critical debate, Agbabi's writing most certainly reflects it. Even though her early poems display the overtly rebellious spirit of dub so indebted to Brathwaite's Afro-centric griot poetics, Agbabi's later work recognizes, as Brathwaite's did, the limitations of a poetry that does not take itself seriously as text, and Agbabi's increasing concern with performance on the page shows that she understands the limits of an oral fixation. Her lack of inhibitions regarding the Western literary tradition and her daring revisions of conventional forms, together with the complexity of the "I" in her writing, reflect the audacious post-colonial prosody of Walcott, who declared "that revolutionary literature is a filial impulse, and that maturity is the assimilation of the features of every ancestor."[3]

Bringing together the political activism of Brathwaite with the poetic acuity of Walcott, Agbabi blurs the boundary between the stereotypical notions of public poet and private poet, and more importantly, between public poetry and private poetry. Determined to complicate the easy distinctions many critics have tried to make between populist and elitist literature, between engagement and edification, Agbabi's project is to heal the chasm between the seemingly private world of the page and the ostensibly more public performance of the stage. For Agbabi, as for Walcott, healing comes in and through a full appreciation (and subsequent appropriation) of the depth and breath of language and tradition. Whether in Standard English or slang, referring to high culture or pop culture, Agbabi's work is about the art and excitement of wordplay. Aligning this with Brathwaite's activism, Agbabi becomes a self-proclaimed "Poetical Activist," determined to tackle the divide between "spoken word" and "real poetry" by bringing a reconfigured sense of performance to the page and the stage. The progression from her first to her third collection of poems testifies to an increasingly vigorous engagement with the public-private divide, and her most recent work speaks specifically to the private implications of public consciousness, as well as to the public ramifications of what may or may not be privately shaped experience.

It is not possible to appreciate the significance of Agbabi's work and its relevance to the public-private divide without addressing the complexity of labels within b/Black British poetry.[4] The labels that are applied to (or by) writers of color in Britain speak to the extent to which such writers feel free to choose between being private individuals or public persons. This situation forces a series of questions: who creates and who legitimates labels in black British poetry; how does such labeling keep certain writers in or out of the public-private spheres, and why? While some British writers describe themselves as black British, others are unsatisfied with such a designation and think of themselves in more specific terms, such as African British.[5] The issue is not one of mere terminology, but rather of the reductive power of essentializing signifiers. In her discussion of retheorizing British identity, R. Victoria Arana references Stuart Hall, who makes the point explicit:

> What is at issue here is the recognition of the extraordinary diversity of subjective positions, social experiences and cultural identities which compose the category "Black"; that is the recognition that "Black" is essentially a politically and culturally *constructed* category, which cannot be grounded on a set of fixed trans-cultural or transcendental racial categories and which therefore has no guarantees in Nature.[6]

In other words, poets of color writing in Britain have faced a set of publicly defined ideas about who they are as a group rather than who they might be as individuals. These characterizations have often created a stultifying sense of what their poetic concerns can validly be. Ethnic identity and poetic identity have not easily been untangled, and consequently poets of color in Britain face not only demands on their senses of themselves, but also expectations as to whom their intended audience should or could be. While rarely articulated in terms of the public-private divide, the debate around labels in b/Black British poetry illustrates how race complicates a poet's positioning along public-private lines of demarcation.

One's private choices about how to grapple with identity politics have serious implications for one's public reception, and nowhere is this more evident than with regard to one's publishing opportunities.[7] Agbabi laments what she considers a prevailing myopia in the publishing world: "It's as if all black writers are supposed to be the same, whereas white writers, of course, they're allowed to write lots of different styles and genres."[8] Agbabi's work pushes against such preconceived notions. She refuses to satisfy the expectations of any audience, white or black, and it is important to note that expectations about style, form, and content come not just from the publishing world, but also from within the black community. In a paper on the problem of recognition and publishing opportunities for black writers, Mahlete-Tsigé Getachew begins by announcing that anyone interested in these issues must seriously consider whether Black literature shares a goal with wider literary activity; if so, whether it successfully contributes to this collective goal; and finally, whether and why this contribution is being systematically marginalized. Getachew's analysis proceeds by methodically interrogating the concepts of Black authorship, Black readership, Black content, and Black experience. She finds each of these concepts wanting and blames an attachment to such flawed concepts for the problematic commercial and cultural status of black writing.[9]

Getachew's position is provocative, if not confrontational, especially given its placement in a collection of essays called *Write Black, Write British*; Kwame Dawes's contribution to this collection invokes Langston Hughes' seminal essay "The Negro and the Racial Mountain," which calls for a distinctively racial art. Agbabi is as skeptical about the idea of a "black aesthetic" as she is about the idea that black expression is or *should be* political. In her view, the demand for a performance poet to be political is not "the case *any more*. I turned around and I think *the times have turned* around as well."[10] She opposes the idea that a poet has a responsibility to reflect a fixed agenda or aesthetic based on a socially imposed identity. Her insistent interrogation of categories calls into question the very notion of any poet having a purely public duty or a purely private interest.

Agbabi tackles head-on what Dawes describes as the unfortunate assumption that performance poetry is synonymous with black poetry.[11] Dawes argues that the label "performance poet" is problematic because for many, it marks a distinction from a "book poet." For him, such a distinction is not only restrictive, but also sets up as authoritative a false dichotomy grounded in lazy acts of analysis. In Dawes' view, "[t]he labels are misguided and deeply inscribed in questions of aesthetics, the politics of race and the function of poetry in society."[12] Ultimately, the relevance of such labeling to the public/private divide is its illustration of what's at stake: does calling poetry "Black" British poetry make a public statement that gives it added weight and power, or does such a label limit it to a narrow readership, thereby diminishing its significance? As Agbabi re-examines the meaning of performance poetry in order to redress the confused labels surrounding race, aesthetics, and the poet in society, she illustrates the importance of re-conceptualizing "public" and "private" as part of asserting the freedom to occupy multiple positions in these realms.

Nevertheless, Agbabi's unrestrained approach to identity in her writing, and its critical reception on its own terms, is possible only because of the cultural strains that preceded it. An earlier generation of black British writers faced entirely different social and political circumstances. Their ability to consider, as Getachew advocates, a responsibility to "wider literary activity" was complicated by the more immediate duty of reflecting and protesting the injustices they saw around them.[13] If one accepts Fred D'Aguiar's assertion that 1970–1980 was "the decade in which recent black poetry established itself," the coming-of-age of black poetry in Britain is firmly anchored in a time when many poets coming to England from the Caribbean *very much* wanted their race recognized as central to their identity. Anything less would have seemed like a personal capitulation in the face of the public ostracism of their people.[14]

It was in this context that dub poetry became the dominant expression of black poetry in Britain. Born out of the turmoil of Jamaica's emergence in the 1970s as an independent nation, and in keeping with the syncretic nature of Caribbean culture, dub poetry bubbled out of a heady mix of radical politics, new ideas about an Afro-centric literature, and new musical technologies and trends.[15] Born out of change, dub wanted to further effect change. Dawes has noted that much of dub poetry derives its attitude and form from "the obscure discourse" of Rastafarianism, which Dawes credits as having "perfected the process of constructing a secret language of codes, puns and word play to both befuddle and distance the establishment."[16] Rasta discourse (or "dread talk") not only departs from the standard English lexis, but also distinguishes itself from standard English grammar: "I" is used as both subject and object in both singular and plural forms, as well as being a translation of the second person pronoun "you," "thereby breaking down the distinction between the self and others."[17] Elaine Savory has pointed out how important this sense of a communal "I" has been for Brathwaite's poetics, in which it represents "simultaneously the fragment of community which is a single individual and the necessity of that fragment taking its place as part of the recuperation of the whole."[18] Brathwaite and the dub poets who found inspiration in his work have thus been acutely aware of the communal significance of a literary text and of its potential to unlock collective memory and identity.[19] Dub drew from Brathwaite's writing this sense of the poet as griot, or public teller of the story of a people: the poet as living, breathing, and representative history. Dub poets, whether Rasta or not, sought to bring the ideas of Black Power to young black people in the Caribbean and to the Caribbean diaspora. They insisted on the validity of Creole as an expressive medium, refusing to accept that Standard English was the only valid medium of poetic expression and relishing the incomprehension of the literary establishment.

Such a conscious separation from the cultural and political "powers that be" is an important part of dub's form and message. It is typical of post-colonial literatures to complicate the comprehension of outsiders by way of exclusionary devices such as dialects, colloquialisms, or culturally specific stories and symbols. Doris Somner calls these "strategies of readerly incompetence" that more careful reading will not overcome.[20] She says that limiting access is the point, essentially announcing to outsiders they can come this close, but no closer. Such strategies of resistance show how post-colonial literature in particular introduces private modes of expression within public modes of expression. The question is whether these strategies of resistance keep this very public-oriented poetry private by limiting its audience and consequently excluding it from mainstream public discourse where it might exert more power.

One prominent criticism of dub and by extension, performance poetry, is that it was (and perhaps still is) overly focused on the stage as a vehicle for transmitting a political message. The stage has been seen as an arena for the public exchange of burning social and political ideas, while the page has been seen as a place for matters less immediately pressing, a place of private rumination for poet and reader. Dub poetry sought to make things happen, and arguably, this intensity of intention was a problem. Dennis Walder points out that Brathwaite always had a broader and more inclusive agenda than the dub poets. Despite his germinal role in dub, Brathwaite was concerned about the lack of interest the dub poets showed in the page. He warned of what he called the "riddum prison"; "sound poetry is one thing pun stage / another on the page Both must perform."[21] However, if the point of dub poetry is to communicate a clear message to the community, a concern with the page is unnecessary, even frivolous.[22] As Walder puts it, the limitations of dub poetry "are the limitations of the time, when the frustrations of urban black communities were especially acute, and the sounds and speech of the streets important to use in solidarity against the oppressor."[23] Agbabi's work is a response to this very real concern that dub and performance poets were limiting their vision of performance to public performance and therefore not taking the page, and the real possibility of a private engagement with political text, seriously.

Agbabi's development of existing conceptions of performance, however, might not have been possible had Jean "Binta" Breeze, one of its key practitioners, not called dub's core philosophy into question. Despite shunning the overt politics of dub, Breeze retained a fundamental sense of poetry as testimony. Further, her experiences as a female dub artist show how gender affects the perception of public and private domains. Breeze's ideas were crucial for Agbabi's reconfiguring of the role and responsibility of the poet in black British poetry.

In her essay "Can a Dub Poet be a Woman?," Jean "Binta" Breeze explains why dub became not only formally constraining for her, but also strongly gendered and therefore limited in its sense of identity.[24] Breeze grew skeptical about the public duty of the poet to deliver a political message and became more interested in exploring language itself, as well as personal experiences of womanhood. In contrast, dub "seemed to suggest that it was much more masculine to achieve distance from the subjective or personal"[25]; indeed, some male dub poets had chastised Breeze for what they considered sexually provocative stage performances, which they felt had distracted from the political relevance of her message. The divide between the public and the private in dub was one that Breeze could no longer tolerate. That she extracted herself from the world of dub, however, did not mean that Breeze rejected the idea of poet as public figure or that she saw no duty in poetry; she simply changed the focus and shape of that duty. Breeze does not write for herself, of her own musings, but rather sees her poetry as a desire to begin a *conversation*. She believes in a poetry of exchange, and that depends very much on a relationship with her readers.[26] Like Breeze, Agbabi became increasingly concerned with finding what is most universal in what is most specific, with what is most publicly relevant in the world of the shared private experience, and Breeze's rejection of dub paved the way for Agbabi's development of the poetic conversation.

A significant point of departure between the two poets is Breeze's lack of interest in the accusation that she is not literary enough and she claims to be unperturbed by the lack of interest the literary establishment might have in her work.[27] Speaking at the same round table discussion, Agbabi announced that she, on the other hand, "will be banging on some doors." While Breeze is content to remain in relatively private realms, Agbabi demands recognition in a broad public sphere.

Given her biography, it is fitting that Patience Agbabi would find any one identifying category a tight squeeze. Born in Britain to Nigerian parents and fostered to a white family, Agbabi's childhood was spent in Sussex and North Wales. She was educated at Oxford and schooled herself in punk, rap, and northern soul before hitting the performance circuit in London. Her first collection, *R.A.W.* (1995), showcased a poet in the guise of "friction" writer, one chafing from the indignities of historical and cultural wrongs.[28] The title poem doesn't lie; the thrust of the work is "rhythm and word / uncooked uncut / uncaged unchained / uncensored."[29] Identity is the main theme of the work, but Agbabi stomps across some refreshingly unhinged terrain, with race, gender, sexuality, subculture, and class all jockeying for position. Amidst her frantic movement across multiple markers of self, there are only two moments in the book where one feels a strident sense of authorial identity unmasked. Significantly, that identity is as public poet provocateur. In the title poem "R.A.W.," Agbabi announces "I'm a poet / it's a four-letter word," and in "Rappin It Up," she initials a memo declaring her poetics; "I am PA and I am rappin it up."[30] In a nod to the influence of dub and its sound systems, this poet is a PA, a public address system. Not only is the title of "Rappin It Up" a clever play on its position as final poem, it is a declaration of allegiance to performance poetry, whose roots are in dub's politics and anti-establish-ment protest. Like the dub poets, Agbabi rejects the influence of the "Great tradition," meaning specifically Shakespeare, Milton, Wordsworth, and Eliot, "all you poets I don't give a fuck."[31]

Although "R.A.W." declares that black people have to re-claim the his-tory and language stolen from them, the poems that immediately follow "R.A.W." problematize any stable reading of images and stereotypes in black culture; "Rap 'Trap," for example, accuses the rapper of squandering Nina Simone's designation as young, gifted, and black and of becoming instead "Uncle Tom with a hard on / disgracing the race."[32] *R.A.W.* makes the implicit point that liberty is not just a racial issue, positing marriage, drugs addic-tion, poverty, and the selfish, materialistic "I" of Thatcherism all as forms of enslavement. Coming as she does after Breeze's critique of dub's focus, Agbabi is not limited by a narrowly politicized agenda. In her explorations of class, race, gender, and sexuality, no one version of self or aspect of identity is priv-ileged or promoted, making hybridity a core theme of the collection. Never-theless, the work itself is not hybrid, poetically speaking, and the primary significance of the volume is not a new vision of performance, but rather Agbabi's refusal to center her performance pieces around public expectations about the politics of race.

The poems in *Transformatrix* (2000), Agbabi's second collection, *appear* to pick up where *R.A.W.* left off.[33] "Prologue" is, as Agbabi intended, per-formance-oriented, "very rappy very in-your-face."[34] The poem begins play-fully, inviting the image of tossing words in and out of one's mouth like licorice allsorts: "let it roll across your tongue / like a dolly mixture," but this rap ends up doing something different from the run-of-the-mill social com-mentary; instead, Agbabi "struts in extravagant metalinguistic play"[35]:

> I got more skills than I got melanin
> I'm fired by adrenaline
> if you wanna know what rhyme it is
> it's feminine.
> Cos I'm Eve on an Apple Mac
> this is a rap attack.[36]

By the end of the collection, Agbabi has left the public performance poetry of *R.A.W.* behind; when she arrives at the eponymous final poem, she's re-casting all the old roles. "Transformatrix" is an exquisitely crafted sonnet that tantalizingly subverts the typically feminist interpretation of this form as corset. This poet is not feeling any unwelcome coercion in the restraints of the poem, reveling instead in the excitement of toying with limits: "Salt pep-pers my lips as the door clicks shut."[37] In effect, the collection is couched in two big statements; "Prologue" and "Transformatrix" can each be seen as an *ars poetica* announcing a postmodern engagement with traditions — rap and literary — and displaying a staunch refusal to obey limiting categories. Drawing on Breeze's reconfiguration of poetry in performance as a space for private experience available through public encounter, Agbabi seeks a new kind of poetry. Crucially, her new concern with the wealth of formal experimentation possible in the privacy of the page has not sapped her politics of its verve. These bookend poems are sites of struggle, and there is a dynamic exchange with language, self, and the very concept of the public-private engagement.

Over the course of this appropriately transformative collection, Agbabi explores the irony of her opening declaration: "I wanna do poetic things in poetic places."[38] The desire to meet literary expectations is complicated by a parallel desire to transgress, to misbehave, to buck the saddle of tradition; the poet is playing on the idea of doing private things in public places. "Transformatrix" takes us into deeper into this norm-violating territory. As the poet waits "pen poised over a blank page," the excitement of the poet's anticipation "for madam's orders, her strict consonants" is intensified by the awareness that someone on the outside of this private fantasy is peering in.[39] The voyeuristic element introduced by putting this S&M prosody on public display heightens the private experience of both the poet and the reader/listener. It is an exchange whereby privacy is willingly compromised in order to question boundaries publicly, not just between the poet and the muse, not only between freedom/pleasure and restraint/pain, but also between the literate, and some might suggest sterile, page and the physicality and excitement of the stage. The page has become the stage. This is the climactic fulfillment of the explicit promise made in "Prologue":

> Give me a stage and I'll cut form on it
> Give me a page and I'll perform on it.[40]

The new kind of page poetry Agbabi espouses can only happen if the reader/listener participates in the staging of the event of the poem. The phrase "Give me" is crucial and is repeated throughout: the poem is a promise of what the poet can do, will do, given the chance. Agbabi insists that public listening can have a private dimension, just as reading in private can begin to feel like participation in a public event. Having attended a number of her live appearances, Broom declares, "after Agbabi's performances, the audience *is* left with a sense that some kind of positive and enlivening bond between audience and poet has been achieved on an interpersonal level."[41]

Whether one accepts the idea that a public performance has the power to create an intensely private experience depends on one's conception of orality and its function. As already noted, Breeze certainly believes in such a public-private encounter. Nicky Marsh points out that although Brathwaite and Mervyn Morris both use the term "submerge" to discuss the voice in oral or performance poetry, they posit contrasting interpretations of what that means: a personal identity (private) submerged in the presence of shared (public) voice versus a cultural history (public) submerged in particularly political (public) voicing. Marsh explains that "[f]or Morris, the performed voice embodies the poet's identity, whereas for Brathwaite, the linking of voice to a larger historical perspective functions as much to depersonalize this poetry as the reverse."[42]

Agbabi's sense of poetry in performance moves away from the Brathwaite/dub sense, that performance is about the collective experience as a forum for raising historical and political consciousness. Instead, drawing on Breeze's idea of *poems as conversations*, Agbabi's sense of engagement with an audience moves towards the kind of performance Morris emphasizes, one through which there can be a connection between poet and audience as people, *with public and private identities*. Paradoxically, a public performance on an actual stage can feel like a private experience *if the poems themselves question the public-private boundary*. That is to say, if the poetry does not seek to promulgate a pre-defined manifesto as part of a publicly determined collective identity politics, but instead allows language to explore the multiplicities of identity and experience shared by everyone, the power of the physical voice can insinuate an intimate, intensely private-feeling experience with an audience.

While the power of Agbabi's oral performance in person is generally recognized, more critical attention should be paid to how Agbabi's dedication to bringing her performance into the text has reduced the presumptive isolation of the page and opened it up as a forum for public interaction. While both Broom and Ramey look at Agbabi in the context of the avant-garde, neither seems to appreciate the full extent of her rigorous engagement with the text as a place of physical and metaphysical activity.[43] By honoring her pledge to re-unite the page and stage, Agbabi has opened up the text as a forum for meaningful public exchange, as opposed to an isolated place for individual bursts of lyricism or rarefied linguistic and/or allusive displays of intellectual pomposity — both serious accusations that have fuelled the passions of those who see a divide between the literary and the oral and prize the latter.

In his discussion of the problem of the "them" and "us" dichotomy inherent in the oral/literary division, Mervyn Morris appeals to performance poets to "prepare their publications with an eye to the imperatives of print."[44] Noting the discrepancy between the attention many dub performers pay to the oral and textual presentation of their work, Morris suggests that "performance poets would do well to regard translation into print as a challenge and an opportunity to be thoughtfully approached."[45] The implication is that a poetry so conceived would not be susceptible to the accusations of inferiority hurled from both sides of the page/stage divide; it would not exist simply as a vehicle to transmit a clear and distinct message to the public, and neither would it exist solely as a well-crafted but isolated artifact, detached from the world outside. Morris emphasizes the importance of the accusation that texts are isolating, quoting both Walter Ong and Brathwaite, some of whose statements privilege the oral tradition over the literary tradition on this very basis.[46] Ong argues, "written words are *isolated* from the fuller context in which the spoken word comes into being. The word in its natural, oral habitat is part of a real, existential present."[47] Similarly, Brathwaite argues that reading is "an *isolated* individualistic expression" whereas the oral tradition requires not only the poet but the audience "to complete the community."[48] Agbabi's recent work defends the page against the accusations that it is a place of isolation and, by implication, sterility. Rather, beginning with *Transformatrix* and intensifying in her third collection *Bloodshot Monochrome*, Agbabi's poems are evidence that text can effectively open itself for participation in readings that aim "to complete the community" that potentially exists between a poem and an audience, regardless of whether that audience is a reader experiencing a poem in private or a group of listeners gathered in a public space. While congratulating Agbabi for her intent to bring page and stage together, critics have sometimes failed to see the poems as shapes of meaning, with forms that mean more than scaffold, and language that is as slippery as it is direct. That is, they fail to read the poems as linguistic structures. It is as if they applaud her idea of being serious about text, but ironically fail to take her text seriously because they are still busy talking about her themes.

In fact, Agbabi's second collection, *Transformatrix*, enacts an enormous shift in poetics. Agbabi's journey from rap to sonnet involves passage through a middle section titled "Seven Sisters," composed of seven sestinas. Sarah Broom notes the skill with which Agbabi presents these sestinas in person, and she also acknowledges the impressive feat of having all seven sestinas use the same six end words while simultaneously maintaining a "radically different tone and setting" for each poem.[49] However, what does not register with this critic is how this particular sequence also creates a sense of exchange within and between the poems that has vital implications for the relationship between private reading and public experience. The sestinas are not just an exercise in prosodic virtuosity but a textual refutation of isolation and individuality, a structural embrace of some kind of underlying order, a repudiation of post-modern cynicism using the post-modern death of the author. In constructing a set of seven sestinas, each one evoking very particular and separate identities, yet all of which echo each other in their circling motion and recycled language, the poet is making a claim about the human condition; each very different individuals, we are nonetheless of one essential form and substance. This sense that no one identity can ever be entirely satisfactory, this questioning of a reliable, stable, and authoritative voice telling "our" story, is central to Walcott's vision and was absolutely absent from dub poetry.[50] Agbabi's insistence on a decentered identity, thematically in *R.A.W.*, and textually in *Transformatrix*, suggests a movement into a more Walcottian sensibility, one which insists that any sense of self, public or private, is constructed, and that therefore an identity is always going to require fluid interaction between the two spheres.

Bloodshot Monochrome (2008) further intensifies the project of boundary breaking so explicitly laid out in "Prologue" and revealed in *Transformatrix*.[51] Agbabi dispenses measured doses of tradition and pop culture with equal dollops of erudition and entertainment. The collection is obsessed with the sonnet and features them in three out of its five sections, proving that this PA is no longer concerned only with public address but truly is a Poetical Activist on many levels; by activating old forms, she brings the page and the stage together in a new conception, a performance space where the main activity is personal and public interrogation of poetics and politics. Agbabi boldly declares her intention to "enter the public-private debate" ("Not Death But Love"), cries out in frustration "when will people stop categorising" ("Two Loves I Have"), declares that "meticulously crafted poetry can appeal to the élite *and* the masses if accessible" ("Not Love But Money"), and snubs the politics versus art argument by reducing its charges to the facile equations "poetry + politics = propaganda" and "blackpoet + sonnet = sellout" ("Knew White Speech").[52] *Bloodshot Monochrome* is a sucker punch to anyone who doubts that performance poetry has to sacrifice erudition in order to be entertaining or that performance is limited to the stage or page. On the one hand, it utilizes the page as a space that encourages both audience and poet to explore the conceptual subtleties and multiple significations of language and meaning permitted by the increased level of attention that the reading process allows. On the other hand, because it is composed with a poetics of exchange based on social and political relevance, it is not boring, sterile, or isolating.

The collection's centerpiece is the sonnet sequence "Problem Pages," whose title ingeniously combines the accusation that there is a problem with the private space of the page with the rebuttal that the page can in fact be a forum where seemingly private dilemmas becomes sites of public exchange and potential resolution. The poems are engaging conceptually, politically, and poetically, and are a particularly daring embodiment of tradition and experiment. Insofar as they each have fourteen lines, they at least echo sonnet form, thus evoking a rich history reaching back to the fourteenth-century poet Francesco Petrarca, himself influenced by Dante. However, in a playful adaptation of the Petrarchan format of using the octave to lay out the predicament and the sestet to provide a resolution, Agbabi has each poem adopt the call and response of a modern day agony aunt or advice column: the octave is the letter to Agbabi from a troubled party, and the sestet is her response. Tradition is also brought to bear on each poem by contriving to have each letter/octave written by a famous poet from the past. The experimentation is not simply in the fun of making up lively letters from dead poets, but in the sequence's implication that there is no one author and really no one poem.

Predictably, there are fourteen sonnets in the sequence, or so it seems. The first page in the sequence has a heading under which are fourteen lines of text. The heading reads "Contributors," and each of the fourteen lines lists a poet who had a particular association with the sonnet form and a phrase from one of his or her poems.[53] Each poet plays a major part in the sonnets that follow, and a phrase from each poet's poems serves as the title for the sonnet. The fact that there are fourteen separate poetic snippets suggests that the text on this page is itself a sonnet, a collage, and a two column cut-up, where reading down one column is a litany of men and women involved in the history and evolution of the sonnet itself, and reading down the other column is a non-linear narrative on the issues of race, gender, sexuality, intellectual snobbery, and poetry. Does the odd presence of some lyricism in this arrangement provide a strong enough whiff of the poetic to warrant calling it a poem? Does thoughtful content merit calling a portion of text a poem? Does assigning a great poet's name to some words make it a poem? Does structure confer poetic value? Does the audacious experimental artistry in lining up a list of poets and implying it could be a poem with the title "Contributors" make it a poem? The section is, in effect, a series of questions and answers on the relationship between tradition and experimentation, artistry and entertainment. The questions demand a level of participation on the part of the reader in determining the validity of the poems and their poetics that undermines the idea of authorship residing in any one poet. The composition of the poem and the determination of its content are thrown open to the public, and yet each member of the public is free to make these determinations privately.

The sequence's play on the idea of the letter, usually an intimate and private communication that is published in this case, reinforces this sense of ongoing exchange between private and public. Sometimes Agbabi's response offers writing and publishing advice, seemingly practical. Often, however, the answers are poetic riffs on the issues the expired poet inspired. Either way, the responses are not meant to be resolutions. They signal not the end of a discussion, but a beginning of a more thoroughgoing debate.

In "Queen of Shadows," Agbabi lifts from a famous passage of T.S. Eliot's critical writing:

> Immature poets imitate; mature poets steal; bad poets deface what they take, and good poets make it into something better, or at least something different. *The good poet welds his theft into a whole of feeling which is unique, utterly different from that from which it was torn; the bad poet throws it into something which has no cohesion.*[54]

Strikingly, Agbabi left out the italicized sentence, perhaps because she is uncertain about the possibility of uniqueness. The engagement of multiple writers in the creation of a sequence of poems, which may in fact amount to parts of a single long poem, reinforces the interrogation of separation and unity that the "Seven Sisters" sequence began in *Transformatrix*. The difference is that *Bloodshot Monochrome*, and "Problem Pages" in particular, is a direct attack on limiting lines of poetic demarcation, and her most exhilarating combination of tradition and experiment to date. It is as if Agbabi saw the rowdy spirit of the avant-garde that's been running around with the cool kids from modernist and postmodernist schools, grabbed it by the scruff of its neck, roughed it up a bit, and reminded it how long it's really been around. "Act your age," Agbabi says to her own experimentation and to that of other poetries, and by that she means, be contemporary, be traditional, and be self-aware. In other words, experimentation *is* traditional *and* contemporary, and it happens in response to the internal private life of the poet and the external public social, political, and artistic climate.

Agbabi is not alone among contemporary British poets in her desire to bring a performance and identity poetics to the page as much as to the stage.[55] However, what sets Agbabi apart from her contemporaries is that she is not content to use the conventional tools of the avant-garde and the experimentalists. Her rebellion is more comprehensive. Rather than using unstable forms and splintered words to explore new and unstable identities, Agbabi calls on the power of old poetic forms to explore contemporary questions of provenance. In decrying the convention among performance poets to shun traditional forms and rigorous concern for the appearance of the poem on the page, Agbabi argues that while poetry is one of the oldest forms of artistic expression and the printed page a recent technology, "each can empower the other for both possess unassailable strengths," and calling for open dialogue and critical debate, Agbabi declares that "it is time for an integrated, holistic 21st century poetics."[56]

Agbabi admits to having felt some pressure to write in a black idiom that was unnatural to her, lacking as she did any direct link to Creole.[57] She found her way out of this impasse thanks, in no small part, to T.S. Eliot:

I like the essay "Traditional and the Individual Talent" a lot. It made me realise, why not use the standard classics if I like them and can use them? I think it's a shame to make distinctions between R & B, Northern Soul and English classics — if they give you pleasure, go for it.[58]

One hears echoes of Walcott and his similar determination to make as much use of as broad a poetic inheritance he felt possible:

I do not consider English to be the language of my masters. I consider language to be my birthright [...]. It is mine to do what other poets before me did, Dante, Chaucer, Villon, Burns, which is to fuse the noble and the common language.[59]

In blending the street-wise slang, the sex, drugs, rock 'n' roll/punk/Northern Soul of present-day Britain with twenty-first century contortions in the sonnet and sestina, Agbabi pioneers her own fusion of the noble and the common.

Exposed to the seemingly irreconcilable traditions of dub and T.S. Eliot, Agbabi re-writes her own rebellion. In the vernacular of contemporary life, she riffs on class, sexuality, gender, and race, unafraid of being "street" or making a statement. Socially accessible and socially relevant — does that make her public enough to be a public poet? She composes elegant sonnets and complex sestinas that speak of their maker's personal history, their own materiality as texts, and the existence of both poem and poet as constructions; she's a formalist and a thoroughly modern postmodernist exploring herself and her place on and off the page. Erudite, experimental, personally present — does this make her private enough to be a private poet? The answers to these questions are yes, no, and both. As in "Knew White Speech," Agbabi makes it clear that for her, the over-riding question is, "Am I poet enough?"[60]

NOTES

1. British Council website for on Contemporary Writers, "Patience Agbabi," <http://www.contemporarywriters.com/authors/?p=auth163>.

2. Patricia Ismond, "Walcott versus Brathwaite," *Critical Perspectives on Derek Walcott,* ed. Robert D. Hamner (Washington, D.C.: Three Continents Press, 1993, 220–236). Reprinted from *Caribbean Quarterly* 17 (Dec. 1971) 54–57. Ismond's article crystallized the opening of the debate, which has continued for decades.

3. Walcott, "The Muse of History," 354.

4. Even the term "Black British" was a contentious and highly contested ascription until halfway through the 1990s. As much as I can, I will follow the usage of whichever critic I am discussing. Otherwise, I will use the lower case.

5. See Mike Philips ("black British"), "Foreword: Migration, Modernity and English Writing — Reflections on Migrant Identity and Canon Formation," *A Black British Canon?* ed. Gail Low and Marion Wynne Davies (London: Palgrave Macmillan, 2006), 13, and Kadjia Sesay ("African British"), *Write Black, Write British: From Post Colonial to Black British Literature* (London: Hansib, 2005).

6. Stuart Hall, "New Ethnicities," *Black Film, British Cinema* (London: ICA Documents #6, 1988), quoted in Arana, "The 1980s: Retheorising and Refashioning British Identity," 236.

7. See Dawes in Sesay and Mahlete-Tsigé Getachew, "Marginalia: Black Literature and the Problem of Recognition," Sesay (ed.), 323–345, for detailed discussion of the publishing of black writers, especially poets, in Britain.

8. Patience Agbabi from Molly Thompson, "An Interview with Patience Agbabi," *Write Black, Write British*, ed. Sesay, 161,

9. Getachew, "Marginalia," 323–324.

10. Patience Agbabi in Thompson, "Interview," 161, emphasis added.

11. Kwame Dawes, "Black British Poetry: Some Considerations," *Write Black, Write British*, ed. Sesay.

12. Ibid., 283. See also Kwame Dawes, "Dichotomies of reading 'street poetry' and 'book poetry,'" *Critical Quarterly* 38:4 (Dec. 1996, 1–20).

13. Getachew, "Marginalia," 243.

14. D'Aguiar, 53. West Indians who came to Britain, beginning with the landing of *Empire Windrush* in 1948, were first greeted by the veiled hostility of tolerance. Later, as the numbers of arrivals grew, outright prejudice was followed quickly by institutionalized bigotry, the reaction to which culminated in the race riots of the 1980s. See Maria Couto, "To be Black and in Brixton," *Economic and Political Weekly* 16:9 (9 May 1981, 846–47).

15. Dub has been described as the "most original poetic form to have emerged in the English language in the last quarter century" (Fred D'Aguiar, quoted in Maya Jaggi, "Poet on the Front Line," The Guardian Profile: Linton Kwesi Johnson, *The Guardian* [4 May 2002]. <http://www.guardian.co.uk/books/2002/may/04/poetry.book>). G. A. Elmer Griffen defines the form succinctly:

> [D]ub poetry is a highly developed, politically charged rhythmic art form which merges local musical folk idioms (initially reggae) with political commentary and analysis. It combines the values of poetry, the properties of voice as instrument, and the power of the vernacular, spoken in the context of political resistance and identity assertion. It places itself subtly and elusively between political speech, dramatic recitation, and song.

G.A. Elmer Griffen, "Word Bullets: Dub in the postcolonial language debate," Rev. of *Verbal Riddim: The Politics and Aesthetics of African-Caribbean Dub Poetry* by Christian Habekost (Amsterdam and Atlanta: Rodopi, 1993) in *Transition* 6 (1995, 57–65), 60.

16. Dawes, "Dichotomies," 16.

17. Walder, *Post-colonial Literatures*, 134.

18. As Savory explains, "Self has an important contradictory identity in his writing, being both a particular moment of existence and part of the collective *nam* of African-descended peoples." Elaine Savory, "The Word becomes nam: Self and Community in the Poetry of Kamau Braithwaite, and its relation to Caribbean Culture and Postmodern Theory," *Writing the Nation: Self and Country in the Post-colonial Imagination*, ed. John C. Hawley (Amsterdam and Atlanta: Rodopi, 1996, 23–41), 24.

19. Ibid., 27.

20. Doris Somner, "Who can tell?: Filling in blanks for Cirilo Villaverde," *Writing the Nation*, 88–107.

21. Kamau Brathwaite, "What Marcus Tellin Us," introduction to Marc Matthews' *Guyana My Altar* (London: Karnak House), quoted in Donnell and Lawson Welsh, 366.

22. See Mutabaruka, "Only a revolution can bring about a solution," an interview with Gerhard Dilger in *Collier*, 249–255.

23. Walder, *Post-colonial Literatures*, 143.

24. Jean Binta Breeze, "Can a Dub Poet be a Woman," *The Routledge Reader in Caribbean Literature*, ed. Donnell and Lawson Welsh, 498–500. Reprinted from *Women: A Cultural Review* I:I (1990), 47–49.

25. Breeze, "Can a Dub Poet be a Woman," 499.

26. Jean Binta Breeze, Patience Agbabi, Jillian Tipene, Ruth Harrison, and Vicki Bertram, "A Round-Table Discussion on Poetry in Performance," *Feminist Review* 62, Contemporary Women Poets (Summer 1999, 24–54), 40.

27. Breeze et al., "Roundtable," 45.

28. Patience Agbabi, *R.A.W.* (London: Izon Amazon in Association with Gecko Press, 1995).

29. Ibid., 48.

30. Ibid., 48, 63.

31. Ibid., 63.

32. Ibid., 52.

33. Patience Agbabi, *Transformatrix* (Edinburgh: Canongate, 2000).

34. Agbabi in Thompson, "Interview," 163.

35. Agbabi, *Transformatrix*, 9; Lauri Ramey, "Patience Agbabi: Freedom in Form," *Sable Litmag* 11 (Autumn 2007, 75–77, 93–96) 75.

36. Agbabi, *Transformatrix*, 10.

37. Ibid., 78.

38. Ibid., 11.

39. Ibid., 78.

40. Ibid., 11.

41. Sarah Broom, *Contemporary British and Irish Poetry: An Introduction* (London: Palgrave/Macmillan 2006), 255–56.

42. Nicky Marsh, "'Peddlin Noh Puerile Parchment of Ethnicity': Questioning Performance in New Black British Poetry," *Wasafiri* 45 (2005), 46–51 (46).

43. Lauri Ramey, "Situating a 'Black' British Poetic Avant-Garde," "*Black*" *British Aesthetics Today*, ed. Arana, 79–100.

44. Morris, "Printing the Performance," 247. Morris was specifically criticizing the decision of Paula Burnett to organize her anthology into sections entitled "The Oral Tradition" and "The Literary Tradition." Paula Burnett (ed.), *The Penguin Book of Caribbean Verse in English* (Harmondsworth: Penguin, 1986).

45. Ibid., 246.
46. Ibid., 242.
47. Walter J. Ong, *Orality and Literacy: The Technologizing of the Word* (London: Methuen, 1982) 101, quoted in Morris, "Printing the Performance," 242.
48. Brathwaite, *History of the Voice*, 18, quoted in Morris, 242, emphasis added.
49. Ibid., quoted in Morris, 254.
50. "every 'I' is a // fiction finally. Phantom narrator, resume" (28, V, ii). Derek Walcott, *Omeros* (New York: Farrar, Straus and Giroux, 1990).
51. Patience Agbabi, *Bloodshot Monochrome* (Edinburgh: Canongate, 2008).
52. Ibid., 40, 34, 42, 45.
53. Ibid., 31; the names of the "Contributors" are arranged chronologically: Henry Howard, Earl of Surrey; William Shakespeare; Lady Mary Wroth; John Milton; Charlotte Smith; William Wordsworth; John Keats; Elizabeth Barrett Browning; Gerard Manley Hopkins; Robert Frost; Claude McKay; Edna St Vincent Millay; Gwendolyn Brooks; June Jordan.
54. Ibid., 37; T. S. Eliot, "Philip Massinger," Kermode (153–160), 153.
55. Commending Agbabi's work, Nicky Marsh notes that Mallissa Read and Akure Wall also explore relationships to their culture and their art on the page ("'Peddlin,'" 50).
56. Agbabi, "Word of Mouth," 29.
57. Ramey, "Patience Agbabi," 94.
58. Agbabi, quoted in Ramey, "Patience Agbabi," 77.
59. Walcott, quoted in Sjoberg, 82 (reprinted in Walder, 127).
60. Agbabi, *Bloodshot Monochrome*, 45.

WORKS CITED

Agbabi, Patience (1995). *R.A.W.* London: Izon Amazon in Association with Gecko Press.
_____ (2000). *Transformatrix.* Edinburgh: Payback Press.
_____ (2002). "Word of Mouth: Deconstructing the 'p' words: 'performance,' 'page' and 'poetry.'" MA Thesis. University of Sussex.
_____ (2008). *Bloodshot Monochrome.* Edinburgh: Canongate.
Arana, R. Victoria (2005). "The 1980s: Retheorising and Refashioning British Identity." *Write Black, Write British: From Post Colonial to Black British Literature.* Ed. Kadjia Sesay. London: Hansib, 230–240.
_____, ed. (2007). *"Black" British Aesthetics Today.* Newcastle: Cambridge Scholars Publishing.
Brathwaite, Kamau (1984). *The History of the Voice.* London: New Beacon Books.
_____ (1987). "What Marcus Tellin Us." Introduction to Mark Matthews' *Guyana My Altar.* London: Karnak House.
_____ (1996). "Jazz and the West Indian Novel, I, II, and III." *The Routledge Reader in Caribbean Literature.* Ed. Alison Donnell and Sarah Lawson Welsh. London: Routledge, 336–343. Reprinted from *Bim* 12:44 (1967, 275–84), *Bim* 12:45 (1967, 39–51), and *Bim* 12:46 (1968, 115–26).
Breeze, Jean Binta, Patience Agbabi, Jillian Tipene, Ruth Harrison, and Vicki Bertram (1999). "A Round-Table Discussion on Poetry in Performance." *Feminist Review,* 62, 24–54.
Breeze, Jean Binta (1996). "Can a Dub Poet be a Woman." *The Routledge Reader in Caribbean Literature.* Ed. Alison Donnell and Sarah Lawson Welsh. London: Routledge, 498–500. Reprinted from *Women: A Cultural Review,* 1:1 (1990), 47–49.
British Council Website on Contemporary Writers. "Patience Agbabi." <http://www.contemporarywriters.com/authors/?p=auth163>.
Broom, Sarah (2006). *Contemporary British and Irish Poetry: An Introduction.* London: Palgrave (Macmillan).
Brown, Stewart, and Mark McWatt (eds.) (2005). *The Oxford Book of Caribbean Verse.* Oxford: Oxford University Press.
Burnett, Paula (ed.) (1986). *The Penguin Book of Caribbean Verse in English.* Harmondsworth: Penguin.
Collier, Gordon (ed.) (1992). *Us / Them: Translation, Transcription and Identity in Post-Colonial Literary Cultures.* Amsterdam and Atlanta: Rodopi.
Couto, Maria (1981). "To be Black and in Brixton." *Economic and Political Weekly,* 16:9, 846–847.
D'Aguiar, Fred (1993). "Have you been here long? Black Poetry in Britain." *New British Poetries: The Scope of the Possible.* Eds. Robert Hampson and Peter Barry. Manchester and New York: Manchester University Press, 51–71.
Dawes, Kwame (2005). "Black British Poetry: Some Considerations." *Write Black, Write British: From Post Colonial to Black British Literature.* Ed. Kadjia Sesay. London: Hansib, 282–299.
_____ (1996). "Dichotomies of reading 'street poetry' and 'book poetry.'" *Critical Quarterly,* 38:4, 1–20.
Donnell, Alison, and Sarah Lawson Welsh (eds.) (1996). *The Routledge Reader in Caribbean Literature.* London: Routledge.

Eliot, T.S. (1975). "Philip Massinger." *Selected Prose of T.S. Eliot.* Ed. Frank Kermode. New York: Farrar, Straus and Giroux, 153–160.

_____ (1975). "Tradition and the Individual Talent." *Selected Prose of T.S. Eliot.* Ed. Frank Kermode. New York: Farrar, Straus and Giroux, 37–44.

Getachew, Mahlete-Tsigé (2005). "Marginalia: Black Literature and the Problem of Recognition." *Write Black, Write British: From Post Colonial to Black British Literature.* Ed. Kadjia Sesay. London: Hansib, 323–345.

Griffen, G. A. Elmer (1995). "Word Bullets: Dub in the postcolonial language debate." Rev. of *Verbal Riddim: The Politics and Aesthetics African-Caribbean Dub Poetry,* by Christian Habekost. Amsterdam and Atlanta: Rodopi, 1993. *Transition,* 6, 57–65.

Hall, Stuart (1988). "New Ethnicities." *Black Film, British Cinema.* London: ICA Documents #6.

Hamner, Robert D. (ed.). (1997). *Critical Perspectives on Derek Walcott.* Washington, D.C.: Three Continents Press.

Hawley, John C. (ed.) (1996). *Writing the Nation: Self and Country in the Post-colonial Imagination.* Amsterdam and Atlanta: Rodopi.

Hughes, Langston (2004). "The Negro Artist and the Racial Mountain." *Twentieth Century American Poetics.* Ed. Dana Gioia, David Mason, and Meg Schoerke. New York: McGraw-Hill, 148–15. Reprinted from *The Nation,* 1926.

Ismond, Patricia (1993). "Walcott versus Brathwaite." *Critical Perspectives on Derek Walcott.* Ed. Robert D. Hamner. Washington, D.C.: Three Continents Press, 220–236. Reprinted from *Caribbean Quarterly* 17:3–4 (Dec. 1971), 54–57.

Jaggi, Maya (2002). "Poet on the Front Line." The Guardian Profile: Linton Kwesi Johnson. *The Guardian* (May 4). <http://www.guardian.co.uk/books/2002/may/04/poetry.book>.

Kermode, Frank (ed.) (1975). *Selected Prose of T.S. Eliot.* New York: Farrar, Straus and Giroux.

Low, Gail, and Marion Wynne Davies (eds.) (2006). *A Black British Canon?* London: Palgrave Macmillan.

Marsh, Nicky (2005). "'Peddlin Noh Puerile Parchment of Etninicity': Questioning Performance in New Black British Poetry." *Wasafiri,* 45, 46–51.

Morris, Mervyn (1992). "Printing the Performance: 'Them' and 'Us'?" *Us / Them: Translation, Transcription and Identity in Post-Colonial Literary Cultures.* Ed. Gordon Collier. Amsterdam and Atlanta: Rodopi, 241–47.

Mutabaruka (1992). "Only a revolution can bring about a solution." Interview with Gerhard Dilger. *Us / Them: Translation, Transcription and Identity in Post-Colonial Literary Cultures.* Ed. Gordon Collier. Amsterdam and Atlanta: Rodopi, 249–255.

Ong, Walter J. (1982). *Orality and Literacy: The Technologizing of the Word.* London: Methuen.

Phillips, Mike (2006). "Foreword: Migration, Modernity and English Writing — Reflections on Migrant Identity and Canon Formation." *A Black British Canon?* Ed. Gail Low and Wynne Davies. London: Palgrave Macmillan, 13–31.

Ramey, Lauri (2007). "Situating a 'Black' British Poetic Avant-Garde." *"Black" British Aesthetics Today.* Ed. R. Victoria Arana. Newcastle: Cambridge Scholars Publishing, 79–100.

_____ (2007). "Patience Agbabi: Freedom in Form." *Sable Litmag* (Autumn 11), 75–77, 93–96.

Savory, Elaine (1996). "The Word becomes nam: Self and Community in the Poetry of Kamau Braithwaite, and its relation to Caribbean Culture and Postmodern Theory." *Writing the Nation: Self and Country in the Post-colonial Imagination.* Ed. John C. Hawley. Amsterdam and Atlanta: Rodopi, 23–41.

Sesay, Kadjia (ed.) (2005). *Write Black, Write British: From Post Colonial to Black British Literature.* London: Hansib.

Sjoberg, Leif (1996). "An Interview with Derek Walcott." *Conversations with Derek Walcott.* Ed. William Baer. University Press of Mississippi.

Thompson, Molly (2005). "An Interview with Patience Agbabi." *Write Black, Write British: From Post Colonial to Black British Literature.* Ed. Kadjia Sesay. London: Hansib, 146–64.

Walcott, Derek (1990). *Omeros.* New York: Farrar, Straus and Giroux.

_____ (1996). "The Muse of History." *The Routledge Reader in Caribbean Literature.* Ed. Alison Donnell and Sarah Lawson Welsh. London: Routledge, 354–358. Reprinted from O. Coombs (ed.) (1974). *Is Massa Day Dead.* New York: Doubleday/Anchor Press.

Walder, Dennis (1998). *Post-colonial Literatures in English: History Language Theory.* Oxford: Blackwell.

6. Strictly Private? Stephen Romer's "Les Portes de la Nuit"

Adrian Grafe

Dante's assertion that the most elevated or worthy subjects for poetry are love, virtue and war is sometimes taken to mean that love and virtue are concerns for the private sphere alone, while it is war which is fittest for public speech. These three concerns — all of which are capable of both private and public enactments and interpretations — come together in one and the same poem: "Les Portes de la Nuit," by Stephen Romer.[1]

However, before exploring poetry and this poem in particular, it is worth stating that there is a tension between public and private, and that behind this tension lies that between the particular and the universal. Privacy (the particular) is in fact a space on which history (the universal) impacts, and which also affects history. Do such considerations have any bearing in turn on the act of authorship, especially the authorship of poetry and of the genre of the diary, a strictly private mode of expression which is nevertheless concerned with the exposure, presentation, or performance, of the self to the self? And which, if it falls into the wrong hands — or the poet's — can be published for all the world to read in what is a singularly beautiful poem of loneliness and longing like "Les Portes de la Nuit"?

Before turning to the poem itself, it might be worth glancing first at Romer's previous work from the public-private aspect, though it should be said that only in *Yellow Studio* does this dimension become crucial, and then exploring the context of the poem within the volume on the one hand and the historical context of the events referred to in the poem on the other. In his first published collection, *Idols* (1986), dedicated to his parents, Stephen Romer paid homage to his grandparents in "Wellingtonia," his grandfather "full of facts and detail," his grandmother "an upstairs painter."[2] In his second collection, *Plato's Ladder* (1992), he wrote of his painter sister, calling her "my Proserpine of summer," while in "A Studio in the Mountains" — the title anticipates *Yellow Studio*—from his third volume, *Tribute* (1998), he returns to her, confessing the comparison was wrong, and quoting (without speech-marks) from a letter of hers: "the house/now stinks of loneliness."[3] The cover of *Yellow Studio* is a detail of a picture of the same name painted by his sister, and the "Yellow Studio" of the poem could easily be related to the "yellow room" in "the house/I grew up in" in the poem "Braughing" from the *Tribute* volume. Along with such allusions to Romer's sister and childhood home, his poetry manifests heightened sensitivity to the workings of history, especially the modern period. An example is Part 3 of *Plato's Ladder*, inspired by an extended stay in Poland and making use of accounts of the Lodz ghetto, particularly in "The Satrap" and "All Souls," the former recounting a visit by the poet to the remains and unmarked graves of that ghetto and the latter meditating, more impersonally, on its ambiguous Nazi-appointed "Chairman," Mordecai Rumkowski. Nevertheless, poems like these are necessarily at least at one remove from historical reality.

But because Romer has his father's diary — and precisely because it his father's — his approach to the post–War years as his father experienced them is more immediate, especially to the extent that, according to William Wootten in his review of *Yellow Studio*, these poems of Romer's constitute a "quest to get closer to his father." What Wootten calls the "particular emotional directness" of these poems — which makes them new in Romer's work — is all the same inseparable from their historical backdrop.[4] And the poems in the section of *Yellow Studio* devoted to his father are among Romer's finest because he achieves a confidentiality of tone in them more intense than in any of his previous work.

In relation to poetry Bernard O'Donoghue has talked about responding to the public world in contrast with the poet's inner world.[5] He has argued that it's quite hard to write a public poem as compared to a poem about what's going on in the poet's head. He admires poets like Heaney and Paulin for this reason and says poets should address themselves to events. But in "Les Portes de la Nuit" we are given a variant on this dichotomy: for one thing "the world inside the poet's head" is missing, or only indirectly present, because he concentrates on, gives the poem up to, his father's life and mind; and for another, the public world is present with the references to army life, the London crowds and named public places, the cinema, and the date, which signals Cold War austerity and reminds us of the two million individuals who were conscripted between 1947 and 1963. Stephen Romer says: "[There are] moments when the 'pressure of public events' becomes such that the poet has to confront them (Spender's statement in the '30's). It was important in the poems for my father to give the historical context of the time, however briefly ('India, Lolita, the Marshall Plan'): the private is so often acted out against the larger, overpowering forces of public events."[6] Without the historical, public context, these poems would be all the poorer. Indeed, their intimate side is heightened by that context.

The historical context had an impact on every aspect of people's private lives. In July 1943, a notorious bachelor, Philip Larkin, wrote: "Everything about the ree-lay-shun-ship between men and women makes me *angry*. It's all a fucking balls-up. It might have been organized by the army, or the Ministry of Food."[7] Larkin is probably referring both to emotional chaos and misunderstanding on the one hand, and the austerity or dearth of the war years — the post-war years were little different in this respect — on the other. The Ministry of Food dealt with price control and rationing. Food rationing did not end until 1954.

"Les Portes de la Nuit" is the fourth of twenty-four poems which make up the fifth and final section of *Yellow Studio*. The volume bears comparison with Hugo Williams's *Letters Home* with its numerous poems about the poet's actor father, and both poets versify their fathers' prose: Williams his father's letters and Romer his father's diary. Stephen Romer makes it clear at the beginning of "Les Portes de la Nuit" that he's not going to be outdone by Williams in this respect. Williams's father's letters were not a recent discovery, and indeed have been published in their original (prose) form in a separate volume. The poems about or to Romer's father are characterized by, among other things, the poet's discovery of his father's diary, and quotations from his diary. These poems are also reminiscent of John Mortimer's *A Voyage Round My Father*, another affectionate tribute to a lawyer father of strong if not eccentric character. There is something quintessentially English about Williams's and Mortimer's literary appreciations of their fathers, and the same is true of Romer's, especially as the cultural and geographical setting is so typically English — which makes the references to French language and culture all the more foreign. This last section in Romer's book, by far the longest in the collection, is the only one to carry a title: "An Enthusiast." These poems are dedicated to the memory of the poet's father. They constitute a response to the poet's father and his death on the one hand and, on the other, to the poet's discovery of his father's diary. The poems owe something of their drama and energy to this discovery, disclosing to the poet new sides of his father. In the "Enthusiast" poems he brings the reader into even more intimate contact with his father than he had done in "Wellingtonia" with his grandparents, through the quotations from his father's diaries, rendered by the poet as verse and worked into the warp and weft of the poems. The "Enthusiast" poems — "Les Portes de la Nuit" is no exception in this respect — are, in terms of social and political life and the international context, "full of facts and detail." The drama of the poet's father's life is seen to unfold against this historical backdrop.

The poem centers on the revelation by the poet of a delicate public-private moment that his father consigned to his "Strictly Private" diary: the physical encounter between two strangers — the poet's father when a young man and a young girl — while they are watching *Les Portes de la Nuit*, a French film of the period. From the beginning, the poem draws the reader's attention to these two dimensions of the poem — the physical and the cinematic:

> The matinée looks and height
> set him apart
> in any cinema or theatre foyer
> when we sought my father out
>
> on an evening trip to London:

The way the poem follows the family's and especially the father's steps so closely makes the poem almost a detective novel in itself— one might even mix genres and call it a biographical or autobiographical detective novel. The collocation of "we" and "my father" in the fourth line draws the reader into the poet's family life, while the context is the public one of "any cinema or theatre foyer." Having evoked the matter of family history, the poem delves even further back into the past — this time, the past of the father alone, before he became a father. But the "precedents" the poet speaks of for his family outings to London are drawn not from what the poet has known so far of his father's past, but from his father's *Strictly Private Diary*: by directly quoting the title his father gave to his diary, the poet stresses its intimate nature. More than intimate, in fact, the title of the diary — especially in conjunction with the equally suggestive poem title — evokes taboos and dark, forbidden secrets: the father's experiences and yearnings, his states of mind, his failures perhaps, and his longing for an absolute, expressed in this poem in relation to marriage, and elsewhere in the volume in religious terms. The adverb in the diary title may also reflect a certain kind of repression in the father. The father has come to London from "Camp," we learn in the final stanza. His changing from "clammy khaki into coolest civvies" (the adjectives are telling) and his choice of a French film represent a longing for freedom and a sense of escapism. By the time the film title is mentioned in the poem, "Lyons" has been adverted to twice. Though it is shorthand for Lyons Corner House, the French place-name cannot be overlooked: "had a meal in Lyons." Such details bring the poem into even closer resonance with France as the country Romer has elected to live in (signaled in the biographical presentation in the volume and mentioned frequently in the poems themselves and in previous volumes).

The poem does not allude to the film other than its title. Even though the poem does not refer to the content of the film itself, the film in fact mingles romance, fantasy and the wartime context. Once the reader knows this, the content of the film cannot but resonate within the poem. The film, then, provides the romantic, very French setting for the encounter in the cinema. By entering "the doors of night," the father and the girl, within the darkness of the cinema, find themselves set free to engage in romance with a stranger. The core of the poem is the father's remarkable description of the way contact develops and strengthens between him and the girl. The father's desire and loneliness — both likely intensified by the film — meet with a reciprocal response from the girl, her bare arms — a detail the father insists upon — seeming to be an invitation in this sense. The way in which the two almost-lovers feel their way into contact with each other is like a ballet: "my left elbow/her right arm," "my hand/her arm," "my grasp/she clasped/my hand in hers," "her shoulders/my left arm," all this leading to: "we sat/clasped together like lovers." No amount of description or paraphrase can match the intricate, gradually-found reciprocity of these stanzas.

Part of the fascination of the poem lies in the poet's versifying his father's prose: it is an act of ventriloquism by which the father becomes the poet and vice versa. The reciprocal intimacy into which the father and the girl enter is somehow mirrored by the intimacy into which the poet enables the reader to enter with his father — and therefore with himself.

When the two intimate strangers come out of the cinema, the poem also shifts. The loose free-verse rhythms — kept under tight control by the four-line stanza pattern and the regular number of stanzas — make way, for one line, for the shadow of an iambic pentameter rhythm: "there was no desire stronger in his mind" — as the father reveals to his diary, and therefore to himself, and as the poet reveals to the reader, what the experience in the cinema means to the father.

The second half of the poem also shifts, then, to the extent that the poem highlights that most private of spaces — even more private than matters of sexuality — the mind: "no desire stronger in his mind," "mentally dazed," "his mind elsewhere," "my mind disturbed," "he's... / reading Wundt's *Psychology.*"

After his experience in and outside the cinema, the father takes refuge in reading Wundt's *Psychology*— in his mind, in other words. The father follows a trajectory that takes him from army camp to the outside world of city streets and restaurants to the inside world of the cinema and back outside again: it is possible to see in this trajectory a weaving in and out of public and private spaces. The father's visit to a private space, his grandmother's in Kensington, shows him wearing a mask: he reveals nothing to her of what he has just experienced (of what he will only consign to his diary) and his mind is "elsewhere." He only takes off this public face for the diary.

The "pleasant" nature of the contact with the girl is offset by mental turbulence — some might see the father as repressed or over-scrupulous. The poem might therefore be considered as being structured about a cluster of opposites calling for reconciliation or equilibrium, in order to resolve a state of disturbance: body/mind, man/woman, tumultuousness/steadiness, single-hood/marriage, loneliness/integration, army life/civvy street, England/France. The first line of the last stanza — "One page later" — brings the father "back [to] Camp," and the poet back into the poem. For it is he who turns the pages of his father's diary, publishing a poem made out of material his father so wished to keep private. For, if what gives the poem its "urgency," to use Romer's word, is the poet's response to the diary, what gives the diary material its intensity is precisely its private nature and, even more precisely, the father's wish to keep it private.

The function of the father's diary, in as far as we can speculate on it, is worth considering. It is as though the recording of daily events and even thoughts and feelings in order to look back on them later to jog the diarist's memory were not necessarily the main purpose of the diary. The diary as found here is a form of introspection in which the writer works through his conflicting feelings and thoughts, and decides what is right for him and what is not, what he wants and doesn't want, however "pleasant" it may be. In this particular case, the diary writer's introspection leads him to a kind of extro-spection, by which he turns his gaze outward to society.

The father's behavior as presented to us by the son, the poet, is explic-itly informed by the tension between public and private. In conversation with his grandmother, as said above, he shows her a public face or mask while his "mind" is "elsewhere"; incidentally, the fact that the body of a human being can be in one place and his mind in another is a psychological mark of the public-private divide. Thus there is a perfect analogy between the father's absent-minded conversation with his grandmother and his keeping his strictly private diary. The poem's public dimension relates it to the social history of the post-war years. The poem begins and ends in two social worlds: that of the family seen as a unit and the army camp to which the father returns at the end. The privacy of the diary is not simply due to the potentially shame-ful or sexual nature of the material it holds, but due to the fact that it reflects the inner life of the diary writer, who was struggling to keep his private and inner lives intact in circumstances (doing his National Service at Camp) in which he had so little privacy. The poem enables us to witness the father within different public settings, but also within the inner world of his experience as filtered through his diary and the poem.

If private and public lives are both present, in fact several lives come together in the poem, including civil life, with the "civvies" and crowded city streets, the moral life with the father's demanding and troubled conscience, and what might be called the examined life, with the diary and the poem itself. The father's "*Strictly Private Diary*/of 1947" is a means of resistance within the excessively corporate, public life he was leading as a National Service conscript in 1947, the year conscription was brought in. The necessity for a private life was intensified by the conditions in which the conscripts lived:

> National Service afforded a unique opportunity to experience communal living [...]. There were approximately forty of us in one barrack-room, so one had to learn how to live with people. Everyone developed a remarkable frankness and honesty. People used to often leave their money on the bed after pay parade, knowing it would be there when they came back after tea. We also had wonderful discussions in bed at night on the "usual subjects" and also our future plans after demob.[8]

Army Camps had their own cinemas and one might conclude that if the father was going to the cinema outside camp it was not for the film but for the possibility of just such an encounter, brief or otherwise. At the camps themselves, what sex there was tended to be particularly public:

> The small town of Wetherby was invaded every week-end by hordes of girls from Leeds, known as "The Leeds Commandos," because they were "in action in all weathers." Some even operated through the wire fence of the camp. Taff Bish and I often had the duty of patrol and used to hide until some poor trainee and his lady friend achieved a near climax. Then we would leap out and beat the fence with our sticks, making the whole structure rattle and spoiling the final ecstasy.[9]

The fact that the father is searching for the "firm friendship" he has not yet found, combined with the fact that he lives a public life, means that his firm friend is the diary itself: "[On] the surface I seem to have everything," writes Anne Frank, "except my one true friend. [...] This is why I've started the diary. [...] I don't want to jot down the facts in this diary the way most people would do, but I want the diary to be my friend [...]."[10] Although published diaries are plentiful and one can find examples of diary poems — Louis MacNeice's *Autumn Journal* comes to mind — it is less common to find someone else's diary than the author's transformed into a poem. If the poem owes its thematic singularity to one thing in particular, it is to the fact that it reflects on the behavior of a man who was living his own private life as a bachelor before he had his children, and who is the poet's father: it is therefore a reflection on what it means to be the son of a father. To their children parents are naturally public figures. But they had lives — private lives — before their children were born, and continue to have them after they are born. The poem then is a reflection on sonship if not fatherhood, both relationships, because familial, that we can situate on the cusp between public and private: the family being both a private space and a founding societal institution. The poem gives us a poetic insight into the father's private experience and into his mind, as well as a poetic insight into the son's discovery of his father: to discover his father's early strictly private diary is to discover his father. And it is another stage to make both the private diary and its discovery public. The poem on the one hand and the diary contained within the poem on the other give rise to the question of authorship: here are two authors with private things to say, albeit in different ways. The poem is the mirror of the father's diary: it is a diary, too, of family life and of the discovery of the diary ("I now find"):

> [...] our family dinner
> at Lyons or the Golden Egg
> had precedents, I now find,
>
> from his *Strictly Private Diary*
> of 1947 [...].

But the poem shares its name with a film — *Les Portes de la Nuit*, an aesthetic, imaginative, emotional, imaginative experience with, like any film shown at a cinema, a public, collective dimension, both in terms of the making and reception of it, while writing and reading are supposedly more solitary, private activities. But language — the very stuff of reading and writing — is interactive. "[...] [P]henomena [such as language] gain the necessary degree of constancy only when they become collective."[11]

The film itself came out in December 1946, and is pitched perfectly between public and private. The film takes place just after World War II and briefly follows a cast of mainly rather louche characters several of whom have made illicit fortunes during the war. This includes a spiv played by an oily Pierre Brasseur who drives a Rolls with a GB number-plate, probably to cock a snook at the British. The film has excellent poetic credentials, as the screenplay was written by Jacques Prévert. It doesn't hang together entirely logically, as it blends social realism regarding the war and its aftermath with darker, tragic tones such as the figure of Fate played by Jean Vilar as a tramp who follows the characters about, telling them what's going to happen to them. The film has some charming chat-up lines typical of the time, such as when the leading female character, Malou, played by Nathalie Nattier, says to Yves Montand, "*Vous croyez vraiment au bonheur?*" (Do you really believe in happiness?) he replies, "*Oui, quand je vous regarde.*" (I do when I gaze upon you). The first time the father is mentioned in the poem it is already in theatrical or cinematic terms: he is compared to a matinée idol. He then becomes associated with the shady, foreign, indeed French, social and magic realism of *Les Portes de la Nuit*.[12] Therefore the idea of performance might be relevant to an understanding of the poem and of the question of the public-private divide.

The poem is pitched formally between regularity and irregularity. The free verse, relative absence of rhyme, and vast number of run-on lines and stanzas make it irregular, while the quatrains, reflected in the number of stanzas (sixteen), give it a semblance of regularity. The poet gives over five whole stanzas, the fifth to the eighth, and later the fifteenth, to the diary. These stanzas, and all the diary quotes, are contained within the poet's own words, as though the strictly private material were encased within the outer husk — one might call it the public presentation — offered by the poet's words. The private world of the diary recounts the father's experience in ways which go beyond appearances. The initially pleasant experience with the girl is found to be unsettling because incompatible with the father's idea of friendship and marriage. We learn in the second line that the father is "set apart." This fact, along with his loneliness, is at one with his strong desire for marriage. The experience with the girl in the cinema is a watershed in the man's life: "from this time on," the poem says, the man's strongest desire was marriage. This information is given in poetically particular terms. When Kafka broke off his engagement to Felice he argued that it was because neither of them was single enough to marry.[13] Whatever Kafka meant by that, the father in the Romer poem declines to make a firm arrangement with the girl in the cinema because he himself isn't single enough. He's already climbing Plato's ladder; he's already married, in fact — wedded to his ideal of the girl he wants to marry.

The energy of the poem derives partly from the father's perception of himself as a moral being. One notices first of all the number of doubts and hesitations that enter the poem once he has left the girl: "but nevertheless decided.../ though from this time on.../ But they kissed on the lips / though his mind elsewhere / but my mind disturbed." Was the pleasure disturbing? Nietzsche wrote in *Human, All too Human*: "In morality man treats himself not as *individuum* but as *dividuum*."[14] One dimension of this *dividuum* is arguably the public-private divide: the idea that morality is a space where the human being is either divided between public and private or is both those things. The phrase "*the* girl" with the italicized definite article indicates the father's search for the right girl — right as in romantically suited, and also just, moral. That girl and not the one in the cinema (or the poem) turned out to be the poet's mother, to whom *Yellow Studio* is dedicated, and who appears in other poems in the volume. There is a sense in "Les Portes de la Nuit" that the events and emotions recounted in it are of the deepest concern to the poet, to the extent that his own life is bound up with them.

The transition from private to public is effected through words, speech (poetic speech): the encounter related in the diary happens in a public place but remains private, not because of the half-light in the cinema but because no words are exchanged. The beautiful, forensically detailed description of the complex interlacing of hands, arms and shoulders, the response of hand to hand, pressure to pressure, is an image of the interlacing effect of the way in which the different elements and run-on lines of the poem come to form a whole. If the father decides against making a "firm arrangement" with the girl, the girl is nevertheless an excellent muse, as the description of the development of the physical contact between them shows. It is the poem itself that comes to be the "firm arrangement" (mirrored later by the desire for the "firm friendship") — sixteen quatrains, moving on several temporal levels — the poet's father declines to make with the girl. The adjective "firm" is almost analogous to the word "strict": the latter is derived etymologically from the verb past participle *strictus* of the verb *stringere*, to tighten. The description of the gradually intensifying physical contact between the two characters (the father and the girl) is given in terms of increasing tightness: "... increased the pressure.../...extended/my grasp... she clasped/my hand.../...we sat/clasped together..." The development of the poem through the quatrain form, and the fact that sixteen is a multiple of four, give the poem relentlessness, a kind of tightness that is satisfying aesthetically and also corresponds to dimensions of the poem's meaning. The father's single-minded — strict — pursuit of an ideal of love — an ideal in the name of which he rejects the idea of any further meeting with the girl in the cinema, despite her acknowledged qualities — is not the least of these dimensions. And there is an analogy between the experience in the cinema and the strictly private diary: they go hand in hand, the enclosed world of the cinema and the strictly private nature of the diary. Yet the cinema is a particular context: semi-dark, half-lit, public but intimate.

The poet italicizes and capitalizes the words *Strictly Private Diary* thus giving the diary title a similar kind of referential or artistic status as *Les Portes de la Nuit* in the poem. The title is both a deterrent and an attraction: a deterrent because it is a notice of the "Keep Off the Grass" or "Beware of the Dog" type; and an attraction precisely because it suggests that its author has something to hide and arouses one's curiosity as to what it could be. In an essay entitled "Public and Private Art," the American poet Anthony Hecht argues that even "that supremely public art of architecture [...] can be exclusive and private." One of the ways it can be so, according to Hecht, is "those ostentations of wealth and power exhibited in the palaces and villas that are calculated to excite our envy and emulation but from which we are firmly denied access by posted signs saying 'Private Property.'"[15] Not only envy or emulation, I would add, but curiosity: the passer-by is made to feel all the more intrigued by the building because of the notice.

This kind of writing depends on privacy for its quality. That is, the words *Strictly Private Diary* are strictly tautological: how can a diary worth its salt be anything but private? A diary with nothing private in it would be superficial or exterior autobiography or history, if that. Because it is so strictly private, reading the diary has the feel of transgression about it: crossing forbidden frontiers. If reading the diary is forbidden, is writing it equally so? There may indeed be something transgressive about the very acts of reading and writing, whatever the material itself. The French writer and novelist Pierre Michon says that his book about Watteau is his most autobiographical text: "*J'y rends compte de l'inavouable, étant entendu que l'inavouable est d'ordre évidemment sexuel.*"[16] [I discuss in it what is too shameful to mention, it being understood that what is too shameful to mention is obviously sexual]. Is the father's diary, then, so strictly private because it contains sexual material, material too shameful to mention? Another poem in the "Enthusiast" section of *Yellow Studio* has Romer's father confessing "'a vast list!'" to a chaplain at Cambridge in the same stanza as "'amorous conduct'" (the father's, as noted in his diary) is mentioned.[17] A diary that goes beyond the recording of historical event — a diary of the kind written by Romer's father — may have a confessional dimension: "'confession' is not the sum of admissions, nor content as such, but Janus-faced form: it probes the recesses to reveal whatever both shuns release and also yearns to be released."[18] Because the diary is so strictly private by definition it shuns publication, yet its contents demand to be said — and if they demand to be said, don't they also demand to be made public, strictly public? The success of a diary depends on how far the author is prepared to adopt a no-holds-barred approach: the less he holds back, the less reservedly he confides in it, the more successful will it be. By calling the Diary *Strictly Private*, doesn't its author actually advertise the privacy of its contents, thereby making their nature public, so that in truth they demand to be read? "Only the quality of the poem, its sense of urgency, can 'justify' the material it is made from," says Stephen Romer. "If readers recognize, empathize with the intensity of the encounter with my father through his 'strictly private diaries,' then that goes some way to justifying my transgression of his privacy; but the recognition of the reader is also a 'by-product' of the encounter, I am not writing to please or to appeal. I think it is precisely the private and 'urgent' nature of the encounter that most readers have responded to."[19] The strictly private nature of the diary adds an additional frisson of excitement to the reading of these poems, the diary reflecting its privacy back onto the poem. The reader shares in the sense of discovery and revelation communicated by the poet.

It was Hugo Williams who in a *TLS* Freelance column once wrote: "I remember something Martin Amis said, about writing his first novel: if you're writing under the desk, you're probably on to something. I have always held that up as an ideal. I even put it into a poem: 'I was a lovesick crammer-candidate, / writing poetry under the desk in History.'"[20] If Stephen Romer has taken up the title of the film *Les Portes de la Nuit* seen by his father and given the poem the same title, couldn't the diary title also be applied to the poem? It's strictly private, it's writing under the desk. (Incidentally, Martin Amis made some telling comments on poetry, saying that "what the poet does is slow things down and really examines the moment with meticulous care and meticulous meaning, and really tries and locates a moment of significance."[21] The "moment of significance" Amis writes of could be either private or public [or indeed something else again]. But in the case of "Les Portes de la Nuit" and many of the other poems in *Yellow Studio*, the point is that the "moment" in question is both private and public. In "Les Portes de la Nuit" that moment is not merely reported on by the poet. Rather, Romer's intense meticulousness *creates* the moment for the reader).

To return, too, to the idea of acting mentioned in connection with Williams and his father: apart from the poem sharing its title with the French film in question, the father himself is a "matinée" idol, acting in his own film—and no more so than when he is in the chiaroscuro of the cinema watching *Les Portes de la Nuit*. The social historian Alain Corbin writes: "At the theatre, there used to be two stages, for the audience itself was giving a performance. Nowadays, what with dark cinemas and the intimacy of television, the spectator is no longer part of the show, but rather reduced to the status of a voyeur."[22] However, the man in the cinema in the poem is not a voyeur but an actor, in some sense performing like the actors in the film. There's something public about this intimacy. It is of a piece with the diary title and the way in which a diary is a representation of the self to the self. In the eleventh stanza of the poem, the one beginning "though from this time on," the way of quoting the diary changes. Instead of quoting the four lines of diary together, as in stanzas five to eight, the poet divides the four lines into two and two, with the blank between the stanzas in the middle:

> [...] from this time on
> there was no desire stronger in his mind
> "than to meet and make
> the firm friendship
>
> of a girl who might later
> become my wife."

This is to clinch the stress on the man's strong desire, and to stress that this desire concerns marriage. Isn't this statement more private than the encounter in the cinema? The meeting with the girl literally *con-firmed* (that is, made firm with) the desire "in [the man's] mind": it henceforth inhabits, indeed animates his inner life. Furthermore, the division here, the blank between the two pairs of lines, might somehow be taken to represent the public-private divide and the crossing from a socially uncommitted relationship to a socially-committed one. Man is not only, according to Aristotle, a political animal (and therefore a public one), but also (among other things) a conjugal one (conjugality, lying as it does at the heart of the poem, is as much a social phenomenon as a private one, a sometimes forgotten fact). Incidentally, the father envisages marriage not primarily as an erotic or religious bond but as a "friendship," a relationship which is by definition more social than erotic. Marriage would enable the father to move from the strictly private world of the diary and the flickering, shadowy half-light in the cinema to participation in social life, no longer an isolated Baudelairean figure in the crowd.

The meeting, then, confirmed the man's desire to marry (though not to marry the girl in the cinema). But is this so? Is it the experience that has confirmed the father's desire to marry? Or is it not rather the writing of the diary, the working through of the experience and its ramifications in words, that has done so?

One more question: why does the poem leave the man reading Wundt's *Psychology?* The reference to the textbook comes in the last stanza of the poem, while in the penultimate one the father writes: "my mind disturbed" after the experience in the cinema. Is he, then, searching for the reasons for the agitation in his mind, brought on by a subtle moment of encounter and contact both private and public? Through the poet's skill, that subtle moment becomes a similar one — both private and public, too — between reader and poem.

NOTES

1. Stephen Romer, *Yellow Studio* (Manchester: Oxford Poets/Carcanet, 2008), 85–87.

2. Stephen Romer, *Idols* (Oxford and New York: Oxford University Press, 1986), 43–44.

3. Stephen Romer, *Tribute* (Oxford and New York: Oxford University Press, 1998), 74.

4. William Wootten, *Times Literary Supplement* (27 June 2008), consulted at <http://www.carca net.co.uk/cgi-bin/scribe?showdoc=571;doctype= review>.

5. On BBC Radio 4, "Start the Week with Andrew Marr," 14 April 2008.

6. Stephen Romer in his presentation of *Yellow Studio* at the Sorbonne Poetry Conference, 28 June 2008. I am indebted to Stephen Romer for granting me access to the notes, hereafter referred to as Romer SPC, on which he based his presentation.

7. Used by Stephen Romer as the epigraph to the previous poem, in *Yellow Studio* (Manchester: Oxford/Carcanet, 2008), 84.

8. Trevor Royle, *The Best Years of Their Lives: The National Service Experience 1945–1963* (London: John Murray, 1997; first edition 1986), 109. The speaker is one Lance-Corporal M. Jones.

9. Ibid., 118.

10. Anne Frank, *The Diary of a Young Girl: The Definitive Version,* edited by Otto H. Frank and Mirjam Pressler, translated by Susan Massotty (London: Penguin, 1995), 7.

11. Wilhelm Wundt, *Outlines of Psychology,* trans. with the cooperation of the author by Charles Hubbard Judd, Ph.D. (Leipzig: Wilhelm Engelmann; London: Williams and Norgate; New York: Gustav E. Stechert, 1897; republished Bristol, UK: Thoemmes Press and Tokyo: Manzen Co. Ltd, 1998), 23.

12. Apart from the title and its allusion to the eponymous film, the father, as said above, also has "a meal in Lyons," which further underscores, at least on the page, this disreputable Gallic flavor.

13. Cf. Gillian Rose, *The Broken Middle: Out of our Ancient Society* (Oxford, UK, and Cambridge, MA: Blackwell, 1992), 59: "Kafka emphasizes that neither he nor Felice were single enough to marry."

14. Ibid., 57.

15. Anthony Hecht, *On the Laws of the Poetic Art* (Princeton: Princeton University Press, 1993), 97.

16. Pierre Michon, *Le roi vient quand il veut:*

propos sur la littérature (Paris: Albin Michel, 2007), 181.

17. "Cambridge," *Yellow Studio*, 89–90 (90).

18. Rose, *The Broken Middle*, 52: "not the sum of admissions" despite Romer's father's "'vast list.'"

19. Romer, Sorbonne Poetry Conference.

20. Hugo Williams, "Freelance" column in *Times Literary Supplement* (30 May 2003), 16.

21. Martin Amis interviewed by Ramona Koval, 9 April 1999.

22. Cf. Quoted by Martin Legros in "*Histoire de la bulle*" ("History of the Cocoon"), part of a special report on 'Private Life, Public Life: What Limits?' *Philosophie Magazine* (Paris), May 2008, 45. I wish to thank Emily Taylor Merriman for her help in editing this essay.

WORKS CITED

Amis, Martin (1999). Interview with Ramona Koval (9 April). www.abc.net.au/rn/arts/bwriting/stories/s2168.htm

Frank, Anne (1995). *The Diary of a Young Girl: The Definitive Version*. Ed. Otto H. Frank and Mirjam Pressler, trans. Susan Massotty. London: Penguin.

Hecht, Anthony (1993). *On the Laws of the Poetic Art*. Princeton: Princeton University Press.

Legros, Martin (2008). "Histoire de la bulle" ("History of the Cocoon"). *Philosophie Magazine* (May), 43–45.

Michon, Pierre (2007). *Le roi vient quand il veut: propos sur la littérature*. Paris: Albin Michel.

Rémond, Alain (2008). "Les 12 carnets intimes." *La Croix*, (21 May), 28.

Romer, Stephen (1986). *Idols*. Oxford and New York: Oxford University Press.

_____ (1992). *Plato's Ladder*. Oxford and New York: Oxford University Press.

_____ (1998). *Tribute*. Oxford and New York: Oxford University Press.

_____ (2008). *Yellow Studio*. Manchester: Oxford Poets/Carcanet.

Rose, Gillian (1992). *The Broken Middle: Out of our Ancient Society*. Oxford, UK, and Cambridge, MA: Blackwell.

Royle, Trevor (1997; first edition 1986). *The Best Years of Their Lives: The National Service Experience 1945–1963*. London: John Murray.

Williams, Hugo (2003). "Freelance" column. *TLS* (30 May), 16.

Wootten, William (2008). Review of *Yellow Studio*. *TLS* (27 June) <http://www.carcanet.co.uk/cgi-bin/scribe?showdoc=571;doctype=review>

Wundt, Wilhelm (1998; first edition 1969; first published in German 1897). *Outlines of Psychology*. Trans. Charles Hubbard Judd, Ph.D., with the cooperation of the author. Leipzig: Wilhelm Engelmann; London: Williams and Norgate; New York: Gustav E. Stechert; republished Bristol, UK: Thoemmes Press, and Tokyo: Manzen Co. Ltd.

PART III

Heaney and the Privateness of the Human Condition

7. Joseph Brodsky and Seamus Heaney in the Birch Grove of Art

Daniella Jancsó

Seamus Heaney's poem "The Birch Grove" in *District and Circle* (2006) ends with a quotation: "'If art teaches us anything [...] it's that the human condition is private.'"[1] The lines cited are from Joseph Brodsky's 1987 Nobel Lecture, in which Brodsky addressed issues that are at the heart of the "public-private divide": what can art do for the individual, and what can it do for society? Should the language of poetry conform to public taste? And perhaps most importantly: why write poetry at all in a world where most contemporary poems meet with a curious blend of disapproval, incomprehension, and apathy? That Brodsky's questions also preoccupied Heaney, Brodsky's fellow poet and friend, is evinced not only by the direct quote in "The Birch Grove," but also by the agenda of Heaney's own Nobel Lecture from 1995. All three texts — the two Nobel Lectures and the poem — arrive at answers that deserve attention in their own right. At the same time, these texts illustrate the inevitable difficulties that poets face when they engage with these issues. The comparison of the prose texts with the poem also shows that there are significant generic differences in the way these problems are resolved. These differences bear on the validity and authority of the views advanced.

The immediate context of the lines from Brodsky's Nobel Lecture that Heaney quotes in "The Birch Grove" offers a concise introduction to Brodsky's views on art:

> If art teaches anything (to the artist, in the first place), it is the privateness of the human condition. Being the most ancient as well as the most literal form of private enterprise, it fosters in a man, knowingly or unwittingly, a sense of his uniqueness, of individuality, of separateness — thus turning him from a social animal into an autonomous "I." Lots of things can be shared; a bed, a piece of bread, convictions, a mistress, but not a poem by, say, Rainer Maria Rilke. A

work of art, of literature especially, and a poem in particular, addresses a man tête-à-tête, entering with him into direct — free of any go-betweens — relations.[2]

For Brodsky, art is primarily a private affair. It is through art that one becomes aware of the human condition; it is art that creates the individual. Aesthetic experience is unmediated; it cannot be shared and, what is equally important, "aesthetic choice is a highly individual matter."[3] On philosophical and literary theoretical grounds, Brodsky's claims can be disputed, it is true. Their psychological truth, however, remains unaffected. For a man of letters whose personal history bears a tragic resemblance to that of Solzhenitsyn and Shostakovich, the only consolation available is the privacy of the aesthetic experience — meaning that no security police agent is spying over his shoulder while he is absorbed in Rilke. Against this background, the trust in the power of art to transform the "social animal" into an "autonomous I" becomes more than just another manifestation of poetic idealism. It is probably the only source of hope for change in a totalitarian system. Brodsky argues that this is why literature, especially poetry, is disliked by those "the champions of the common good, masters of the masses." For Brodsky, the poem resists general consenting unanimity in favor of the individual, human voice of dissent, figuratively characterized by marks of punctuation that turn a zero into a face.[4]

Logically, this process would lead to the disappearance of the "masses." Since "masses" for Brodsky means a manipulable mass of bodies, the stuff that dictatorships are made on, he propagates their elimination. He envisions the transformation of the featureless member of society into a unique individual through art — and on a grand scale. Although aesthetic experience is absolutely private, it should be a "mass private experience."

Brodsky's position could be summarized by the apparently paradoxical insight that art has to be absolutely private in order to become public. In other words, art can exert an effect in public only through multiple private aesthetic experiences. The implication is that aesthetic experience cannot be institutionalized. Perhaps that is Brodsky's reason why art alone can be credited. Only aesthetic experience can guarantee a life worth living, and its absence leads inevitably to oppression and terror: "[F]or a human being there is no other future save that outlined by art. Otherwise, what lies ahead is the past — the political one, first of all, with all its mass police entertainments."[5] Brodsky is convinced that the transformative power of art could redeem the individual person; what is more, despite serious doubts, he still sees a chance not only for the individual, but also for the human race. In the spirit of the Enlightenment, he believes that art can promote the progress of humanity.[6]

An important part of Brodsky's "reformation programme" is the cultivation of language. Rather than making concessions to public taste, the poet should strive to raise the public to his own linguistic level. He disputes the view that poetry, in an apparently laudable effort to be democratic, should use ordinary language. Such a choice, says Brodsky, places poetry at the mercy of history — when in fact, if language is what distinguishes the human animal, "poetry in particular, being the highest form of locution — is, to put it bluntly, the goal of our species."[7] Here is, in typical Brodskyan fashion, "Everything against the grain" — to quote Seamus Heaney's characterization of his friend in his tribute "Audenesque — in memory of Joseph Brodsky."[8] Against the grain, Brodsky acted upon this provocation: if people are to speak the language of literature, poetry should be made "available to everyone in this country and at a low cost,"[9] which is what he suggested in "An Immodest Proposal" as Poet Laureate in his October 1991 address to the Library of Congress.

To realize these aims, Brodsky founded the American Poetry and Literacy Project: hundreds of thousands of books of poetry were given away for free in motel rooms, supermarkets, gas stations, and post offices. No wonder that Heaney saw Brodsky's "impersonal importance" in his "total conviction about poetry as a force for good — not so much 'for the good of society' as for the health of the individual mind and soul."[10] In the same commemorative essay, "Joseph Brodsky 1940–1996," Heaney gives a vivid summary of Brodsky's guiding principles:

> He was resolutely against any idea that put the social cart before the personal horse, anything that clad original response in a common uniform. "Herd" for Joseph would have been the opposite of "heard," but that did not lessen his passion to reinstate poetry as an integral part of the common culture of the United States.[11]

Heaney's analysis is related to Brodsky's Nobel Lecture in that it yokes together two different, if not mutually exclusive, ideals: intensive individual aesthetic experience on the one hand, and large-scale impact on the other. (That Heaney sensed this contradiction is suggested by his careful phrasing: "but that did not lessen his passion..."). It seems to me that these ideals are shared by the majority of twentieth-century poets — for understandable reasons. The difficulty they face is to reconcile these ideals and yet arrive at consistent arguments. Brodsky's solution in his Nobel Lecture was to call for the paradox of "mass private experiences."

The closing sentences of Brodsky's lecture call attention to the source of another contradiction. After his high-principled arguments about art as the only future for mankind, his final word on the *raison d'être* of poetry may cause some astonishment:

> The one who writes a poem writes it *above all* because verse writing is an extraordinary accelerator of conscience, of thinking, of comprehending the universe.

> Having experienced this acceleration once, one is no longer capable of abandoning the chance to repeat this experience; one falls into dependency on this process, the way others fall into dependency on drugs or on alcohol. One who finds himself in this sort of dependency on language is, I guess, what they call a poet.[12]

Brodsky's chief motivation for writing poetry is deeply personal: it is a psychological necessity, an addiction. The surprising implication here is that at some point in the creative process, it no longer matters whether poetry has any public (or private) appeal. Against this background, Brodsky's own arguments that poetry is a force for good, "the only insurance available against the vulgarity of the human heart,"[13] appear secondary at best. While he could reconcile the ideal of the privacy of art with the ideal of maximal effect by opting for a "mass private experience," in Brodsky's Nobel Lecture there is no resolution of the conflicting views on why one writes poetry. Though the rhetorical force and virtuosity of his speech remain unaffected by this inconsistency, the validity of his arguments becomes too easily questioned.

In his own Nobel Lecture, "Crediting Poetry," Seamus Heaney confronts the same questions that occupied Brodsky some eight years earlier: what is the use of art in a world "of devastating and repeated acts of massacre, assassination and extirpation"? What should the language of poetry be like? Why write and why read poems? As a poet from Northern Ireland, Heaney is well aware of conflicting ideals and expectations concerning poetry.[14] But rather than arguing with equal passion for opposing sides or leaving conflicts unresolved as Brodsky did, Heaney claims that the very nature of poetry is to be able to reconcile contradictory positions. In a programmatic passage of his lecture, he *defines* poetry as follows:

> But I credit [poetry] ultimately because poetry can make an order as true to the impact of external reality and as sensitive to the inner laws of the poet's being as the ripples that rippled in and rippled out across the water in that scullery bucket fifty years ago. An order where we can at last grow up to that which we stored up as we grew. An order which satisfies all that is appetitive in the intelligence and prehensile in the affections. I credit poetry, in other words, both for being itself and for being a help, for making possible a fluid and restorative relationship between the mind's centre and its circumference, between the child gazing at the word "Stockholm" on the face of the radio dial and the man facing the faces that he meets in Stockholm at this most privileged moment. I credit it because credit is due to it, in our time and in all time, for its truth to life, in every sense of that phrase.[15]

It is an ingenious rhetorical move to define poetry as an assemblage of principally contradictory features: reflecting the external world as well as the internal reality of the poet; being itself and at the same time being there for

others; having artistic autonomy and yet being responsive to social and political issues. Though this strategy is observable throughout Heaney's Nobel
Lecture, the following passage is perhaps its clearest manifestation:

> Poetic form is both the ship and the anchor. It is at once a buoyancy and a
> steadying, allowing for the simultaneous gratification of whatever is centrifugal
> and whatever is centripetal in mind and body. And it is by such means that
> Yeats's work does what the necessary poetry always does, which is to touch the
> base of our sympathetic nature while taking in at the same time the unsympa-
> thetic nature of the world to which that nature is constantly exposed.[16]

In a similar manner, Heaney argues in the frequently anthologized essay
"The Redress of Poetry" (originally given as a lecture at Oxford in 1989) that
poetry is autonomous and self-referential *and* at the same time reflects the
external environment:

> Poetry cannot afford to lose its fundamentally self-delighting inventiveness, its
> joy in being a process of language *as well as* a representation of things in the
> world.[17]

Heaney counters Plato's well-known critique by presenting poetry as a means
of redressing wrongs through balancing the scales and giving voice to the
wretched and the oppressed. But a few paragraphs later, he quotes Borges and
ends his essay (as Brodsky did his Nobel Lecture) with a celebration of poetry
as a source of intense pleasure, a "drug" that can bring about moments of rapture — the very condition Plato was wary of. Here, we may presume, Heaney's
views converge with Brodsky's on the privacy of art:

> Borges is talking about the fluid, exhilarating moment which lies at the heart of
> any memorable reading, the undisappointed joy of finding that everything holds
> up and answers the desire that it awakens. At such moments, the delight of hav-
> ing all one's faculties simultaneously provoked and gratified is like gaining an
> upper hand over all that is contingent and (as Borges says) "inconsequential."[18]

In the light of Heaney's definition of poetry as an art which can fulfill very
different — if not contradictory — designs and desires, such inconsistencies do
not in fact invalidate the argument. Logically, if one accepts the all-inclusive
definition of poetry, what follows is indisputable. The only point of attack
left in Heaney's Nobel Lecture (and in the forerunner essay, "The Redress of
Poetry") is the definition. With that, Heaney's arguments stand or fall.

But what is the use of laying bare the logical inconsistencies in these texts?
Why worry about the stringency of argumentation? Do they not "work" after
all? The prose is powerfully written, absorbing, provocative, and most of all,
persuasive about the import of poetry — as one would expect from a speech
given on such a prominent occasion. If it is *belief* in the force of poetry that
we are seeking, we need look no further than these lectures. Yet if we are

looking for valid and authoritative statements about poetry, the inconsistencies become problematic.

The continuing demand for such binding statements, despite all postmodernist efforts, is indicated by the introduction to a recent anthology of poetic theory. After considering the overwhelming variety of modern poems and poetologies, the editor comes to the following conclusion:

> The temptation here is to say that in the twentieth century there is not poetry but "poetries"; that there is no longer a single state of the art, but many different states. While this may be true it is in danger of ignoring a risk and a possibility. The risk is that the conviction and seriousness of poets, critics, and theorists in arguing their case for a poetry will be met with indifference. These arguments do not invite their readers to respond with a shrug of the shoulders as they gather another item in the checklist of "poetries," but with articulate agreement or disagreement. The possibility is that there is an alternative to the "literary historian's nightmare." There are patterns in the ways that modern poetry's past has been imagined, just as there are differences in judgement about the nature of poetic language or the characteristics of modern poetry that can speak to and against each other.[19]

Consistency and soundness of argument can be only beneficial to a dialogue among different "poetries." These are — to use Wittgenstein's terms — the rules of the language game, whether discussed in a lecture given at the Nobel Foundation or at a university. The suspicion that the subject matter (what is poetry? why write?) might make a consistent argument impossible cannot be pursued here further, although it certainly deserves investigation.

There is, however, another language game that poets play in which such rules are not mandatory. In a *poem*, "moves" that cause problems in argumentative prose texts are allowed, or even welcome. While contradictions and inconsistencies provide points of attack in non-literary prose writings, in lyrical texts they are considered enriching. This observation brings us back to the "The Birch Grove." How does the Brodsky quotation — "'If art teaches us anything [...] it's that the human condition is private'" — function in Seamus Heaney's poem? On a first reading, it is the peaceful retirement evocative of a Virgilian idyll that catches our attention. Who would not be seduced by these delightful images: purling water, birch saplings shimmering white in the sunlight, red brick and slate, plum and apple? A woman in a white satin nightdress pouring tea; a man relaxing to the sound of Bach's music. A perfect world, nature and art in harmony with man and woman in concord. Affluence, harmoniousness, hope in the freshly planted future. No sign of hardship, no sign of despair. We are tempted to believe that a fulfilled, meaningful, gratifying life is still possible after all. There may be just one obstacle preventing us from yielding completely to the charms of this idyllic scene — a single word, Brodsky's word: *private*. The meaning of this unexpected, perplexing, ambiguous word is dependent on the perspective we adopt.

From the point of view of the male figure who utters the last words of the poem, the meaning of *private* is absolutely positive: it is the source of satisfaction. He is satisfied with his settled upper-middle class life: his private property, his private birch grove, his private life. For him, privacy means security, peace, and comfort, the exclusive club of family. He has apparently realized his dream of an ideal life, to live in seclusion as totally apart from the public sphere as if it did not exist. But therein lies the rub: the public realm looms large over this private utopia.

The utopian nature of the scene is clear for the speaker of the poem, who is well aware of the limitedness of the male figure's view. The description of the couple as "grown-up selves" is slightly condescending, and the phrase "common or garden air" has a touch of irony. The puzzling statement emphasizing that "plum tree and apple retain their credibility" is perhaps a subtle way of saying that in contrast, the man and the woman do not remain credible. Significantly, art figures more as a commodity than a source of aesthetic experience: in the reference to Bach's music, the emphasis is not on its aesthetic value, but on its commercial quality. Bach is a product, a *CD*, ready to be consumed along with the breakfast tea. This "transubstantiation" is surely not what Brodsky had in mind when he argued for the transformative power of art.

From the speaker's perspective, the closing quotation is no longer a self-congratulatory remark, but acquires a different meaning. It becomes a biting criticism of the attitude represented by the couple, who are ignorant of— or rather, choosing to ignore — their larger environment, and who are concerned merely with providing for themselves. Their vanity is pointed out by the evocation of past civilizations' ruins, the "unroofed abbey" and the "broken-floored Roman villa," which are reminders of transitoriness and function as *memento mori*: *Et in arcadia ego*. Indeed. The image of the seemingly harmless jet trail that is "like a willow wand or taper," of which the couple is unaware, is a herald of death in a post–9/11 world. Ian McEwan points out in *Saturday*, a novel published two months prior to the first publication of Heaney's poem in March 2005, that in the case of the sign *airplane*, a process of semantic reshuffling has taken place:

> It's already almost eighteen months since half the planet watched, and watched again the unseen captives driven through the sky to the slaughter, at which time there gathered round the innocent silhouette of any jet plane a novel association.[20]

A similar point is made in a recent poem by Stephen Romer, "A Transcendental Weekend," where the poet implies — as in Heaney's poem — that peace of mind is only attainable by the deliberate exclusion of information about the external world:

> It seemed the best was a weekend ban
> on images and news, when every time
> a plane came over we saw the towers
> gashed and smoking.... A ban on CNN.[21]

In "The Birch Grove," the symbolic potential of the jet trail is emphasized by the epanalepsis: the trail "tapers" and is in turn compared to a "taper," an odd comparison. The conspicuous framing of the line, established by the words *tapers* and *taper*, creates a sense of confinement and could signal a willful short circuiting of associations. The claim that this line is an evocation of September 11 is reinforced by the fact that the terrorist attacks are explicitly discussed in other poems in *District and Circle*. The destruction of New York's "tallest towers" is the central image in "Anything Can Happen," a "post–9/11 adaptation of a Horatian ode," as one critic called it,[22] and the plight of firemen is described in "Helmet," the poem immediately following "Anything Can Happen."

That the image of the jet trail in "The Birch Grove" terminates the description of the garden scene also suggests a sense of finality characteristic of the aftermath of catastrophes: one is at a loss, not knowing how to continue. The Brodsky quotation immediately following the sinister image of the jet trail could then be regarded as an indication (or as a reminder) of the redemptive power of art. When one is at a loss, when one does not know how to go on, one may turn to art to save the situation. This interpretation is in line with Brodsky's own thoughts on art as an *ultimum refugium*.

Yet there is still more to the concluding lines of "The Birch Grove." While in Brodsky's lecture the experience of privacy was considered absolutely positive, Heaney's poem challenges this view. After the meticulous description of the couple in harmony — however complacent they may be — the last statement comes as an anticlimax, if not as a shock. The force of the final line emphasizes the state of privacy instead of the act of sharing. Looking at it this way, the final word of the poem is to be understood in the sense of isolation and is a weighty counterbalance to the utopian idyll of the preceding fifteen lines. From this perspective, the condition of privateness that art brings to awareness appears as inevitable as it is lamentable. Despite the harmonious atmosphere, despite the charms of nature and culture, the last word on the human condition is "private": isolation instead of integration. Privacy, in Brodsky still a pleasurable (or at least not unpleasant) state, is shown to be a potentially distressing condition in Heaney's poem.

In "The Birch Grove," the Brodsky quotation functions as the intersection of different interpretations: the poem can be read as the positive vision of a private utopia; it can be taken as a criticism of this ideal; or it may show the ultimate vanity of all efforts to overcome isolation. That none of these interpretations prevails is due to the ambiguity of every image and situation in the poem, from the planting of the trees to the white satin nightdress to the participial *trumping*. The planting of the birch grove is an action emblematic of hope and trust in the future; however, this action takes place in an emphatically confined area: "at the back of a garden," "in a corner walled off." That *birches* are planted is ambiguous, too. Birches are the first to sprout in the spring and suggest birth, hope, and a new beginning; at the same time, being the national tree of Brodsky's native country, they evoke Brodsky's experience of Russia, including the "mass police entertainments" and persecution. These negative associations are reinforced by the fact that in Norse mythology, birches symbolize the end of the world, with the last battle being fought around a birch tree.[23] And if we read the phrase "dandles a sandal" as an allusion to Gerard Manley Hopkins's poem "The Binsey Poplars (felled 1879)," where the trees "dandled a sandalled / shadow that swam or sank," the sad fate of the newly planted birch grove is also anticipated in Heaney's poem.[24] Similarly, the female figure's white satin nightdress — as suffused and cool as "the white of the bark" — is on the one hand a status symbol, a sign of affluence and sophistication. On the other hand, its coolness and whiteness may imply something about the character of the woman, or even something about the emotional intensity of the couple's relationship.[25] The balancing of contrasting moods is also accomplished with the phrase "trumping life with a quote," where *trumping* may be read either at face value or ironically.

With these different interpretations come contrasting views on the role of art. Art can function as any consumer good that can be purchased and owned; it can be a redemptive force offering solace in times of crises; or art can itself trigger a crisis by making the reader aware of his or her own isolation. It is an obvious fact of literary criticism that a single work of art can give rise to multiple — at times conflicting — interpretations. What is more interesting is to recognize that "The Birch Grove" exemplifies Heaney's definition of poetry as an assemblage of principally contradictory positions. Although the Nobel Lectures by Brodsky and Heaney set out to validate poetry, it is poetry, in this case "The Birch Grove," that validates the propositions in the essays.

Brodsky's central claim about the transformative power of art — that art can transform a member of the masses into an individual — does not figure prominently in Heaney's poem. Yet this does not mean that Brodsky's admittedly idealistic view is dismissed. On the contrary, the existence of the poem already confirms Brodsky's position: although "The Birch Grove" describes (and subtly criticizes) an unappealing, consumer-oriented approach to art, it does so in a work of art. As a work of art, it has an aesthetic potential, can exert an artistic effect, and may become a transformative force. There is no guarantee that this transformation will ever happen, obviously. But it may happen, and that is what matters for Brodsky and Heaney. Brodsky's views reappear in a similar form in Heaney's own Nobel Lecture. For all his skepticism, for all his serious doubts about both the state of the world and the present status of poetry, Heaney ends with the following creed:

> The form of the poem [...] is crucial to poetry's power to do the thing which always is and always will be to poetry's credit: the power to persuade that vulnerable part of our consciousness of its rightness in spite of the evidence of wrongness all around it, the power to remind us that we are hunters and gatherers of values, that our very solitudes and distresses are creditable, in so far as they, too, are an earnest of our veritable human being.[26]

Despite reservations about the power of art and the widespread conviction that, as Auden said, "Poetry makes nothing happen," *poetry* still happens. Although well aware that poetry has little public resonance, poets keep writing poems and continue to appeal to the public — they go on planting birches of literature "at the back of a garden," "in a corner walled off."

In addition to Brodsky, the more recent Nobel Laureate Doris Lessing also pleaded in her lecture for reading the classics, deplored the growing ignorance of literature in Western societies, and called for a change.[27] This insistence is perhaps the most intriguing attribute of twentieth-century writers and poets, a precious common denominator of otherwise divergent convictions about what literature should be. Heaney's resoluteness can be traced back to a *belief* in the credibility of poetry and in that of human beings, while Brodsky's motivation comes from a very different source, a form of *addiction*. Yet both their poetries of perseverance are beyond reason.

NOTES

1. Seamus Heaney, *District and Circle* (London: Faber and Faber, 2006), 72. "The Birch Grove" first appeared in *Times Literary Supplement* in March 2005. Available online in *The Guardian* (1 April 2006) <http://www.guardian.co.uk/books/2006/apr/01/poetry.seamusheaney>.

2. Joseph Brodsky, Nobel Lecture, *Les Prix Nobel. The Nobel Prizes, 1987.* Trans. Barry Rubin (The Nobel Foundation. Stockholm: Almqvist and Wiksell International, 1987), 240.

3. Ibid.

4. Ibid.

5. Ibid., 243–44.

6. Ibid., 242.

7. Ibid., 241–242.

8. Seamus Heaney, *Electric Light* (London: Faber and Faber, 2001), 64.

9. Joseph Brodsky, *On Grief and Reason. Essays* (New York: Farrar Straus Giroux, 1995), 210.

10. Seamus Heaney, *Finders Keepers. Selected Prose 1971–2001* (London: Faber and Faber, 2002), 404.

11. Ibid.

12. Brodsky, Nobel Lecture, 247; emphasis mine.

13. Brodsky, *On Grief and Reason*, 210.

14. Heaney was repeatedly and virulently attacked for his treatment of political issues in his poems, above all in his 1975 collection *North*. Ciaran Carson reproached him for taking an anthro-

pological approach to sectarian violence, and the critic James Simmons accused him of "endorsing a tribal position or making vague gestures towards the inevitability of carnage" (Andrews 1992, 3).

15. Seamus Heaney, "Crediting Poetry," *Les Prix Nobel. The Nobel Prizes. 1995* (The Nobel Foundation. Stockholm: Almqvist and Wiksell International, 1995), 322.

16. Ibid., 333.

17. Seamus Heaney, *The Redress of Poetry.* Oxford Lectures (London and Boston: Faber and Faber), 5, emphasis mine.

18. Ibid., 9.

19. Jon Cook, *Poetry in Theory. An Anthology 1900–2000* (Oxford: Blackwell, 2004), 2.

20. Ian McEwan, *Saturday* (London: Jonathan Cape, 2005), 16.

21. Stephen Romer, *The Yellow Studio* (Manchester: Carcanet, 2008), 68.

22. William Wootten, "A gentle simmer," *Times Literary Supplement* (2 June 2006).

23. Cf. also the well-known poem "Birches" by Robert Frost, whom the young Heaney "loved for his farmer's accuracy and his wily down-to-earthness," as he recalled in his Nobel Lecture (Heaney, "Crediting Poetry," 323).

24. Hopkins, Gerard Manley. *The Poetical Works of Gerard Manley Hopkins,* ed. Norman H. Mackenzie (Oxford: Clarendon, 1990), 156.

25. The female figure in an enclosed garden also evokes the *hortus conclusus* motive; the Christian symbolism (see also the references to an *abbey* and an *abbot*) establishes yet another layer of meaning in the poem. Within this framework, the jet trail could be interpreted (perhaps not without irony) as the Holy Spirit.

26. Heaney, "Crediting Poetry," 333.

27. Doris Lessing, "On not winning the Nobel Prize" (7 Dec. 2007), <http://nobelprize.org/nobel_prizes/literature/laureates/2007/lessing-lecture_en.html>

WORKS CITED

Andrews, Elmer (ed.) (1992). *Seamus Heaney: A Collection of Critical Essays.* Houndmills: Macmillan.

Brodsky, Joseph (1987). Nobel Lecture. *Les Prix Nobel. The Nobel Prizes. 1987.* Trans. Barry Rubin. The Nobel Foundation. Stockholm: Almqvist and Wiksell International, 239–247.

_____ (1995). *On Grief and Reason.* Essays. New York: Farrar Straus Giroux.

Cook, Jon (ed.) (2004). *Poetry in Theory. An Anthology 1900–2000.* Oxford: Blackwell.

Hardy, Barbara (2007). "Literary Allusions, Appropriations and Assimilations." *Seamus Heaney: Poet, Critic, Translator.* Houndmills: Palgrave Macmillan, 189–210.

Heaney, Seamus (1995). "Crediting Poetry." *Les Prix Nobel. The Nobel Prizes. 1995.* The Nobel Foundation. Stockholm: Almqvist and Wiksell International, 317–335.

_____ (1995). *The Redress of Poetry. Oxford Lectures.* London and Boston: Faber and Faber.

_____ (2001). *Electric Light.* London: Faber and Faber.

_____ (2002). *Finders Keepers. Selected Prose 1971–2001.* London: Faber and Faber.

_____ (2006). *District and Circle.* London: Faber and Faber.

Hopkins, Gerard Manley (1990). *The Poetical Works of Gerard Manley Hopkins,* ed. Norman H. Makenzie. Oxford: Clarendon.

McEwan, Ian (2005). *Saturday.* London: Jonathan Cape.

Romer, Stephen (2008). *The Yellow Studio.* Manchester: Carcanet.

Wootten, William (2006). "A gentle simmer." *Times Literary Supplement* (2 June).

8. "We men [...] must vanish"[1] — Heaney's Wordsworth: Toward the Configuration of an Event Form

Pascale Guibert

Through his readings and rewritings of Wordsworth, Seamus Heaney has pondered the relation between the public and the private as far as the writing self is concerned. The uses and the forms of this inheritance have continually evolved in Heaney's œuvre, both critical and poetic. At the beginning of his career, when he still had a reputation to make, the most widespread images of iconic Wordsworth particularly interested Heaney. Later, formal idiosyncrasies accessible only through intimate reading-contact with the Wordsworthian text came to inspirit the writings of "Famous Seamus." Since public renown is no longer sought, spectacular manifestations of poetic craft and well-tried formulaic prowesses are no longer required. In fact, public renown is no longer at stake at all for the international, trans-temporal, trans-individual, utterly public poetic figure that Seamus Heaney has become.

The uses that the private has been put to in order to configure both Heaney's and Wordsworth's public figures have gradually and consequentially evolved. Tracing this development chronologically will enable us to follow the modalities and implications of Heaney's travail of inheritance — a travail that, in the opening to events that his poems display and operate, will prove to have consequences far beyond private achievement.

In this regard, Heaney's choice of reading Wordsworth is telling; Wordsworth's expressly private enterprise, even in an autobiographical text like *The Prelude* (which claims to disclose "the history of a poet's mind"[2]), has a didactic and even a broadly anthropological purpose: "what we have loved,/ Others will love, and we may teach them how," as Wordsworth prophetically assures Coleridge.[3] This avowed purpose of exemplarity in what Wordsworth already sees as a joint task transforms anecdotes into paradigms, past private occurrences into hoped-for universal schemes for the future:

> Blessed with true happiness if we may be
> United helpers forward of a day
> Of firmer trust, joint labourers in the work —[4]

A consciousness of expression as an embracing gesture, as acting toward others, animates Wordsworth's whole œuvre, as it also animates Heaney's own œuvre for different purposes and in different ways. Though recognized early in Heaney's career, this concern was not always seen as positive, as this damning criticism from 1975 demonstrates:

> [...] Heaney seems to have moved — unwillingly, perhaps — from being a writer with the gift of precision, to become the laureate of violence — a mythmaker, an anthropologist of ritual killing, an apologist of "the situation," in the last resort, a mystifier.[5]

It is true that all gestures toward universality, directed at an utterly public stance or figure, may smack of essentialism and imperialism. We will see how Heaney's poems evolve from such a temptation and poetic pitfall to another definition of the utterly public — through painstaking consideration, year after year, of Wordsworth's poeticization of the private.

This constant questioning of the role of expression in both poets considered here, the doubts and the trust formalized in their poetry and their prose, has prompted my own approach to the public-private divide in Heaney's continuations of Wordsworth. The present exploration of the public-private divide will concern itself not with books and readers, with numbers, or with actualized facts and situations. Instead, it will deal solely with expression as a (non)place. The text of the poem, its printed trace before my eyes, will be considered as the very (non)place where "one" or "many" can appear, where the interplays of the singular and the plural are staged, where the private and the public will part and re-form. The poem is shown as what Jacques Derrida calls a "stage"[6] and Alain Badiou a "presentative structure"[7] — for both, the (non)place where an event can happen. The event, in the perspective of the analysis conducted here, is a "one-multiple" poetic subject, an "overhuman" being,[8] utterly public in its being utterly opened. It is a becoming rather than a being: singular and made up of private voices, situated places, moments, and occurrences.

In his recent *The Century* (2005, trans. 2007), Alain Badiou set himself the task of reading a number of representative twentieth-century Western literary texts in search of whatever new thought emerged in that literature:

> What did the men of this century think, over and above merely developing the thought of their predecessors? In other words, what are the century's uninherited thoughts? What was thought in the century that was previously unthought — or even unthinkable?[9]

To conduct his research, Badiou confronts the achievements of twentieth-century works of art with what those of the nineteenth century had "announced, dreamed, and promised."[10] While he recognizes that the decisive break with Romanticism that the Moderns claimed never actually happened,[11] Badiou analyses the New Man that twentieth-century works of art have produced, "compelling humanity to some excess with regard to itself"[12] on its way to the "overhuman." This New Man, this "overhuman" figure revealed in the literary texts considered by Badiou, develops from the Romantic subject and yet also breaks with its singularity, a singularity that was gradually magnified from the second generation Romantics onward and reflected the progress of capitalism.[13]

Heaney's inheriting of Wordsworth works toward the inventive construction of an "overhuman," de-temporalized, utterly public poetic subject, through the elaboration of a form necessary to its advent, or event. Such a form, called an "event form," is conceived along the principles determining Badiou's "event site." In *Being and Event* (1988), the "event site" (or "evental site," in Oliver Feltham's translation) is the historical construction that conditions the possibility of an event. To Badiou, both mathemes (Jacques Lacan's symbolic formulae) and poems can constitute in themselves the historicized structures from which an event can be delivered into being.[14] Heaney's particular and repeated soundings of the private in Wordsworth have led him to formulate, in his latest poetry, an event form that makes an inter-personal poetic subject possible. The logic of advent of this "overhuman" corresponds to what Derrida calls "*la logique du fantôme*" / "the logic of the ghost" in that its very event "exceeds a binary dialectical logic."[15] Its composition is specter-like, or spectral: a spirit, but a spirit with a body. As "the furtive and ungraspable visibility of the invisible,"[16] the spectral in Derrida refers to the written trace. In the context of the public-private issue, the poetic expression analyzed here (Heaney's, continuing Wordsworth's) is obsessed with the question of spectrality in its travail of inheritance aspect, as well as in its avowed preoccupation with crossing human borders. Hence, it will not be difficult to see why a specter should haunt the question of the public-private divide: "the logic of the ghost" is political, though it may appear through the most private, self-reflexive voice (Hamlet is one of the familiar ghosts of *Specters of Marx*) and even interlace two private voices (in a poem, moreover). Since it ignores all man-made restrictions and previsions, it concerns the public sphere at its largest, "recogniz[ing] in its principle the respect for those others who are no longer or for those others who are not yet *there*, presently living, whether they are already dead or not yet born."[17] It is this respect which we will see at work in Heaney's poetry.

"Follower"?

This subtitle questions the titular affirmation of an early Heaney poem from the 1966 *Death of a Naturalist*. As a manifestation of (poetic) autonomy and status, "Follower" allegorizes this archetypal moment of revolution when, having grown from a child stumbling behind his father, the now-manly poet goes on ahead, shadowed by a fragile father figure. Premature as we may deem this early representation of the poetic self, it can also only be considered proleptic with very strict restrictions: Heaney's poetic fathers will never have been "stumbling," and certainly never precisely "behind" him. "Before" seems far more appropriate to the poetic situation under analysis, to this poetic "following" that will lead Heaney's texts to re-explore the frontier between the private and the public and question the appearance that they stand apart.

As Blake Morrison recognized, in 1982 Seamus Heaney was, through his lectures, readings, and pieces of criticism, still largely and willingly responsible for producing "a considerably simplified version of his achievement" and for presenting himself as

> a simple, straightforward, readily accessible writer whose methods and ideas owe more to the nineteenth century than the twentieth. A backwater all to himself, he is seen as lying outside the main currents of contemporary European and Anglo-American intellectual life; a throwback to an earlier age, he is admired precisely for not being a "modern"

— an assessment that Morrison carefully and convincingly disproves.[18] Indeed, Heaney's first two volumes of poetry, *Death of a Naturalist* (1966) and *Door into the Dark* (1969), tapping as they do a vein that Robert Mayo, in his appreciation of Wordsworth's themes in the *Lyrical Ballads*, says was "already stale"[19] at the end of the eighteenth century, go a long way toward explaining both — and at the same time — the foul criticism from some poetry specialists and the lavish praise from the lay public.[20] In these volumes and in his interviews of the period, Heaney (like Wordsworth) takes subjects that, Mayo shows, were "*commonplace* in the *minor* verse of the last years of the *eighteenth century*."[21] Heaney hammers home his intentions and method by repeatedly going back to the past in his writings: mostly to his own childhood, but beyond that, also to Wordsworth's past and Wordsworth's childhood. Whole episodes poetically retraced in these early Heaney volumes can easily be seen as refractions of similar Wordsworthian scenes.

Even acknowledging the consequential differences between a Wordsworth and a Heaney poem — for how could it be otherwise? — "Death of a Naturalist" (1966), for instance, can be read as a rewriting of lines 27–49 of the first book of the 1799 *Prelude*.[22] Superficially, the poaching scene ending in a young

boy running away, as well as the atmosphere of guilt and images of punishment through a familiar world becoming *unheimlich*, are transposed from
Cumbrian fells to Northern Irish fields. The game caught by others' snares
dwindles to frogspawn in the later poem, in undaring accordance with our
contemporary concern for the animal cause. The movement and rhythm of
the narration is similar in both poems, which both unfold as re-effectuations
of a "spot of time" — even if we must admit, with Nicholas Roe, the distinction between a Heaneyan and a Wordsworthian spot of time: "The imaginative life of Wordsworth's spot of time is internal, in 'Death of a Naturalist' it
is disengaged and external to the child."[23] In this difference can already be
read, so early in Heaney's career, the outward, exterior-bound movement at
work in Heaney's poetry of the private. Later, and further off, Heaney's solitary fiddler in "The Given Note" (1969) seems to have caught his "spirit
music" — not, as "he maintains, from nowhere"[24] — but from Wordsworth's
"Solitary Reaper," of which it looks like a Hibernicized quasi-calque. The
"Highland Lass"'s voice, already strange-sounding in 1805, disincarnates
the girl from whom it must have come and prolongs her unnaturally in the
process, lingering "Long after it was heard no more."[25] This voice now passes
through Heaney's nameless and invisible alter ego, a mere relaying station for
melodies, further disincarnated and dispersed into more northern-and-west-
ern breezes.

Field Work's Glanmore Sonnets (1979) insistently draw on Wordsworth's
poems' atmosphere and terminology when they do not directly quote them.[26]
Written shortly after the Heaneys' move south to the Republic, as the poet
was starting another life and configuring a new poetic figure for himself in
the lush countryside at the foot of the Wicklow hills, they inherit the sense
of liberation and confidence of Wordsworth's second (1805) opening of the
Prelude. Whereas the Wordsworthian self, "enfranchised," exults: "I breathe
again," Heaney's first sonnet opens the surrounding land as already soaked in
this life and diffusing it: "the turned-up acres breathe."[27] The rich fields of
Heaney's borrowed habitation reveal the roots in both the natural and the
metaphoric "subsoil," the furrows having for a long time in Heaney consciously referred to poetic activity. This connection is made through the turning back and inward imagining of the actual plowing of a field, and through
the Latin name of the activity considered by the poet in a now famous parallel, first pondered and evoked by Heaney (can it be a coincidence?) in
"Reflections on Wordsworth and Yeats."[28] All these early forms of transposition, as they open the private self onto a broad public context, also de-privatize what was given as specifically Heaneyan and turn Heaney-land into
collective poetic ground.

At the end of what can be seen as his first period, in the second half of the 1980s, Heaney published his *William Wordsworth: Poems Selected* with Faber. There, the first words of his introduction concern the child, the first two paragraphs develop the role of childhood in Wordsworth's poetry, and the third paragraph emphatically reaffirms Wordsworth's monumentality:

> his achievement [...] is the largest and most securely founded in the canon of native English poetry since Milton. He is an indispensable figure in the evolution of modern writing, a finder and keeper of the self-as-subject.[29]

The progression of these paragraphs, from the exposition of private childhood to the establishment of international fame, presents a formula for success as it reconstructs Wordsworth's way to canonization at the same time as it synthesizes Heaney's own achievement thus far. If many of Heaney's early poems do indeed verify such formulae for success by continuing Wordsworth, Heaney's prose, while directing our readings, also corroborates his writings. His 1978 essay "The Makings of a Music: Reflections on Wordsworth and Yeats" makes sure we follow Heaney correctly in the way he first followed Wordsworth to fame through giving expression to what is most intensely intimate. He then exults in unearthing and listing "all the typical Wordsworthian verbs": "powers sink in, mould, impress, frame, minister, enter unawares."[30] The drive inward and downward that determines his own critical approach ("I want to see how far we can go in seeking the origins of a poet's characteristic 'music,'" Heaney states at the beginning of this essay) also "moulds" his poetic practice. This is the time of the bog poems, which bring him further back and down than pre–Freudian Wordsworth could, in his own days: Heaney almost dis-closes the "outback of [his] mind" when he opens the bog as the representation of the unconscious — personal and collective — in "Kinship."[31]

Beyond warranting Heaney wide — if mixed — renown, this first series of texts purports to follow the deeper-inward Wordsworthian drive that interested Heaney at the time and raises the question of the contemporary poet's poetic and political courage. A mark of his escapism to Hugh Haughton,[32] of his "double betrayal" to Al Alvarez,[33] of conservatism to Geoffrey Harvey,[34] to me even these early forms of his affiliation to Wordsworth give another image of Heaney's enterprise.

At a time when clear-cut positions and answers were expected from any Northern Irish public figure, the ambiguity that this poetic relation with the English Romantic poet entertains renegotiates frontiers rather than taking sides. The backward drive of such an affiliation reveals what Badiou sees as

> the principle of courage that underlies any cognitive enterprise: to be of one's time through an unprecedented manner of not being in one's time. In Nietzsche's terms, to have the courage to be untimely.[35]

De-stationing

On his way deeper down into an ambivalent unconscious both personal and collective, Heaney encounters Wordsworth again: no longer the Wordsworth for whom the "discovery" of childhood led to his late canonization, but a last stage, territorializing Wordsworth, a "community" Wordsworth. This encounter leads Heaney to configure a new modality of the public, fashioned through the expression of private and exclusive concerns.

Such a poetic pair, one writing at the end of the Franco–English war and the other at the height of the Troubles, may constitute a "we in times of war" at first. Certainly the situations are not conducive to questioning and giving form to what will become a "we in times of peace," the "disparate 'we' of togetherness" that Badiou has seen art works of the end of the twentieth century striving to formulate.[36]

Yet the construction of the myth of the bog through Heaney's bog poems of the 1970s leads Heaney to start realizing the possibility of such a "we." This "we" takes shape as Heaney links his bog with a number of wests: the west of Ireland (where the most extensive and productive bogs of Ireland are to be found) as a quintessential zone or national *topos*; "the frontier of the west" of the United States that Heaney tells us gave rise to his desire to construct such a myth for Ireland[37]; and Wordsworth's west. Notably, the Faber publication features the 1805 "Stepping Westward" among the fifty or so Wordsworth poems that Heaney selected. At the heart of this poem, the voice declaims:

> And stepping westward seemed to be
> A kind of heavenly destiny.[38]

Such an encounter of metaphysical, mythic wests may well look like unholy ground for a dangerous conjuration of conservatives, nationalists, preservationists, and community-installers by whatever name one wishes to call them. Considering the two poets' sometimes defensive works, there is room for such suspicion. We might think of Wordsworth erecting his Lake District as a stronghold against what he saw as the invasion of the hordes of factory-workers in his 1844 expostulations against the projected Kendal and Windermere Railway. We might also think of Heaney's 1972 "A New Song" that expresses an ambivalent dream of submerging (with love, maybe) the architectural, military, and linguistic signs of British presence on his "home ground."[39]

But this suspicion would neglect the fact that Wordsworth's voice does not vibrate then from his native Cumbria, but from the Scottish banks of Lake Katarine. It would also ignore the insistent reiteration of the directional phrase in the continuous aspect of its verb: in the phrase "stepping westward," the geographical locality becomes "loco-motive." Lastly, it would disregard the relation between Wordsworth's and Heaney's wests, which is established through Wordsworth's west being included within the contemporary Irish poet's work and blended with it. Rather than confirming the cardinal point, Heaney disorients it by atomizing and disseminating it. "The west" is thus demystified as it is de-privatized and un-singularized. An instance of the later Freudian *unheimlich*, it contains within itself the principle of its pleasurable unfixity. Its grotesque form is conceived according to the celebrated formula that Wordsworth gives in his 1800 Preface to the *Lyrical Ballads*:

> I mean the pleasure which the mind derives from the perception of similitude in dissimilitude. This principle is the great spring of the activity of our minds and their chief feeder. From this principle the direction of the sexual appetite, and all the passions connected with it take their origin: It is the life of our ordinary conversation; and upon the accuracy with which similitude in dissimilitude, and dissimilitude in similitude are perceived, depend our taste and our moral feelings.[40]

Such disengaging "The West" from solely anecdotal or circumstantial private preoccupations amounts to moving from a community "we"— or "we in times of war"— toward an assembled "we," the overhuman "we" of those twentieth-century works of art that, according to Badiou, claim that "No, there is no individual wisdom. Under the twinned words Life and History, thought is always related to far more than the individual."[41]

"The Gutteral Muse"[42]

In his 1986 essay on Sylvia Plath, Heaney reads Wordsworth's "There Was a Boy" as an allegory reflecting the three stages of a poet's career. After the first stage — consisting in learning the craft, which is compared by Wordsworth to learning to whistle — Heaney sees the poet, like Wordsworth's "boy," able to "call up answering calls."[43] "This," Heaney writes, "represents the poetry of relation, of ripple-and-wave effect upon audience; at this point, the poet's art has found ways by which distinctively personal subjects and emotional necessities can be made a common possession of the reader's." In other words, the possibility of relation — or of creating a plural entity, a "one-multiple" beyond borders — lies in the concomitant achievement of disjunction. The distinct stationing of two active presences, that of a poet and that of a listener/reader, forms the divide conditioning the "we." This "divide," significantly covered with ripple and wave traces, calls for attention, for "the interpretative intervention" that will have "to both detain and decide" the effectiveness of an event.[44] Before we come to the formalization proper of the event in

Heaney's poetry, let us now focus on this divide that is part of the event site structure.

As early as 1975, the prose poems of *Stations* had revealed this necessity of disjunction to Heaney as he felt and explored its lack. Experiencing the welded, compact, and stationary world of "The Stations of the West," he had to admit its dead end and the necessity of imagining a world out of joint, with room for passages and new forms of relations:

> Neither did any gift of tongues descend in my days in that upper room when all around me seemed to prophesy. But still I would recall the stations of the west, white sand, hard rock, light ascending like its definition over Rannafast and Errigal, Annaghry and Kincaslagh: names portable as altar stones, unleavened elements.[45]

Is this the reason why this volume remained confidential until, when Heaney no longer had to strive for publicity, nine poems out of the original seventeen were more widely disseminated in the *Opened Ground* collection of 1988? Is it because Heaney felt that he had to conform to the needs of a community "we," to stick to the clichés and discourses that made him part of a certain public world? Perhaps at that time he did not want to expose such explicit reservations about the necessity of disjunction for the possibility of relation. What "The Stations of the West" retraces is the sum total of the denials of such a "poetry of relation." Eleven years later, in his essay on Sylvia Plath's poetry, Heaney formulates this denial as the goal to be reached.

Meanwhile, the fixed, unsurprising, compact, and absolute presence of each element composing the world of "The Stations of the West" leaves no room for the "creation-in-relation" factor that Heaney discovers at Grasmere and in Wordsworth in his 1984 Pete Laver Memorial Lecture, "Place and Displacement." This essay begins with a long quotation from *The Prelude* 1805, where Wordsworth retraces his "conflict of sensations without name" at the break of the Franco–English war in 1793.[46] Heaney reads this pulling-apart of Wordsworth's feelings as the matter that his poetic world is made of. A whole lexicon of painful torture is deployed in Heaney's text ("trauma" [114], "strain" [115], "riven" [115], "stretched" [119]), which draws him to extend Wordsworth's experience to the contemporary Northern Irish poets' predicament: then living and creating in "demeaning conditions" and "tak[ing] the strain of being in two places at once."[47] By so doing, Heaney conforms once again to the principle formulated in the 1800 Preface to *The Lyrical Ballads*, namely to perceive, expose, and analyze the "similitude in dissimilitude, and dissimilitude in similitude." By expressing such junction in disjunction, he creates the space where the "ripple-and-wave effect" of "the poetry of relation" takes place. There, in Grasmere, Heaney no longer blends in Wordsworth in a way that confuses the public as to what part the private plays in his poetry. He can then confidently take his distance with Wordsworth — that is, depart *with* him, not depart *from* him — in order to establish an absolutely public space beyond all possible actualizations.

In 1991, Heaney again expresses a model of rupture leading to the creation of a space of relation when he rereads the 1799 *Prelude* skating scene.[48] This scene haunts Heaney's whole œuvre differently through the years, manifesting through the multiple ruptures that the Wordsworthian text imposes, the event of the poet and the bearings it has on the world. Heaney's furthering and scattering of the scene in his own œuvre expands the forms of disjunction, proving their creativeness. These reapparitions in Heaney's volumes detemporalize the sequence as he further deterritorializes it in each dis-placement and re-placement. Then, by insisting on the textuality of his own continuation, Heaney marks an epochal break, separating the times of creation and the artistic periods. Whereas he keeps intact Wordworth's utter silence in his second stanza as well as the darkness that has been made to fall upon it,[49] Heaney deforms "the shadow of a star" as he revives it.[50] By making its own blackened lines reconfigure in negative "the narrow milky way in the black ice," the 1991 continuation squeezes and flattens the material aspect conveyed to the star in *The Prelude*. The writing insists on its textuality by (dis)joining the Romantic and the contemporary modes of apprehension and expression of the universe. Lastly, this second Heaneyan skating scene expands the opening in the final comparison of *The Prelude* passage. With his "Till all was tranquil as a summer sea."[51] Wordsworth both breaks away from the frozen lake of Windermere and displaces the "sea" by making it into a metaphor. Heaney continues this double retirement in his own last line by erasing the visible mark of comparison and replacing it with a catachresis, and also by further re-forming and de-forming the "sea" evoked by Wordsworth: "We knew we'd come through and kept sailing towards."[52]

Three moments of rupture are recalled and staged in Wordsworth's paradigmatic scene. In the inaugural one, Wordsworth states that he "cares not for [his] home" and indeed turns away from it, all the while accompanied by the death of "The orange sky of evening."[53] The blank between the two stanzas accentuates both this first and the second break, when Wordsworth evokes his "Not seldom [...] retir[ing] / Into a silent bay [...]."[54] This blank is closely followed by the third break, lines 179–180, represented as the skating Wordsworth "reclining back upon [his] heels / Stopped short —[...]."

The dash in line 180, accompanying Wordsworth's stopping short, transcribes the moment of event: the persona's sudden and surprising retirement, the advent of the poet and the possibilities that advent opens. It is a passage made clear — cleared and rendered visible. Heaney seizes it as such and pushes it forward into a formulated absence. Absence is created and dispersed in the lines of the 1991 poem by an insistent lexicon of abandon ("farewell," "Beyond our usual hold," "from grip to give") and by the agglutinating abstractions composed with the use of suffixation. These abstractions pull us upward and away from the ground to realize Heaney's intention that inflating compounds should make balloons of his words:

> Heaney has been talking for some time, Jonathan Allison reminds us in 1991, not only about his heart being lighter but his poetry too: "I would like to be able to be less heavy," he told Tom Adair, "to transform things more ... to be lighter." [...] While this trope of lightness is rehearsed repeatedly in *Seeing Things* in the image of floating, casting, and spinning, Heaney's language has itself become "less heavy" since *North*. [...] We can see this easy-going quality in his hyphenated phrases [...].[55]

Absence is also made by the organization of the spacing, suspense-creating blanks of enjambments and stanza breaks. Notably, the heart of this poem — as in all the poems of the second part of *Seeing Things*, "Squarings" — is void. This hollowed-out conduit at the heart of the Heaneyan poem is what Muldoon, in his *End of the Poem* essay, playfully calls the "gutteral muse."[56] It is also what Jessica Stephens rightly detects as the very principle of Heaney's poetry, calling it "a gap of a different, powerful, life-affirming nature."[57]

Continuing Wordsworth, this poem, which explores the possibilities of disjunction, produces what Badiou calls a "*site événementiel.*" An event site is a constructed structure (Badiou says "historicized")[58] through which an event can happen. Mathemes and poems are such evident "non-natural"[59] architectures. Yet in order to be "foundational," the site has to be formed "*on the edge of the void.*"[60] The undecidability warranted and represented by the void is the condition of an event.[61] The different ruptures we have seen Heaney's poem multiply and expand from Wordsworth's give form to such a void. It remains for our "interpretative interventions"[62] to apprehend the event and truly express it from its site: the event of an innumerable "we," in this continuation of Wordsworth.

"We knew we'd come through [...]," writes Heaney at the end of "Crossings xxviii." How many does that "we" of the last line make, do you think? All the more so as, in his introduction to his *William Wordsworth: Poems Selected*, Heaney sees in the former's poems "the songs of a man who has come through."[63]

"Spirit[ing one]self"[64]

As Marc Porée writes:

> Thus it appears to the profane observer of Wordsworth's poetry that it keeps returning, implicitly or explicitly, to the spectral condition that follows the death

of the body [...]. It has never done anything else, to the point of being literally haunted by it, than pose the terms of the impossible interrogation: "What is a ghost?"[65]

Wordsworth's poetry "pores over" dead bodies, problematically "modelling the act of reading."[66] If the phrase "There Was a Boy" can indeed sum up what Wordsworth's poetry is so often about, thus linking reading and writing with dead bodies, "There Was a Boy," both as a phrase and as a poem, also conjures up the image of Heaney's "wreader" (both reader and writer, writer because reader) of Wordsworth.

When, in 1986, Heaney reads the poem "There Was a Boy" as an allegory of the three stages of a poet's career, death — not semantically named, but syntactically evoked — appears to be the definitive achievement of the poet, the perfection he must strive for while alive and in full possession of his art. At this (third) stage, Heaney writes, "skill is no use any more,"[67] thus denying and obliterating the conscious and conscientious poetic effect. He goes on: "As he [the poet represented by 'the boy'] stands open like an eye or an ear, he becomes imprinted with all the melodies and hieroglyphs of the world." Here death penetrates the active senses through the dismemberment expressed in the sentence, and it touches the creative self as formulated in the passive imprints that the "he" is subjected to. What more effective "divide" than death can be imagined?

Heaney's latest poetic achievements extend the Wordsworthian gesture of ultimate retirement or disincarnation, producing an event form through which such vanishings can occur. *District and Circle* (2006) is the volume of this achievement: giving voices to so many still-life and eclipsed figures of past volumes; recalling the dead; conjuring ghosts and inheriting so many voices, the voices of Rilke, Seferis, Horace, Eohan Rua Ò Súillebháin, Chaucer, Milosz, Hughes, and Auden, to name but a few. This is yet without naming Wordsworth's, who reappears — as all true ghosts should — without being presently there, in the negated and neglected "bootless runners" presented in the cenotaph of the poem "Wordsworth's Skates."[68] Having composed and multiplied expressions of disjunction, the forms of a divide, Heaney elaborates the possibility of forming an event site. In *District and Circle*, each poem is a structure painstakingly creating disjunctions *en abyme* so that an event or events can be expressed. It remains for us to reconstruct and express the event concerning the subject that this particular poetic site makes possible.

We can easily notice how the poem "Wordsworth's Skates" produces opening forms *en abyme*: to the small frames of the ellipses at the beginning and the *vedute* that they open is added the "display case" of the second stanza, at the almost-heart of the poem. This display case — of the stanza and in the stanza — is a replica of the material display case in Grasmere's Dove Cottage, where Wordsworth's "bootless runners [lie] toppled / In dust."[69] What this redoubled opening form makes happen is death, death conveyed through the meaning of the verbs selected for this middle stanza, to which can be super-added the effect of the passive voice when it is applied to them — not to say anything about the "dust" (line 6) and the "bindings" (line 7), which seem to secure the *rigor mortis* of the emblematic relic contained there.

We can say that in their various forms, these forms determine the definite finitude, if not the definitive *finis*, of the object that they embalm. Surrounding or "binding" the dead object, the form itself must be seen as imbued with a strange life of its own — a spectral life, haunted by the death of its own making *and* constituting the event of the absolute other that death is. This event form appears, for example, when an extraordinary interlacing of Heaneyan suffixation and Wordsworthian negation simultaneously asserts the retirement of the individual and the advent of a unique plural voice, as in "Not the boot-less runners [...]." It is also there in the first line-in-three of "Wordsworth's Skates," which so deftly plays on visibility and invisibility. In its visual de-composition, it visually and aurally re-composes the "star" that Wordsworth had brought down and incised in the ice in his 1799 *Prelude*, and which Heaney squeezes and textualizes into a "narrow milky way" in his 1991 "Cross-ings xxviii."

Here, we are in an altogether different time and space from the one explored in the 1978 essay called "The Makings of a Music: Reflections on Wordsworth and Yeats," where Heaney's first published "wreading" of the skating scene appears. There, early Heaneyan "gravity"[70] is projected onto the sequence and materialized in the vocabulary, the imagination, and the sounds with which Heaney presents his reading before he quotes the second stanza of Wordsworth's 1799 skating scene: "As his poetic feet repeat his footfalls, the earth seems to be a treadmill that he turns; the big diurnal roll is sensed through the poetic beat and the world moves like a waterwheel under the fall of his voice."[71] There, a private voice redoubles a private concern, folding back another private voice on its own self; here, two voices are distinctly heard, both gathered and let free. Then and only then, does the text open as a space of spectrality.[72] The poem is made to appear haunted by the voices it both reverberates and announces,[73] its phenomenality as text made to present itself as a visible sign of the invisible.[74]

Through such an achievement of the death-of-the-object as well as that of the anecdotal and the individual performed in this composition, poetry attains "the pure transparency of the act."[75] The energetic iambic antepenul-timate line (with its anacrusis giving the necessary run off) makes us hear, and see, and feel the cold breeze from the skater sliding by, flashing "from the clutch of earth along its curve," and leaving it "scored."[76]

What seems to have been "[brought] to perfection" is not so much "the long slide" as in the 1991 skating scene, but the "letting go"[77] of the undefined figure, which we would be wrong to limit too hastily to an apparition of Wordsworth. The "he" that flashes past, shining with the intermittent "gleam" of the star of Wordsworth's inaugural poem, is soon to vanish altogether in his imprinting the longest and airiest line in this poem. "He" is doomed to disappear, leaving definitive marks that trace both the actual and the virtual. The lines left incised by the passages of pens and skates are not two, not four, but at least five: those of a score, tracing the possibility of music.

As Derrida wrote in *Specters of Marx,* "There where man, a certain determined concept of man, is finished, there the pure humanity of man, of the *other man* and of man *as other* begins or has finally the chance of heralding itself— of promising itself. In an apparently inhuman or else a-human fashion."[78]

In these configurations of the poetic self retraced through the Wordsworth-Heaney modes of assemblage displayed in Heaney's "wreadings," it is possible to apprehend the form — and the *movement* in it — given to Wordsworth's intuition of a "Man [...] greater than he seems."[79] Heaney's event forms have eventually made way for this figure, far beyond private incarnation and more than public: a-personal.

Because of these constant and polymorphous goings-beyond "the animal datum of the body"[80] that the poet testifies to in his creation, it would not be proper to say that Heaney constitutes a supplementary link in Wordsworth's chain of poets, "each with each / Connected."[81] Combining Wordsworth's singular expressions of the private with his own, Heaney here gives shape to a uniquely plural, composite formalization of an utterly opened, absolutely a-personal event (beyond the public, even, which can still be considered as fixed, being there): the divide foundational of an event site. Thus, filled with the spirit of Wordsworth, what Heaney gradually perfects in his writing is the representation of the void of an absence, a formalization of "retirement" that may be the sign of Romanticism's *relève.*[82]

NOTES

1. William Wordsworth, "The River Duddon, xxxiv, After-Thought" (1820), *William Wordsworth: Poems Selected by Seamus Heaney* (London: Faber & Faber, 2001; first edition 1988), 138. Lines 8–9 read: "We Men, who in our morn of youth defied / The elements, must vanish;— be it so!"

2. William Wordsworth, *The Prelude* (1805), XIII: 408, *The Prelude, 1799, 1805, 1850* ed. Jonathan Wordsworth, H.M. Abrams, Stephen Gill (New York & London: Norton, 1979), 480.

3. Ibid., 444–445, 482. For a detailed analysis of Romantic anthropology in some of its various aspects, cf. René Gallet and Pascale Guibert, eds., *Le sujet romantique et le monde: la voie anglaise* (Caen: Presses Universitaires de Caen, 2009).

4. Wordsworth, *Prelude,* 437–439.

5. Ciaran Carson, "Escaped From the Massacre?" review of *North,* by Seamus Heaney, *The Honest Ulsterman,* 50 (Winter 1975), 183.

6. Jacques Derrida, *Spectres de Marx: L'État de*

la dette, le travail du deuil et la nouvelle Internationale (Paris: Galilée, 1993), 22, for instance. But
this metaphor (in its literal means-of-transporta-
tion sense) of the text as stage runs throughout his
works. Hereafter, references to the French text will
be given first, followed by references to the English translation by Peggy Kamuf.

7. Alain Badiou, L'être et l'événement (Paris:
Seuil, 1988), 204; Being and Event (London and
New York: Continuum, 2005), 183. Hereafter, ref-
erences to the French text will be given first, fol-
lowed by references to the English translation by
Oliver Feltham.

8. Alain Badiou, Le Siècle (Paris: Seuil, 2005),
54; The Century (Malden, MA: Polity Press 2008;
first edition 2007), 32. Hereafter, references to the
French text will be given first, followed by references to the English translation by Alberto Toscano.

9. Ibid., 13 / 3.

10. Ibid., 227 / 161.

11. Ibid., 216 / 153.

12. Ibid., 226 / 160.

13. See Raymond Williams, Culture and Society 1780–1950 (Harmondsworth: Penguin Books,
1968).

14. Badiou, L'être et l'événement, 199 / 178.

15. Derrida, Spectres de Marx, 108 / 63.

16. Ibid., 27 / 7.

17. Ibid., 15 / xix.

18. Blake Morrison, Seamus Heaney (London:
Methuen [Contemporary Writers Series], 1982),
11–12.

19. Robert Mayo, "The Contemporaneity of
the Lyrical Ballads," PMLA 69: 3 (1954, 486–522),
491.

20. See James Fenton's insightful analysis of this
"knack" Heaney seems to have had of "soaking up
all the available attention." "The Orpheus of Ulster," The Strength of Poetry (Oxford: Oxford University Press, 2003; first edition 2001, 85–102),
92.

21. Mayo, "The Contemporaneity of the Lyrical Ballads," 490. My italics.

22. See Nicholas Roe, "'Wordsworth at the
Flax-dam': an early poem by Seamus Heaney,"
Critical Approaches to Anglo-Irish Literature, Irish
Literary Studies vol. 29, ed. Michael Allen and
Angela Wilcox (Gerrards Cross: Colin Smythe,
1989), 166–170.

23. Ibid., 168.

24. Seamus Heaney, "The Given Note," l. 13
and 16, Door into the Dark (London: Faber &
Faber, 1969), 46.

25. Wordsworth, "The Solitary Reaper" (1805),
l. 32, William Wordsworth: Poems Selected by Seamus Heaney, 133.

26. See Hugh Haughton, "Power and Hiding
Places: Wordsworth and Seamus Heaney," The

Monstrous Debt. Modalities of Romantic Influence
in Twentieth-Century Literature, ed. Damian Walford Davies and Richard Marggraf Turley (Detroit:
Wayne University Press, 2006, 61–100), 85–88.

27. William Wordsworth, The Prelude (1805),
I: 19, The Prelude, 1799, 1805, 1850, ed. Jonathan
Wordsworth, M.H. Abrams, Stephen Gill (New
York & London: Norton, 1979), 28; and Seamus
Heaney, "Glanmore Sonnets," I, l. 5, in Field Work
(London: Faber & Faber, 1985; first edition 1979),
33.

28. Heaney, "The Makings of a Music: Reflections on Wordsworth and Yeats," Preoccupations.
Selected Prose 1968–1978 (London: Faber & Faber,
1984; first edition 1980, 61–78), 65.

29. Heaney, William Wordsworth. Poems Selected by Seamus Heaney, vii.

30. Heaney, Preoccupations, 68.

31. Seamus Heaney, "Kinship," ii, l. 48, North
(London: Faber & Faber, 1986; first edition 1975),
82.

32. Haughton, "Power and Hiding Places," 99.
Haughton's reading, intent on showing Heaney's
inclination to borrow so much from the great poetic father, betrays both a narcissistic and an es-
capist tendency: "It may be that Heaney's return to
childhood has its root in the same adult recoil not
just from 'The Troubles' but from the troubling
pressure of accelerating cultural change in Ireland
and elsewhere."

33. Al Alvarez, New York Review, 6 March 1980,
quoted in Fenton, 88.

34. Geoffrey Harvey, The Romantic Tradition
in Modern English Poetry (Basingstoke: Macmillan, 1986), 16 sq. Geoffrey Harvey is then not dealing with Heaney, but with the "modern poets"
Wordsworth, Hardy, and Larkin when he raises
the question of a probable link between one's popularity and the conservatism of one's verse.

35. Badiou, Le Siècle, 38 / 21.

36. Ibid., 139 / 97.

37. Heaney, "Feeling into Words," in Preoccupations, 55.

38. William Wordsworth, "Stepping Westward"
(1805), l. 11–12, in Heaney, William Wordsworth:
Poems Selected by Seamus Heaney, 132.

39. William Wordsworth, "Two Letters Re-
Printed from The Morning Post," Wordsworth's Guide
to the Lakes (1810), Ernest de Sélincourt, ed. (Lon-
don: Henry Frowde, 1906), 147–166; and Heaney,
"A New Song," l. 13–20, Wintering Out (London:
Faber & Faber, 1972), 33.

40. Wordsworth, 1800–1802 Preface to the
Lyrical Ballads (1798), William Wordsworth and
Samuel Taylor Coleridge, Lyrical Ballads, W. J. B.
Owen, ed. (Oxford: Oxford University Press 1996;
first edition 1967), 173.

41. Badiou, Le Siècle, 29 / 14.

42. This subtitle comes from a pun on Heaney's

first line of the poem "Traditions" (*Wintering Out*, 1972) by Paul Muldoon, in his essay on Heaney, Graves, and Day-Lewis in *The End of the Poem: Oxford Lectures* (New York: Farrar, Strauss and Giroux, 2006, 368–395), 394.

43. Seamus Heaney, "The Indefatigable Hoof-taps: Sylvia Plath," *The Government of the Tongue: The 1986 T. S. Eliot Memorial Lectures and Other Critical Writings* (London: Faber & Faber, 1988, 148–170), 159.

44. Badiou, *L'être et l'événement*, 204 / 183.

45. Seamus Heaney, *Stations* (Belfast: Ulsterman Publications, 1975), 22.

46. Wordsworth, *The Prelude* 1805, X: 265, in *The Prelude, 1799, 1805, 1850*, 372.

47. Seamus Heaney, *Place and Displacement: Recent Poetry of Northern Ireland* (Grasmere: Trustees of Dove Cottage, 1985), 4. Reprinted in *Finders Keepers: Selected Prose 1971–2001* (London: Faber & Faber, 2002, 112–33), 117.

48. I refer to this particular state of composition of *The Prelude* since it is also this two-book version that Heaney selected for his *William Wordsworth: Poems Selected*.

49. Wordsworth, *The Prelude* 1799, I: 176–177, *The Prelude, 1799, 1805, 1850*, 5 ("[...] all the shadowy banks on either side / Came sweeping through the darkness [...]").

50. Wordsworth, *The Prelude* 1799, I: l. 173.

51. Ibid., 185.

52. Heaney, "Crossings xxviii," l. 12, *Seeing Things* (London: Faber & Faber, 1991), 86.

53. Wordsworth, *The Prelude* 1799, I: 156 & 169.

54. Ibid., 170–1.

55. Jonathan Allison, rev. of *Seeing Things*, *Éire-Ireland* (1991), 139.

56. Muldoon, *The End of the Poem*, 394.

57. Jessica Stephens, "Obedience. Seamus Heaney's *The Government of the Tongue* and *North*" (unpublished, 2008).

58. Badiou, *L'être et l'événement*, 194 / 174.

59. Ibid., 193 / 173.

60. Ibid., 195 / 175.

61. Ibid., 215 / 193.

62. Ibid., 204 / 183.

63. Heaney, *William Wordsworth: Poems Selected*, ix.

64. This subtitle borrows a phrase from the very last line of Heaney's "The Tollund Man in Springtime," *District and Circle* (London: Faber & Faber, 2006), 55–7. 1972 *Wintering Out*'s "Tollund Man" is the voice not-speaking the 2006 poem. If he introduces himself in quite a fittingly ghostly way in the first stanza, his gradual (de)composition as the "display-case peat" of the text opens (l. 46), where

we see him take on typically Heaneyan traits, complexifies his "presence" until, in the last stanza, it is impossible to say for sure who the international intertemporal traveler "spirit[ing him] self into the street" is.

65. Marc Porée, "'Over her / his dead body': *quelques modalités du spectral chez Wordsworth*," *Wordsworth ou l'autre voix*, ed. Christian la Cassagnère and Adolphe Haberer (Lyon: Presses Universitaires de Lyon, 1999, 75–94), 79. My translation.

66. Porée, "'Over her / his dead body,'" 79.

67. Heaney, "The Indefatigable Hoof-taps: Sylvia Plath," *The Government of the Tongue*, 163.

68. Heaney, *District and Circle*, 22.

69. Heaney, "Wordsworth's Skates," l. 5–6, *District and Circle*, 22.

70. See "Kinship," IV: 95–6, *North* (London: Faber & Faber, 1986; first edition 1975), 43; but one can easily retrace such a bent and its downward-oriented imaginary in all the volumes of Heaney's first period — which will later open onto the obverse upward-soaring movement of the time of the Sweeney poems, in *Sweeney Astray* (1983) and *Station Island* (1984).

71. Heaney, *Preoccupations*, 67.

72. Derrida, *Spectres de Marx*, 111 / 65.

73. Ibid., 15 / xviii–xix.

74. Ibid., 27 / 7.

75. Badiou, *Le Siècle*, 228 / 162.

76. Heaney, "Wordsworth's Skates," l. 9–10, *District and Circle*, 22.

77. Heaney, "Crossings xxviii," l. 3, 2 and 4, *Seeing Things*, 86.

78. Derrida, *Spectres de Marx*, 125 / 74.

79. Wordsworth, "Though narrow be that old Man's cares, and near" (1806–7), *William Wordsworth: Poems Selected*, ed. Heaney, 135.

80. Badiou, *Le Siècle*, 247 / 175.

81. Wordsworth, *The Prelude* 1805, XII: 301–2, in *The Prelude, 1799, 1805, 1850*, 452.

82. Alan Bass, the translator of Derrida's *Margins of Philosophy*, explains the untranslatability of Derrida's translation of Hegel's *"Aufhebung"* as *"relève"* in a very clear and precise note (20, note 43). In his words, it is a "conserving-and-negating lift," a lift in which is inscribed an effect of substitution and difference. The conserving gesture of Heaney's poetry composes the plural utterance of a private self evolved from Romanticism onward, which, in itself, contains its negating gesture of the self. This negating gesture (re)creates the Wordsworthian divide, with Romanticism now, as formalized void where the totally open event of an utterly public, a-personal, "one-multiple" self can take place.

Works Cited

Badiou, Alain (1988). *L'être et l'événement.* Paris: Seuil.

_____ (1997). *Deleuze: la clameur de l'être.* Paris: Hachette Littératures.

_____ (2000). *Deleuze. The Clamor of Being.* Trans. Louise Burchill. Minneapolis: University of Minnesota Press.

_____ (2007; first edition 2005). *Being and Event.* Trans. Oliver Feltham. London & New York: Continuum.

_____ (2005). *Le Siècle.* Paris: Seuil.

_____ (2008). *The Century.* Trans. Alberto Toscano. Malden, MA: Polity Press.

Bushell, Sally, and Tony Pinkney (eds.) (2003). "Wordsworth's 'Second Selves' — The Poetic Afterlife 1789–2002." *The Wordsworth Circle* special issue, 34–1.

Davies, Damian Walford, and Richard Marggraf Turley (2006). *The Monstrous Debt. Modalities of Romantic Influence in Twentieth-Century Literature.* Detroit: Wayne University Press.

Derrida, Jacques (1984). *Margins of Philosophy.* Trans. Alan Bass. Chicago: Chicago University Press.

_____ (1993). *Spectres de Marx. L'État de la dette, le travail du deuil et la nouvelle Internationale.* Paris: Galilée.

_____ (1994). *Specters of Marx: The State of the Debt, The Work of Mourning, and The New International.* Trans. Peggy Kamuf. New York & London: Routledge.

Fenton, James (2003; first edition 2001). *The Strength of Poetry.* Oxford: Oxford University Press.

Friedman, Michael F. (1979). *The Making of a Tory Humanist. Wordsworth and the Idea of Community.* New York: Columbia University Press.

Gallet, René, and Pascale Guibert (eds.) (2009). *Le Sujet romantique et le monde: la voie anglaise.* Caen: Presses Universitaires de Caen.

Genette, Gérard (1982). *Palimpsestes. La littérature au second degré.* Paris: Seuil.

Gravil, Richard (1983). "Wordsworth's Second Selves?" *The Wordsworth Circle* 14–4, 191–201.

Harvey, Geoffrey (1986). *The Romantic Tradition in Modern English Poetry.* Basingstoke: Macmillan.

Haughton, Hugh (2006). "Power and Hiding Places: Wordsworth and Seamus Heaney." *The Monstrous Debt. Modalities of Romantic Influence in Twentieth-Century Literature,* ed. Davies and Turley, 61–100.

_____ (1991; first edition 1966). *Death of a Naturalist.* London: Faber & Faber.

Heaney, Seamus (1969). *Door into the Dark.* London: Faber & Faber.

_____ (1975). *Stations.* Belfast: Ulsterman Publications.

_____ (1986; first edition 1975). *North.* London: Faber & Faber.

_____ (1985; first edition 1979). *Field Work.* London: Faber & Faber.

_____ (1983). *An Open Letter.* Derry: Field Day Pamphlets n° 2.

_____ (1984; first edition 1980). *Preoccupations. Selected Prose 1968–1978.* London: Faber & Faber.

_____ (1984). *Station Island.* London: Faber & Faber.

_____ (1984; first edition 1983). *Sweeney Astray.* London: Faber & Faber.

_____ (1985). *Place and Displacement: Recent Poetry of Northern Ireland.* Grasmere: Trustees of Dove Cottage.

_____ (1985; first edition 1972). *Wintering Out.* London: Faber & Faber.

_____ (1987). *The Haw Lantern.* London: Faber & Faber.

_____ (1988). *The Government of the Tongue. The 1986 T. S. Eliot Memorial Lectures and Other Critical Writings.* London: Faber & Faber.

_____ (1989). *The Place of Writing.* Atlanta: Scholars Press.

_____ (1991). *Seeing Things.* London: Faber & Faber.

_____ (1995). *The Redress of Poetry. Oxford Lectures.* London: Faber & Faber.

_____ (1998). *Opened Ground. Poems 1966–1996.* London: Faber & Faber.

_____ (2001; first edition 1988). *William Wordsworth. Poems Selected by Seamus Heaney.* London: Faber & Faber.

_____ (2002). *Finders Keepers. Selected Prose 1971–2001.* London: Faber & Faber.

_____ (2006). *District and Circle.* London: Faber & Faber.

Heaney, Seamus, and Noel Connor (1979). *Gravities. A Collection of Poems and Drawings.* Newcastle upon Tyne: Charlotte Press Publications.

Mayo, Robert (1954). "The Contemporaneity of the *Lyrical Ballads.*" *PMLA* 69, 486–522.

Morrison, Blake (1982). *Seamus Heaney.* London: Methuen (Contemporary Writers Series).

Muldoon, Paul (2006). "'Welsh Incident' by Robert Graves; 'A Failure' by C. Day-Lewis; 'Keeping Going' by Seamus Heaney." *The End of the Poem. Oxford Lectures.* New York: Farrar, Strauss and Giroux, 368–395.

O'Neill, Michael (2001). "O 'Shining in Modest Glory': Contemporary Northern Irish Poets and Romantic Poetry." *The Wordsworth Circle,* 32, 59–65.

Porée, Marc (1999). "'Over her / his dead body': quelques modalités du spectral chez Wordsworth." *Wordsworth ou l'autre voix,* ed. Christian la Cassagnére and Adolphe Haberer. Lyon: Presses Universitaires de Lyon, 75–94.

Ricks, Christopher (2002). *Allusion to the Poets.* Oxford: Oxford University Press.

Roe, Nicholas (1989). "'Wordsworth at the Flaxdam': an early poem by Seamus Heaney." *Critical Approaches to Anglo-Irish Literature* (Irish Literary Studies vol. 29), ed. Michael Allen and Angela Wilcox. Gerrards Cross: Colin Smythe, 166–170.

Stephens, Jessica (2008). "Obedience. Seamus Heaney's *The Government of the Tongue* and *North.*" Unpublished.

Wordsworth, William (1906). *Wordsworth's Guide to the Lakes* (1810). Ed. Ernest De Sélincourt. London: Henry Frowde.

_____ (1977). *The Poems,* vol. 1. Ed. John O. Hayden. Harmondsworth: Penguin.

_____ (1979). *The Prelude, 1799, 1805, 1850.* Eds. Jonathan Wordsworth, M. H. Abrams and Stephen Gill. New York and London: Norton.

Wordsworth, William, and Samuel Taylor Coleridge (1996). *Lyrical Ballads* (1798), ed. W. J. B. Owen. Oxford: Oxford University Press.

9. "Imagined within the gravitational pull of the actual": The Fusion of the Private and the Public in Seamus Heaney's Poetics

Torsten Caeners

Digging and the archaeology of Bogland: the origin of the public and the private in Heaney's poetry

It would be wrong to label Seamus Heaney as a political poet, but to define his poetry as predominantly lyrical would equally not do it justice. While a great number of poems in Heaney's oeuvre are purely lyrical and private (one need only think of his sonnet sequences "Clearances" and "Glanmore Sonnets"), it is not difficult to find poems that convey a political message as well. The bulk of the Irish poets and writers of Heaney's generation exhibit a clear-cut political agenda in their works, and one would expect the political aspect of Heaney's poetry to be more strongly asserted, considering that he is an Irish poet who lived in Ireland during the political troubles of the twentieth century. This is not the case, however. Heaney's poetry acknowledges the public-private divide in that it chooses neither, gravitating to one side or the other as it sees fit. His poetry refuses to take sides and the dichotomy of the public and the private is constituted in a way that resists extreme political positions.

Heaney has refrained from instrumentalizing his position as the foremost poet of his generation in political terms; instead, his poetical career has always been intricately connected with Irish traditions and Irish history. Before all else, the source of Heaney's poetry lies in the bog lands of rural Derry and his family's history of farming.[1] Heaney's concern in his early poetry is with rural verities and their connection to the human condition. Indeed, the foundation of Heaney's poetry is as far removed from the concerns of Irish politics as can be imagined. Heaney notes that in his genesis as a poet, he developed "a sense of crafting words and for one reason or another, words as bearers of history and mystery began to invite [him]."[2] This statement is programmatic for Heaney and his poetry. The idea of "crafting words" suggests that, for Heaney, poetry is as much a craft or trade as it is a form of art. In his early notion of a fusion between the seemingly contrastive fields of art and craft, we can already trace the poet's conception of and possible resolution to the dialectic of the public and the private.

Etymologically, "art" and "craft" are semantically close; according to the *Oxford English Dictionary*, the two terms "were formerly synonymous and had a nearly parallel sense-development, though they diverge in their leading modern senses."[3] The difference in the contemporary meanings of these terms lies in the fact that "craft" is connected to economic concerns, whereas "art" is not.[4] In this respect, "craft" is closely associated with "trade."[5] This dichotomy describes the basic features of the private and the public domains. If we place "craft" and "art" within the framework of traditional aesthetics, we arrive at an "ivory tower" concept of art-for-art's sake vs. a socially integrated concept of craft. Art, conceived within an "ivory tower" concept of aesthetics, is dissociated from moral, utilitarian, and other public consideration. In order to aspire to true art, artists must renounce their ties to common nature and dedicate themselves wholly to the pursuit of art alone. Oscar Wilde notes:

> A work of art is the unique result of a unique temperament. Its beauty comes from the fact that the author is what he is. It has nothing to do with the fact that other people want what they want. Indeed, the moment that an artist takes notice of what other people want, and tries to supply the demand, he ceases to be an artist, and becomes a dull or an amusing craftsman, an honest or dishonest tradesman. He has no further claim to be considered as an artist. Art is the most intense mood of individualism that the world has known.[6]

Wilde's notion of art is one of total subjectivity. Art is dissociated from the public and confined exclusively to the private sphere in both creation and reception. If artists so much as acknowledge a public demand, Wilde states, they become craftsmen and tradesmen, and any possibility of true art is lost. While his view is extreme, it exemplifies the connection between the concepts of "art" and "craft," as well as the implicit categorization of "art" as private and "craft" as public. In its fundamental utilitarianism, the concept of craft is placed in opposition to art.

By stating that poetic creation is a process of "crafting words," Heaney, in contrast to the above, establishes a definitive social connection for his poetry. In a play of etymological possibilities that is typical for Heaney, the phrase "crafting words" becomes at once constitutive and expressive of his understanding of poetry. For Heaney, the structure of a poem emerges through words that are *crafted*— expertly combined by means of an acquired skill. Rather than arising from some sort of divine inspiration, the poem emerges from a social demand, from the inevitable human connection poets have to their culture. While they are artists, poets also work within a web of socio-cultural discourses that they are dependent on and which are, at the same time, co-dependent on them. This positioning is manifest in the etymological convergence of the meanings of "art" and "craft." By stating that his poetry is a crafting of words, Heaney implies that it fuses aspects of both practices. Any poem, once produced, has a twofold destiny: (1) as an aesthetic object with all the implications of that term, and (2) as a product of "craft" to be traded and distributed socially and culturally. Poetry is an activity, and the poem a commodity that is ingrained in social and public activities and discourses. In this conception, poetry is a hybrid concept oscillating between two spheres; it exists in relationship to (and serves as a bridge between) the private and the public, but is located in neither domain. It negotiates its position in a space in-between.

According to Heaney, the poetic process includes not only a bridging of the private and public divide, but also of the divide between past and present. This interrelatedness of diachronic, synchronic, socio-cultural, and personal influences can be traced and exemplified by two early poems from Heaney's *Death of a Naturalist* (1966) and *Door into the Dark* (1969). In his early poetological poem "Digging," Heaney links the trade of his ancestors with the craft of the poet and portrays the poet's work in terms of farming. While not yet conceptualized strictly as a clash between the private and the public, the poet's conflict is between his family's past — namely potato digging and turf cutting — and his personal future, which is in literature. The poem establishes a divide between the speaker's family history (which by implication is collective and public, as it represents the public legacy of the proverbial Irish tenant farmer) and the contemporary situation of the private individual. The speaker of "Digging" is torn between his sense of duty to his family and his calling to be(come) a writer, a conflict that divides his individuality from the collective of the family and effectively isolates him. This divide is bridged in the poem's final stanza, which suggests a solution as the poet concedes by saying he has "no spade to follow men" like his forebears, but that he will "dig with" his "squat pen."[7] The poet aims to use the writer's pen analogously to the way his ancestors worked with the spade. In this way, art is brought into the realm of craft and trade. The principles of agriculture are transferred onto the practice of poetic writing, re-establishing the connection between the poet, his family, and their combined legacy. For Heaney, writing poetry *is* digging. "Digging" poetically into his own past, the poet is able to continue his family's legacy. The poem's synthesis of past and present as well as of the collective and the individual is programmatic for all of Heaney's subsequent poems.

Heaney's poetic digging unearths not only personal memories, but is extended in "Bogland" to include the public history of Ireland. As the poet remarks in the quote above, words are "bearers of history and mystery." Heaney combines this insight with concepts established in "Digging" and sets up the poet as a type of archaeologist. This move from the farmer to the archaeologist signifies a transition from family history to national history. Speaking of "Bogland," Heaney acknowledges that learning about the frontier West while teaching American literature prompted him to "set up [...] the bog as an answering Irish myth."[8] The concern of "Bogland" is not private, but collective.[9] The archaeologist digs into the history and mythology of Ireland via excavation of the bogs, which contain the preserved treasures of the past. The poet's dig is linguistic in nature, but it nonetheless uncovers previously unrecognized historical and mythological connections. In "Feeling into Words," Heaney explains that he believes in "poetry as divination [...]; poems are elements of continuity, with the aura and authenticity of archaeological finds, where the buried shard has an importance that is not diminished by the importance of the buried city; poetry as a dig [...]."[10] "[T]he buried shard" is not diminished in importance by "the buried city." While "the buried city" represents knowledge and insight into the past on a collective and public level, "the buried shard," which is a household artifact and signifies the private domain, is equally important. "Bogland" exemplifies this reality, and it is here that the metaphor of poet as archaeologist is employed for the first time, as "the Great Irish Elk" is lifted from the peat.[11] Similar to the "buried city," the "Great Irish Elk" represents the public domain. This iconic image of Ireland and its national history enters contemporary culture as an exhibit in a public museum, where it is set up as "an astounding crate full of air." In addition to the Elk, the archaeologist also recovers butter from the dig. Like the "buried shard," butter is an artifact from the private domain of the kitchen, and it is of the same importance to the archaeologist as the iconic elk. The butter, though initially private, becomes a public matter through its rediscovery by the archaeologist.

In setting up the metaphor of poetry as archaeology, Heaney concedes that poetry is as much a private matter as it is a public one. Though conceived in private, publication releases a poem into the public sphere, where it must negotiate between its private origin and public destiny. With regard to "Bogland," Heaney states:

> I began to get an idea of bog as the memory of the landscape, or as a landscape that remembered everything that happened in and to it. [...] I had a tentative unrealized need to make a congruence between memory of bogland and [...] our national consciousness.[12]

The origin of "Bogland" as recounted here reiterates the connections between the individual and the public as well as the past and the present/future. The bogland of Ireland is a storehouse of memory that "remember[s] everything that happened in and to it." By extension, poetry becomes an archive of society, a means of digging up the past and showing its relevance for the present.

Although one can trace Heaney's concern with the public-private divide in his early poetry, it is a concern that remained secondary. This changed dramatically in 1969, which saw a resurgence of violence between the Catholic and Protestant communities in Northern Ireland. British troops were brought in to address the situation and the country's religious tensions were aggravated by political ones. On 30 January 1972, these tensions sparked a violent incident that has entered Irish national history as Bloody Sunday.[13] On that day, a civil rights march escalated into a bloodbath when police fired on the demonstrators. Fourteen unarmed civilians were killed and seventeen wounded. In the aftermath, public support for the IRA grew and terrorist attacks in Ireland as well as England followed.

Irish writers could not ignore the atrocities flaring around them, and most offered some sort of public response. Authors were faced with a difficult situation. It was not simply a matter of Irish vs. English; the situation involved private religious beliefs that were now being aggressively politicized. In the face of religiously indiscriminate violence on the part of the British Army, representing a threat of renewed English occupation, one had to choose sides not only between Catholicism and Protestantism, but also between condemning or condoning the violence that was becoming commonplace.

Heaney felt enormous public pressure to comment on the new Irish predicament, and the public role of political poet was basically forced upon him.[14] As Kieran Quinlan states, the poet "was suddenly faced with the task of diverting his poetic talents from their engagement with rural and domestic verities to confront the dramatically intensified political situation."[15] Heaney followed his own poetology of "Digging" and "Bogland" and extended its implications into the political. The public extension of the predominantly private concern of family and individual in "Bogland" was now pushed further into the national political sphere by means of a coherent poetics that Heaney conceptualized in the wake of continued Irish violence.

Heaney's poetic theory

The so-called bog poems constitute Heaney's poetic answer to the complex situation of Ireland in the late 1960s and early 1970s.[16] Heaney states that from 1969 onwards, "the problems of poetry moved from being simply a matter of achieving the satisfactory verbal icon to being a search for images and symbols adequate to [the] predicament."[17] He found these symbols in Iron Age bodies excavated from bogs throughout Europe, which he discovered in Peter Glob's book *The Bog People*. Glob's book includes detailed case studies of mummified bodies which have been preserved since Iron Age times by the special fluids of the bogs and retain astonishingly human features. According to Glob, the recovered bodies are of people slain by members of their own clan. This was done as punishment for crimes, but also as voluntary sacrifice to the gods. The acts had both public and religious functions. Here Heaney locates a connection to Ireland that he weaves into his poetry, giving it a clearly recognizable political dimension.[18] The bog poems, while political, are not specific to the twentieth-century Troubles and thus avoid taking sides between the Irish factions of that time. Instead, the bog poems comment on the atrocities in a manner that gives them universal and artistic significance while also retaining the intricacies of the religious background and the authenticity of the violence.[19]

In the bog poems, Heaney effects a fusion between the concept of poetic digging and the Jungian notion of the collective unconscious, a key feature of his poetic theory. Writing about the bog poems, Heaney mentions Jungian concepts, especially the notion of the archetype.[20] With regard to his poetics, the phrase "archetypical patterns" is important: it is by means of such patterns that the fate of the bog bodies and that of the victims of Irish violence are linked. Heaney conceptualizes the interrelation of the public and the private in terms of Jungian psychoanalysis. Jung relates archetypes and the collective unconscious as follows:

> The collective unconscious is a part of the psyche which can be negatively distinguished from a personal consciousness by the fact that it does not, like the latter, owe its existence to personal experience and consequently is not a personal acquisition. [...] Whereas the personal unconscious consists for the most part of *complexes*, the content of the collective unconscious is made up essentially of *archetypes*.[21]

Archetypes are the structural matrix of the collective unconscious. Inherited rather than acquired, they constitute a psychic repository that "can become conscious secondarily and which give[s] definite form to certain psychic contents."[22] Repetitions of specific acts and social circumstances during the course of human history have led to the consolidation of archetypes in the collective unconscious.[23] These archetypes are activated in the presence of similar situations and act upon the individual involuntarily.

In facing the political crises in Ireland Heaney looks to avoid the repression of either his public or private concerns. As a solution to the conflict, he appropriates Jung's concept of the collective unconscious and fuses it with his notion of poetry as archaeological digging. Jung's collective unconscious is conceived as a reciprocal conductor between the individual and his or her culture, where the poet's digging unearths unrealized connections that both admonish and potentially unify. In his bog poems, Heaney excavates an archetypical connection between the religiously motivated violence in contemporary Ireland and the religious sacrifices in the Iron Age. This type of violence has been repeated throughout history and has lodged in the collective unconsciousness as an archetype. Heaney acknowledges the archetypical poetically by combining it with the poetic concepts developed in "Digging" and "Bogland," thus escaping a one-sided commitment and a permanent inner displacement. This appropriation of Jungian concepts adapts and evolves Heaney's early poetics in response to the intensified political situation.

As in "Bogland," where the archaeologist does not differentiate between the importance of the "shard" and the "city," Heaney refuses to subordinate the private to the public: in fact, he does not establish a hierarchy between the two concepts at all. Instead, Heaney constitutes the public and the private as "fields of force" that exert ever-changing pressure on the poet's consciousness and demand a fusion in the finished poem. In poetry it is "imperative to discover a field of force."[24] By introducing the concept of "the field of force," Heaney can circumvent the choice between the private and the public and thus escape a permanent displacement of his inner balance. The introduction of the notion of the "fields of force" is the second major aspect of Heaney's poetics and, like the notions of the archetype and the collective unconscious, it is centrally concerned with the public-private divide in poetry.

The advantage of the "field of force" concept is that it does not constitute the public and the private as static. Rather, both the public and the private are dynamic functions that take into account both the amorphous nature of the individual creative process and the changing tensions of reality. By nature, force-fields are not absolute, and neither are their boundaries. Their strength is dependent on the potency of the energy that produces them, and this energy is variable. Therefore, Heaney can describe the process of poetic creation as "the imagination pressing back against the pressures of reality."[25] The imagination, representing the poet's private thoughts — his conscious and unconscious wishes and desires — is "pressing *back*" (emphasis mine) against reality: reality, which is the public, is an intrusive force threatening the private. In response, the private consciousness exerts a fitting counter-pressure necessary to resist the demands of reality:

> [I]n the activity of poetry, too there is a tendency to place a counter-reality in the scales — a reality which may be only imagined but which nevertheless has weight because it is imagined within the gravitational pull of the actual and can therefore hold its own and balance out against the historical situation.[26]

Since poetry is "imagined within the gravitational pull of the actual," it has something to say about and to the "actual." Poetry as a "counter-reality" provides a commentary on the political and cultural situation from which it was created. Consequently, it can help promote change and affect the "historical situation."[27] For Heaney, poetry emerges from the boundary between the private and public fields of force. The public-private divide is not truly bridged, but the tensions that are produced are sublimated creatively into a poetry that does not take sides. Poetry is a creative fusion of aspects from both realms, a space where partly overlapping aspects meet in the threshold between the two "fields of force" and are combined into a new imaginative reality.

This threshold should be imagined as a kind of no-man's land devoid of fixed borders. From this nondescript place emerges a newness that renegotiates the borders on both sides and changes the nature of the private as well as the public. The newly balanced fusion releases poets from their anxieties, because such poetry provides a glimpsed alternative to reality. It "does not intervene in the actual but by offering consciousness a chance to recognize its predicaments, foreknow its capacities and rehearse its comebacks [...] it does constitute a beneficent event, for poet and audience alike."[28] Poetry emerges from the constant contact between the private consciousness of the poet and the public demands of reality, and it allows the poet to "rehearse" possible reactions to reality. This activity has a liberating effect on the individual, because the poet and reader can play with decisions without running the risk of implementing them. For the private individual, the alternative reality created by poetry produces "a distinct sensation that [...] poetry is 'strong enough to help'; it is then that the redress grows palpable."[29] The poetry of redress that Heaney advocates here has therapeutic properties.[30] It establishes a connection between the past and the future and produces, or at least suggests, a course of action that constitutes a viable and positive "prospect."

Mindful of political realities, Heaney is well aware that this would not be enough for a political activist.[31] The poet's duty, as Heaney sees it, is not to produce events, however, but to provide a commentary on events, to "offer consciousness a chance to recognize its predicaments" and find release from the constant demands of a threatening reality. The focus for Heaney is on the private consciousness of the individual. For him, poetry is primarily a private means of dealing with the often troubling realities of existence. Heaney, however, is not blind to the public aspect of poetry. He is very much aware of the "idea of poetry as an answer, and the idea of an answering poetry as a responsible poetry, and the idea of poetry's answer, its responsibility, being given in its own language rather than in the language of the world that provokes it, that too has been one of [his] constant themes."[32] From its effect on the individual, poetry's influence spreads into the public and can secondarily influence the public field of discourse. After all,

> the idea of poetry as a symbolic resolution of opposing truths, the idea of the poem as having its existence in a realm separate from the discourse of politics, does not absolve it or the poet from political responsibility. Nobody is going to advocate an ivory tower address for the poet nor a holier-than-thou attitude.[33]

It is true that the redressing effects of poetry work first upon the individual person (poet and reader), but poetry stems from the individual consciousness that, following Jung, is also a manifestation of the collective psyche. Since poetry is always "imagined in the gravitational pull of the actual," that is under the constant pressure of the public, it has something to contribute to the "actual." Poetry thus conceived has a balancing function. It can nullify the danger of displacement not only for the poet, but also for any reader and, therefore, for the public. It suggests a mediating position, another truth, in the conflicting conditions of reality.[34]

Heaney's poetry of redress is not a private answer to a public demand, nor is it a public statement bereft of individuality; it is always a combination of the two. It covers a middle ground accessible to everyone regardless of political and/or religious affiliations. The public domain exerts constant pressure on the private consciousness, which reacts with a fitting counter-pressure. This counter-pressure takes the form of an imaginative reality modeled upon the "actual" in which the poet's mind can temporarily escape the threatening forces of reality. Due to the intricate relationship between the collective and private consciousnesses as conceived in Jungian terms, the imagined reality created in the poem can provide a similar liberating alternative for the public sphere and may affect civic discourse. Consequently, poetry cannot help but be influenced *by* and partake *in* the public sphere; it is always a fusion of the private and the public.

The Poetics of Redress in a Post-9/11 World

Since the events of 9/11, the issue of terrorism that has long troubled Ireland has become the subject of public discourse around the world. In Heaney's most recent volume of poetry *District and Circle* (2006), a number of poems deal with the international predicaments resulting from 9/11. Two short poems from the collection exemplify Heaney's poetics and their application to the 9/11 context particularly well.[35] Both poems exhibit traces of their conception on the threshold between the private and the public. In response to the events of 9/11, Heaney translated, or perhaps emulated, Horace's Ode. He says about the source poem:

> The poem is [...] tremendous. It is about *terra tremens,* the opposite of *terra firma.* It was written a little over two thousand years ago by the Roman poet Horace, but it could have been written yesterday in Baghdad. In it, Horace expresses the shock he felt when Jupiter [...] drove his chariot across a clear blue sky.[36]

The shock of the speaker in Horace's Ode is linked by Heaney to the shock felt around the world as the events of 9/11 were broadcast live. It is the unpreparedness for the event that makes Horace's Ode contemporary and relevant within the 9/11 context. The experience of the sudden and unexpected catastrophe of 9/11 has historical precursors, of which Horace's Ode is only one specimen. "Anything Can Happen" is a poetic rendering of an archetypal experience that has been ingrained in the collective unconscious by means of repetition. It is through this archetypal relationship that Horace's Ode epitomizes our present, post–9/11 situation, bringing the realization that, indeed, anything can happen at any time.

Heaney's images bear striking resemblances to the ineffaceable images from 9/11. Jupiter galloping "his thunder cart and his horses" in the blue sky conjures up the sunny morning of September 11th, the peaceful background against which the hijacked planes crashed into the Twin Towers. The phrase "the tallest towers / Be overturned" is a direct reference to the collapse of the World Trade Center. Lines 10–12 form a particularly potent image. The image of "Stropped-beaked Fortune" captures the central theme of the poem, namely that dreadful things can happen at any moment. It also evokes the image of American Airlines Flight 11 and United Airlines Flight 175 crashing into the World Trade Center. Endowing "Fortune" with the epithet "stropped-beaked" gives it the properties of a bird, which evokes the image of an airplane. The verb "swoops" lends predatory aspects to Fortune-as-bird thus introducing the idea of violent death. The image is completed by the phrase "making the air gasp," which is a rendering of the explosive impact of the planes in the Twin Towers. The word "crest" opens another level of meaning. "Crest" denotes "corona" or "crown" and would, especially in connection with personified fate, refer to Fortune's power to reverse one's destiny at will. At the same time, "crest" also alludes to the insignia worn by members of the New York Police and Fire Departments and recalls the arbitrary deaths among those in emergency services during the attack and its aftermath.

"Anything Can Happen" was first published in November 2001 under the title "Horace and the Thunder" in *The Irish Times.* There are small, but crucial differences between "Horace and the Thunder" and "Anything Can Happen" that allow a glimpse into the dynamics of the reality-pressure and imaginary counter-pressure from which the poem sprang. Lines 8 and following in "Horace and the Thunder" read, "Anything can happen. The tallest things

[sic] / be overturned." Heaney changed "[The tallest] things" to "towers" in the 2006 version. Obviously, the phrase "tallest things" is semantically much more ambiguous. "Tallest towers," on the other hand — especially after 9/11 and used in the plural — inevitably evokes the Twin Towers and ties the poem closely to the events surrounding the demise of the World Trade Center. Line 16 of "Horace and the Thunder" reads: "Smoke furl and boiling ashes darken day." Though clearly a reference to terrorist attacks, the line in question is born from a place closer to Heaney than the U.S. "Smoke" and "boiling ashes" bring images of terrorist attacks to mind, but these images are not specifically associated with 9/11; they could be connected with many kinds of catastrophes, such as volcanic eruptions. The final line of "Anything Can Happen," with its "Telluric ash and fire-spores," is again tuned more specifically to a 9/11 context. "[F]ire-spores" conjures images both of severed electrical cords and of metal saws cutting through the debris at Ground Zero. "Telluric ash" describes the airborne waves of ashes darkening the streets of New York as enriched with tellurium, a component in metal alloys used in synthetic rubber and gasoline. Thus, the revision of the last line for "Anything Can Happen" also strengthens the identification of the poem's content with the 9/11 events. These revisions show a steady move away from a more open message towards one that a reader can only identify with the September attacks.

In terms of Heaney's poetics, the pressure of reality originally led the poet to emulate Horace's Ode as an act of countering that pressure. In the years following 2001, the reality-pressure was not only sustained, but increased as the implications and ramifications of 9/11 became truly apparent. Within the imaginary realm of the poem, the revisions re-establish the necessary counter-pressure to keep the poem "within the gravitational pull of the actual."

The next poem, "Out of Shot," is in many ways a counter-piece. This sonnet begins peacefully, with the speaker enjoying a late summer's morning standing at "a gate, inspecting livestock." The reader follows the movement of the speaker's thoughts backwards in time. Somewhere on the horizon, the speaker has caught "gleams of the distant Viking *vik* / of Wicklow Bay." The Old Norse word "vik," still present in the name Wicklow, means inlet or bay; "vik" may, however, also stem from the Old English word "wic," deriving from the Latin "vicus" and denoting a camp or trading settlement.[37] This etymological ambiguity spurs the chain of thoughts that follows: the Old English "wic" as settlement leads to thoughts on "scriptorium," while the old Norse "vic" conjures up the "Norse raids" that destroyed monasteries and libraries along the English and Irish coasts. These Viking raids of the late eighth century put the coastal population of Ireland in a similar situation as the speaker of Horace's Ode, namely one of uncertainty where fate could strike at any moment. This fear is conveyed in the poem by the allusion to "night dreads."

The one thing that provides safety for the coastal population is a "storm on the Irish Sea," which the Vikings would not navigate by night. Such storms guaranteed "no attack" during the night or the next morning. This refers to the situation of ancient Irish history. Yet it also serves as a link to the attack reported in the news "last night." Again, the situation described links the events and experiences of eighth-century Ireland with a contemporary situation by means of an archetype. The connection is geographical and historical, as it connects historical Ireland with modern Ireland, but also historical Ireland with contemporary Iraq/Afghanistan. This association is further emphasized in the remaining lines of the poem. The phrase "bazaar district" situates the news report in the war zones of Afghanistan and Iraq, but the sestet draws another connection as well, namely to the IRA mortar attack on 10 Downing Street in 1991. This attack was executed out of the back of a white van and is similar to the one featured in the TV news, in which "mortar shells" were shot from the back of a cart. The terrorist attack of the IRA in the late twentieth century and the insurgent attacks in present-day Afghanistan and Iraq are simultaneously invoked, raising the uneasy question about whether to perceive the bombers as terrorists or freedom fighters.

The speaker's recollection of the attack in the sestet lacks descriptive precision. The only information given is the location and the means of attack. Neither the exact location of the bazaar, nor a specific description of the cart, nor the number of people wounded or killed is provided. These are basic pieces of information included in any TV news report, and one would expect these details to be remembered. As they are not, the lack of descriptive detail is a poetic rendering of the speaker's vague memory of the scene. The uninterrupted flow of similar reports from the war zones has dulled the speaker's senses to their true horror. Because of the sheer number of such reports that are featured in the news every day, they have lost their shocking character and have taken on a sameness that negates their importance. This desensitization is also the reason for the focus on the donkey. The speaker, a farmer, finds the donkey to be the most noteworthy element, and its unusual presence foregrounds the news report.

In contrast to "Anything Can Happen," the political implications are much less specific in "Out of Shot." The poem is far less tightly focused on one historical moment. Rather, the political allusions originate and proceed from the speaker's own private world, from feelings aroused during activities of daily routine. It is from this private core that the historical situation of Ireland is invoked, a situation which forms part of the speaker's own frame of mind. Heaney grounds the poem in the private and personal, but at the same time it discloses the underlying connection of every personal space to the political and public, both historical and contemporary. The imaginary world of the speaker is the ancient history of Ireland. In accordance with Heaney's poetic theory, "Out of Shot" depicts how this imaginary world is created in the context of contemporary reality and how closely these coordinates match. The poem's imagination reflects the specific problems that exert pressure in the real world and transforms this pressure by means of archetypal sublimation. The transformation into the historical reality of eighth-century Ireland helps to alleviate the reality-pressures in that the outcome of the historical situation is known. The contemporary situation can be better endured with the knowledge that a similar situation has once been positively overcome.

Conclusion

In its rural beginnings, Heaney's poetry was implicitly concerned with the public-private divide through the rift between family heritage and individual destiny. This concern was later elaborated into a national one by presenting the bog as a repository of national memory. Heaney's poetry was forced to confront the dialectic between public and private by political developments in Ireland. On the basis of this confrontation, a poetic theory emerged that is not only engaged with the public-private divide, but takes it as its foundation. Heaney's poetic theory, born out of the Irish Troubles of the late 1960s and early 1970s, proposes a process of creation in which the private mind is under the pressure of a harsh reality. Archetypal patterns work on the poet through the Jungian collective unconscious and, once they are acknowledged and discovered, the poet is able to set up an imaginative counter-pressure. The poet reacts in a sublimatory fashion and creates a fictional world, a place where the individual can breathe and take solace. In order for this to be effective, however, the imagined must reflect reality; only then can the mind test alternatives and neutralize psychic pressure. The incorporation of what Heaney calls the "coordinates of reality" makes the poems relevant to the public. Thus, Heaney's theory of poetry inevitably fuses private and public discourses.

In "Anything Can Happen," the pressure of public events caused a revision of the poem's content, leading it away from the personal sphere and linking it specifically to the events of 9/11. "Out of Shot" remains a much more private poem in which the international situation is personalized and no specific event is recounted. Allusions to Irish history and IRA terrorism strengthen the local atmosphere of the poem. While this is so, the political message contained in "Out of Shot" is no less potent than in "Anything Can Happen." Both poems constitute implementations of Heaney's poetics and show that the private and the public can never be separated in art, but inevitably imprint their reciprocal effect on the poetic artifact.

Notes

1. Cf. Torsten Caeners, *"Neither god nor ghost*: The resurrection of the Tollund Man in Seamus Heaney's *District and Circle," LWU: Journal of Academic Research and Education*, 39 (2006, 21–38), 21–23.

2. Seamus Heaney, "Feeling into Words," *Preoccupations: Selected Prose 1968–1978* (New York: Farrar Straus Giroux, 1980), 45.

3. The *Oxford English Dictionary* Online Version <http://dictionary.oed.com/>.

4. The *O.E.D.* defines "craft" as a "branch of skilled work," or more precisely "an art, trade, or profession requiring special skill and knowledge; *esp.* a manual art, a handicraft; sometimes applied to any business, calling, or profession by which a livelihood is earned."

5. "art," *O.E.D*: "5a. The practice of some occupation, business, or profession habitually carried on, esp. when practiced as a means of livelihood or gain; a calling; formerly used very widely, including professions; now usually applied to a mercantile occupation and to a skilled handicraft, as distinct from a profession [...] and *spec.* restricted to a skilled handicraft, as distinguished from a professional or mercantile occupation on the one hand, and from unskilled labour on the other."

6. Oscar Wilde, "The Soul of Man under Socialism," *The Collected Works of Oscar Wilde*, (Hertfordshire: Wordsworth, 1997), 1052.

7. Heaney, "Digging," 3, ll. 29–31. Unless otherwise specified, all quotations of poems are taken from *Opened Ground: Selected Poems 1966–1996* (New York: Farrar Straus Giroux, 1996).

8. Heaney, "Feeling into Words," *Preoccupations: Selected Prose 1968–1978* (New York: Farrar Straus Giroux, 1980), 55.

9. Heaney's comment about "Bogland" suggests that he made a conscious decision to lay down the bog as a national myth and indicates a growing acknowledgement of the public in Heaney's poetry at that time. The fact that "Bogland" is roughly contemporary with the emergence of the bog poems underscores this contention.

10. Heaney, "Feeling into Words," 41.

11. Heaney, "Bogland," 41, ll. 9–15.

12. Heaney, "Feeling into Words," 54.

13. For a closer inspection of the Irish situation of the mid-1960s to mid-1970s, see Arthur Marwick, *A History of the Modern British Isles 1914–1999* (Oxford: Blackwell, 2000), 223–234.

14. See Jeffery Triggs, "Hurt into Poetry: The Political Verses of Seamus Heaney and Robert Bly" in *The New Orleans Review*, 19:3–4 (1992, 162–173), 172.

15. Kieran Quinlan, "Unearthing a Terrible Beauty: Seamus Heaney's Victims of Violence," *World Literature Today* 57:3 (1983, 365–369), 365.

16. The bog poems include "The Tollund Man," "Nerthus," "The Grauballe Man," "Come to the Bower," "Bog Queen," "Punishment," "Strange Fruit," and "Kinship."

17. Heaney, "Feeling into Words," 56.

18. "Punishment" describes the mummified body of a young, undernourished woman who was apparently murdered by her clan as punishment for adultery. A parallel is drawn to the treatment of young, twentieth-century Irish Catholic women who had been involved with British military officers and were subsequently tarred and feathered by members of their own communities. "The Tollund Man" deals with the bog mummy of a sacrificial victim: "The Tollund Man was sacrificed in order to procure a good harvest and renew the seasonal change, [and] the poet prays for the victims of religious and political strife in Ireland to affect a renewal of society and civilised life" (Torsten Caeners, *"Neither god nor ghost,"* 26).

19. Heaney was strongly criticized for not taking a more definitive political stand. See, for instance, Keiran Quinlan's comment on the poem in his essay "Unearthing a Terrible Beauty: Seamus Heaney's Victims of Violence" as well as Ciaran Carson's review of *North*.

20. Heaney, "Feeling into Words," 57–58.

21. C.G. Jung, "The Concept of the Collective Unconscious," *The Portable Jung*, ed. Joseph Campbell (London: Penguin, 1976), 59–60.

22. Ibid., 60.

23. Cf. Jung, "The Concept of the Collective Unconscious," 66–67.

24. Heaney, "Feeling into Words," 56–57.

25. Seamus Heaney, *The Redress of Poetry* (New York: Farrar Straus Giroux, 1996), 1.

26. Heaney, *The Redress of Poetry*, 3–4.

27. One should not underestimate the effectiveness and importance of the commentary function of poetry. Foucault, who takes the dissemination of and control over discourse as the principle foundation of modern culture, ascribes a powerful function to commentary. He states: "I would like to limit myself to pointing out that, in what we generally refer to as commentary, the difference between primary and secondary text plays two interdependent roles. [...] it permits us to create new discourses ad infinitum: the top-heaviness of the original text, its permanence, its status as discourse ever capable of being brought up to date [...] creates an open possibility for discussion. On the other hand, whatever the techniques employed, commentary's only role is to say *finally*, what has silently been articulated *deep down*. It must [...] say, for the first time, what has already been said, and repeat tirelessly what was, nevertheless, never said" (Michel Foucault, "Discourse on Language,"

The Archaeology of Knowledge [New York: Pantheon Books, 1972], 221).

28. Heaney, *The Redress of Poetry*, 2.

29. Ibid., 9.

30. With regard to the meaning of "redress," Heaney notes the different senses of the verb, upon which he calls, including one of its obsolete meanings "'To set (a person or a thing) upright again, to raise again to an erect position. Also *fig.* to set up again, restore, re-establish'" (Seamus Heaney, *The Redress of Poetry* [New York: Farrar Straus Giroux, 1996], 15).

31. Cf. Heaney, *The Redress of Poetry*, 2.

32. Seamus Heaney, "Frontiers of Writing," *The Redress of Poetry* (New York: Farrar Straus Giroux, 1996), 191.

33. Seamus Heaney, "Place and Displacement: Recent Poetry from Northern Ireland," *Finders Keepers: Selected Prose 1971–2001* (London: Faber and Faber, *2002)*,118.

34. Cf. "As long as the coordinates ... empowered way," Heaney, *The Redress of Poetry*, 8.

35. The following two poems are taken from Seamus Heaney, *District and Circle* (London: Faber, 2006): "Anything Can Happen," 13, "Out of Shot," 15.

36. Seamus Heaney, *Anything can happen: a poem and essay by Seamus Heaney with translations in support of art for amnesty* (Dublin: Town House, 2004), 15.

37. The *Oxford English Dictionary* Online Version < http://dictionary.oed.com>.

WORKS CITED

Caeners, Torsten (2006). *"Neither god nor ghost*: The resurrection of the Tollund Man in Seamus Heaney's *District and Circle." LWU: Journal of Academic Research and Education*, 39, 21–38.

Carson, Ciaran (1975). "Review of *North.*" *The Honest Ulsterman*, 50, 184–185.

Foucault, Michel (1972). *The Archaeology of Knowledge.* New York: Pantheon Books.

Glob, Peter V. (1971). *The Bog People.* New York: Ballantine Books.

Heaney, Seamus (1966). *Death of a Naturalist.* London: Faber and Faber.

_____ (1969). *Door into the Dark.* London: Faber and Faber.

_____ (1980). "Feeling into Words." *Preoccupations: Selected Prose 1968–1978.* New York: Farrar Straus Giroux, 41–60.

_____ (1980). *Preoccupations: Selected Prose 1968– 1978.* New York: Farrar Straus Giroux.

_____ (1996). "Frontiers of Writing." *The Redress of Poetry.* New York: Farrar Straus Giroux, 186– 203.

_____ (1996). *The Redress of Poetry.* New York: Farrar Straus Giroux.

_____ (1998). *Opened Ground: Selected Poems 1966– 1996.* New York: Farrar Straus Giroux.

_____ (2002). *Finders Keepers: Selected Prose 1971– 2001.* London: Faber and Faber.

_____ (2002). "Place and Displacement: Recent Poetry from Northern Ireland." *Finders Keepers: Selected Prose 1971–2001.* London: Faber and Faber, 112–133.

_____ (2004). *Anything can happen: a poem and essay by Seamus Heaney with translations in support of Art for Amnesty.* Dublin: Town House.

_____ (2006). *District and Circle.* London: Faber and Faber.

Jung, C.G. (1976). "The Concept of the Collective Unconscious." *The Portable Jung.* Ed. Joseph Campbell. London: Penguin, 59–69.

_____ (1976). *The Portable Jung.* Ed. Joseph Campbell. London: Penguin.

Marwick, Arthur (2000). *A History of the Modern British Isles 1914–1999,* Oxford: Blackwell.

Oxford English Dictionary. Online Version. <http:// dictionary.oed.com>. Terms cited: "craft," "art," "wic."

Quinlan, Kieran (1983). "Unearthing a Terrible Beauty: Seamus Heaney's Victims of Violence." *World Literature Today,* 57:3, 365–369.

Triggs, Jeffery (1992). "Hurt into Poetry: The Political Verses of Seamus Heaney and Robert Bly." *The New Orleans Review,* 19:3–4, 162–173.

Wilde, Oscar (1997). "The Soul of Man under Socialism." *The Collected Works of Oscar Wilde.* Hertfordshire: Wordsworth, 1041–1066.

PART IV

The North, the Nation, and the Public-Private Divide

10. "Inwardness" and the "quest for a public poetry" in the Works of Tony Harrison

Cécile Marshall

The "public versus private" debate makes up the core of Tony Harrison's poetry and informs the poetic genres he chooses. In his choice of subject matter and themes, he is keen to emphasize the constant interplay between individual lives and the larger historical context. In his reflection on poetry as a specific medium, on the role of the poet in modern society, he has explored a wide variety of poetic formats, from poems written for the page to be individually read and re-read at leisure to overtly public forms such as drama, television and public readings that bring different constraints to be directly accessible to the audience. From the beginning, he defined his first major collection of poems, *The Loiners* (1970), as dealing with sex and history; in his most famous poems, the sonnets of *The School of Eloquence* (from the late seventies and early eighties) and the long poem *v.* (1985), personal dilemmas and the larger political context are intrinsically linked.

The unusual destiny of *v.* as a film/poem, on the screen and in the political arena, is emblematic of the public dimension of Tony Harrison's poetry: poetry frees itself from the literary ghetto to annex the mass media. The columns of major British newspapers have become tribunes for his poems, as has the television that, on many occasions, has broadcast rhyming verse to a mass audience. With poems such as "A Cold Coming" (first published in *The Guardian* in 1991), "Poems from Bosnia" (written from the front line and faxed to *The Guardian* in 1995), and *The Shadow of Hiroshima*, a film/poem broadcast on Channel 4 that same year, Tony Harrison constantly tries to redefine and question the role of the individual in the midst of history. His most quoted declaration states his position regarding the public and private divide:

> Poetry is all I write, whether for books, or readings, or for the National Theatre, or for the opera house and concert hall, or even for TV. All these activities are part of the same quest for a public poetry, though in that word "public" I would never want to exclude inwardness. I think how Milton's sonnets range from the directly outward to the tenderly inward, and how the public address of the one makes a clearing for the shared privacy of the other.[1]

For Harrison, poetry is fundamentally a public art / act and it should renew contact with the public (the audience and public themes) if it is to survive in the post–Holocaust world. He firmly believes in the interpenetration of the two dimensions, public and private being for him the two ends of a continuum. Although this statement was written over twenty years ago (1987), his poetry since has continued to explore the frontier between public and private, to find how "inwardness" complements the "quest for a public poetry."

The 1960s: politics and the privates in The Loiners

The Loiners, entitled after James Joyce's *Dubliners*, explores the articulation between sexuality and politics. The title is a pun on "loins" (a reference to the genitals) and "loners" (a reference to loneliness). In an interview with John Haffenden in 1983, Tony Harrison declared: "To go back to *The Loiners*, which dealt with sex and history: the intimacies of the private life are a kind of earthing area for the lightning of history and of political struggles."[2] Private life, especially the intimacy of sexuality, is presented as a key to understanding history and politics. The protagonists of *The Loiners* are indeed emblematic of a society that fears sexuality, and they contribute to placing sexuality at the heart of the political debate. The collection reads as a series of portraits, voices, and encounters, linked by the common theme of loneliness, marginality, and the experiencing of problematic sexual identities.

The collection is largely influenced by the time and place of its production. In the early 1960s, when Tony Harrison was teaching English literature in Nigeria, he worked on an adaptation of Aristophanes' *Lysistrata* (a comedy based on the parallels between war and sexuality). The interest for the link between public and private, which had existed since the Greeks, had been revived by the publication a few years earlier of *Eros and Civilization* by Herbert Marcuse. The poems of *The Loiners* are concerned with sexuality as a potential source of creativity and also as a source of conflict with the forces of repression. The protagonists express their confused or rebellious relations with society through their sexuality. As Luke Spencer acknowledges, *Eros and Civilization*

> had an enormous impact on the politics of private desire and public revolt in the 1960s. Insistence on the political dimension of sexuality was a keynote of

countercultural ideology, and one that sometimes came too readily to hand as an excuse for getting laid instead of engaging in more radical forms of action.[3]

Tony Harrison's Loiners are ordinary, lonely people, crushed by conventions and public morality. Ironically, they are ignorant of Marcuse's theory of the subversive potential of sexuality. Isolated in their personal dilemmas, they appear as victims rather than rebels: ambivalent emblems of resistance with a huge gap between the symbols the poet would like them to be and their lack of political consciousness. A few protagonists venture political diatribes, but only to alleviate their guilt. The use of the first person speaker in these instances betrays the poet's reluctance to underwrite their behavior.

The exploration of the public-private divide in *The Loiners* owes much to African culture, in particular to a belief in the "permanent and various interactions between the body and the social and cultural context."[4] The poems use disease as a metaphor for social dysfunction. The organic body and the body politic correspond with each other in as much as "the body is first and foremost what a culture makes of it."[5] In *The Loiners*, the favorite disease is a sexual one, namely syphilis, which appears right at the beginning of the collection in "Thomas Campey and the Copernican System." It reappears in "Distant Ophir," where it embodies colonial retribution.[6] In "The Death of the PWD Man," which closes the African sequence in *The Loiners*, the color red is a symptom of agonizing Western culture, plagued by colonialism:

> *Anxious, anxious, anxious, anxious, perhaps the train'll crash.*
> *Anxious, anxious, anxious, Doctor Adgie, there's a rash*
> *The shape of bloody Britain and it's starting to spread.*
> *My belly's like a blow-up globe all blotched with Empire red.*
> *Chancres, chancres, Shetlands, spots, boils, Hebrides,*
> *Atlasitis, Atlasitis, British Isles Disease!*[7]

The breeze mentioned in the very first poem of *The Loiners* has turned into a hurricane, morbid and uncontrollable. An overwhelming feeling of urgency and powerlessness is conveyed by the effect of accumulation. The time has come for the PWD Man (the man who works for the Public Works Department) to go back to dreaded *"Worstedopolis"* in the north of England. This is a dramatic as well as a medical crisis; the PWD Man seems to undergo an apoplectic fit. The repetitions, staccato rhythm, and the final punctuation mark (dot dot dot) create the effect of a speaker gasping for breath. Harrison uses the protagonist as a synecdoche of a British malaise and obliquely reaffirms the intrinsic link between abuse of power (colonization/contamination), sexual repression, and social dysfunction.

By always placing the body and sexuality at the core of public life, the poet subverts the modern tendency towards "a certain retreat of the body from the social field."[8] In fact, Tony Harrison adheres to the vision according to which "the body, as an object of research, cannot be separated from a social field of meanings of which it is just one link."[9] Harrison declares: "Separating those issues is done by people who need to separate those issues, people who find culture more comfortable if it is ahistorical and apolitical, and I don't believe it can be."[10] This mutual interaction between public and private spheres is a constant preoccupation, hence the title of the 1981 collection to which Harrison refers, *Continuous*.

"Running up and down the ladder" in Continuous: *privacy and sentimentalism*

Answering John Haffenden about his personal appropriation of "an historical-social resentment" in these sonnets, Tony Harrison replied:

> I see them all as intimately related: the historical, the autobiographical, and the metaphysical if you like. [...] I always remember the way kids at school used to write out their addresses in full, starting with their name and school and going on with "Beeston, Leeds, West Riding, Yorkshire, England, Great Britain, Europe, The World, The Universe": I think I have a mind and sensibility which keeps running up and down that kind of ladder, that scale or spectrum, and it seems to me that what you call the psychological issues are as historical as the historical issues are psychological. I see them as part of the same scale, the same historical spectrum.[11]

As early as 1971, a year after the publication of *The Loiners*, Tony Harrison started writing a sequence of sonnets dealing with language and history. Right from the beginning, *The School of Eloquence* had a strong political content, as the overall structure of the sequence shows. It is composed of three parts. Packed with cultural and literary references, the first is made up of poems with an obvious socio-political and historical content. The second part, largely autobiographical, is devoted to family relationships between father, mother, and son, the latter being the narrator of these dramatic playlets. The third explicitly returns to the historical theme followed by a meditation on art and mortality. The balance between the three parts has considerably varied in the course of publication. In 1978, in one of the first publications of *The School of Eloquence*, the historical poems of the first part outnumber the rest: thirteen sonnets against two in the second part and three in the third.[12] At this early stage, the sequence was clearly a manifesto on political and linguistic oppression. The title of the sequence itself testifies to the poet's ideological sympathies: "The School of Eloquence" had been one of the many names used by the London Corresponding Society, a radical eighteenth- and nineteenth-century organization devoted to educating the working classes and developing political consciousness. This ideological reference is made explicit in *Selected Poems,* which uses a quotation from E. P. Thompson's *The Making of the English Working Class* as an epigraph for the sequence.

With *The School of Eloquence,* Tony Harrison offers a poetic version of *The Making of the English Working Class.* Incorporating anecdotes and quotations directly borrowed from E. P. Thompson, the poet expresses personal feelings with a political edge. The history of the working class is used as a starting point for the exploration of eloquence, language, and the cultural divide. The aesthetic project is strongly influenced by the sociolinguistic theories of the 1960s and 1970s, in particular the theory of linguistic deficit promoted by Basil Bernstein in *Class, Codes, and Control* (1971) to which Tony Harrison refers in an interview with John Haffenden.[13] Moreover, in "On Not Being Milton," the opening sonnet of "The School of Eloquence" sequence, the poet uses a similar metaphor to Bernstein's, namely a linguistic version of Marxism in which the means of production are replaced by the means of expression.

Gradually, the autobiographical sonnets were allowed to expand the sequence. In the 1981 edition of *Continuous,* which followed the death of the poet's father, there are fifty sonnets; sixty-seven appear in the first edition of *Selected Poems* in 1984, and seventy-nine in the second edition in 1987. Each time, the additions were made to Part II, the explicitly autobiographical section. These sonnets urgently reveal the personal dilemmas of a *déclassé* poet: the conflicts of loyalty of an ex-scholarship boy from a Northern working-class family who refuses to forget his origins and is tormented by the awareness of his alienation. Since then, more published sonnets have steadily reinforced the personal dimension.[14] This trend may be associated with a leaning toward sentimentalism. Although Richard Hoggart, one of the co-dedicatees of "Them & [uz]," warned against the risk of self-dramatization in *The Uses of Literacy,* Harrison claims the right to be sentimental and even legitimizes it by quoting Dickens as a successful example: "I got a lot from Dickens. I liked what I think of as something very English about Dickens, also his directness, his vulgarity, his willingness to be almost sentimental."[15]

If sentimentalism is indeed one of the trademarks of popular culture, Tony Harrison does not hesitate to be populist. His anti-intellectual and anti-academic vein sometimes reveals a deliberate tendency towards sentimentalism. From declarations of love ("I can't squeeze more love into their stone"),[16] to intimate confessions ("I'm guilty, and the way I make it up's / in poetry, and that much I confess"),[17] to melodramatic punchlines, tears flow generously in the central part of *The School of Eloquence.* In "Still," the analogy between ink and tears sounds clichéd, which is the point: "And if the page I'm writing on has smears / they're not the sort to lose me marks for mess / being self-examination's grudging tears / soaked into the blotter, Nothingness").[18] In "Isolation," the poet's regression towards the emotional fragility of childhood is dramatized typographically. The sonnet explicitly starts with "I cried once as a boy," which is opposed to "but don't cry now." The negation is repeated until the last quatrain:

> and don't, though the fresh grave's flecked with sleet,
> and dad, with every fire back home switched on, 's
> frozen,
>   and don't
>   until I hear him bleat
> round the ransacked house for his long johns.[19]

The poem suggests that the pleasure of intellectual refinements should be subject to the simple pleasures of exchange and confession and the communication of emotions. In "Marked With D.," the poet establishes a dialogue between intellect and emotion that Douglas Dunn defines as lyricism:

> In the works of writers like Philip Larkin, Norman MacCaig, Tony Harrison and Seamus Heaney, lyricism is drawn from an ability to engage with the materials of ordinary life, and then absorb them [...]. Much more than a tacit acknowledgement of history and reality underlies their poetry; it is built into the poetry itself, which includes facsimile descriptions of what can be seen, heard, felt, smelled and touched, as well as the conclusions that can be drawn from them. Often it is a poetry of subjective dilemmas and dramas which the intuitive procedures of lyric poetry can render impersonal and therefore acceptable for the reader.[20]

The focus has not really changed, however. Exploring personal dilemmas is just a different way of tackling what remains the same issue: a sociopolitical, cultural issue, that of eloquence. Tony Harrison insists that his poetry is not just confessional: "[in poems such as] 'Timer,' for example, [...] there is just deep feeling — poems which are unqualified except for the fact that they are in the sequence ... and therefore they are qualified."[21] The presence of such sonnets in the sequence underlines the continuum between public and private spheres; even the most personal sonnet has a political dimension by the sheer fact of being in a political sequence. The attention given to anecdotes and individual feeling finds its legitimacy in the analogies it creates with the public sphere. Individual dilemmas are rendered impersonal and universal, thanks to the conscious existence of a tangible historical context.

After the success of his dramatic poetry in the 1970s, *The School of Eloquence* was a watershed for Tony Harrison's career as a public poet. He gave more and more public readings in sometimes unexpected places, such as pubs and nursing homes. Paradoxically, even when reading in public, Tony Harrison distinguishes between private and public. Speaking of the appropriate voice for such readings, he notes that "you need to project your voice outward to the audience for the public poetry." He is quick to add, however, that "there are some intimate poems which I'll want to read as if we're talking together. They're meant to be read and re-read quietly at home or in bed."[22] The success was confirmed with the long 1985 poem *v.,* in which the poet reflects on and dramatizes his conflicting identities.

Going public: poetry, the media and the Commons

Whereas the poem's acclaim remained confined to the community of poetry enthusiasts, the film version of *v.* attracted the media's attention and reached a much wider audience. Even before it was broadcast on Channel 4, public opinion had turned it into a political issue that kept the media raging for several weeks. When the broadcast of the thirty-minute film directed by Richard Eyre was announced in 1987, it created such a row that it is now impossible to mention the poem without discussing the political stakes. To testify to the public dimension of *v.,* the second Bloodaxe edition was augmented by forty-five pages of press articles.

Two years after the poem's publication, the film/poem created one of those rare moments in history when a nation becomes passionate about poetry. The polemic started on October 11, 1987: *The Observer,* in an article entitled "Clear road for rude ode," announced the *Independent Broadcasting Authority*'s decision to broadcast *V.* on November 4 at 11:30 P.M., in spite of the sometimes vulgar language. The insults, written in capital letters in the poem, point to the graffiti the poet found on his parents' grave and in the rest of Beeston's cemetery in Leeds during the 1984 miners' strike:

> The language of this graveyard ranges from
> a bit of Latin for a former Mayor
> or those who laid their lives down at the Somme,
> the hymnal fragments and the gilded prayer,
>
> how people "fell asleep in the Good Lord,"
> brief chisellable bits from the good book
> and rhymes whatever length they could afford,
> to CUNT, PISS, SHIT and (mostly) FUCK![23]

The offensive language is also used extensively in a key passage of the poem, the imaginary confrontation between the poet and the vandal with his spray-can. The film alternates images of a public reading of *v.*; Beeston Hill and its cemetery; and black and white newsreels from the Second World War up to the 1980s, including the Falklands War, the miners' strike, and Ulster violence. The article in the *Observer* insisted on the uniqueness of the case, particularly the fact that the IBA made their decision only after they had watched the program, something they rarely do. Soon after, the case was discussed in the press. Conservative MPs, with the support of the *National Viewers' and Listeners' Association*, campaigned for the banning, not only of the broadcast, but also of Tony Harrison's poetry from the school curriculum. On October 27, *V.* was even granted a motion in the House of Commons.[24]

The film raised the question of the impact of poetry on public opinion. Because Harrison addressed his fellow-countrymen with great clarity, his poetry and political ideas became accessible to a wider audience than that of traditional poetry readership. The film focuses on burning issues — social gaps, unemployment, racism — and takes a view that was potentially destabilizing for the Conservative government of the time. Although there may be elements of comedy in the confrontation between the poet and his skinhead alter ego, the film's atmosphere is nonetheless tense and often violent. Moreover, *v.* questions the poet's legitimacy to use his own voice and private experience to speak for the whole nation. The vandal refuses to let the poet speak on his behalf. The latter tries to justify his right to create public poetry, even state-of-the-nation poetry, while at the same time doubting the political efficiency of his enterprise.

Right from the beginning of his career, Tony Harrison alternated writing and public readings. Reflecting on "Art & Extinction" has convinced him that poetry needs to adjust to a changing world if it is to survive at all:

> The poet too is an almost extinct species, and it's an almost extinct idea to think of languages as the carrier of our most important messages. [...] Now the future doesn't look that much of a dead cert for gambling on: we are faced with a very real idea of extinction, not only of personal extinction but of the work and of memory, and it certainly takes away the feeling that you were laying up a readership in heaven for the future. That choice, which in a sense sustained poets for centuries, is no longer open to us.[25]

To confront the modern world, Harrison uses the mass media: television, with now over a dozen film/poems in verse, and also the press, with a particularly successful collaboration with the *Guardian* throughout his career.

War and the individual in the "Gulf War poems," "Poems from Bosnia," The Shadow of Hiroshima

Ezra Pound declared that "literature is news that stays news," and Tony Harrison takes this motto literally. His activities as a dramatist testify to his almost obsessive concern about the reception of his poetry and its impact on contemporary society. The move from the page of a book to the front page of a newspaper such as *The Guardian* is characteristic of his quest for a public poetry tuned in to its times.

In 1991, *The Guardian* published two *Gulf War Poems*. Unlike the dense and complexly structured "Initial Illumination," the first Gulf War poem (March 5), "A Cold Coming" (March 18) is a direct response to a photograph by Kenneth Jarecke published a few days earlier in *The Observer*. It had initially appeared with the following caption: "The charred head of an Iraqi soldier leans through the windscreen of his burned-out vehicle, February 28. He died when a convoy of Iraqi vehicles retreating from Kuwait City was attacked by Allied Forces." "A Cold Coming" immediately became the eponymous poem in a sixteen-page pamphlet published by Bloodaxe Books. The front cover brutally raises the issue of the representation of horror, of the line between informing the public and allowing the public to become voyeurs or perhaps even complicit in violence. The poem's ironic setting seems to be an oblique response to Baudrillard's essay "The Reality Gulf," published two months before in the *Guardian*, in which Baudrillard denounced the mediatic simulacrum generated by the conflict. While he had just as many reservations about the mass media, Harrison chose to fight back in his own way, paradoxically using the press as a forum for his public poems.

In "A Cold Coming," Harrison runs the risk of inauthenticity when he ventriloquizes the voice of the other. Yet he also acknowledges the inherent difficulty of this enterprise and embodies the Western journalist in quest of truth. The poem, set just after the Desert Storm operation, illustrates the horror of the confrontation between Allied and Iraqi forces with post–Holocaust imagery of burnt corpses and barren land. But rather than giving a Western point of view, the poet imagines a dialogue with the Iraqi victim who gives personal details about his life, his aborted family and dreams. The Iraqi envies the American soldiers who have been able to secure a vicarious post-mortem life, thanks to technology and money. In spite of its own doubts about the impact of poetry, "A Cold Coming" truly had a public dimension and inspired another poem by Ian Gregson: "How Does It Feel? Thoughts On Tony Harrison's Poem 'A Cold Coming.'" In that poem, Gregson denounces the inauthenticity of the Iraqi voice. "A Cold Coming" keeps reminding the reader of the poetic artifice, in particular at the end, when the persona wants to play back the recording of his conversation with the Iraqi soldier: "REWIND and PLAY / and I heard the charred man say:," which is followed by a large blank on the page: the Iraqi soldier is dead and his poetic words are mere illusion on the page.

The poet's position in "Three Poems from Bosnia" is different, however.

The question of the authenticity of the vision is no longer a problem, since the poems were written in Sarajevo in September 1995 while Harrison was a special war correspondent for *The Guardian*.[26] He faxed the three poems between September 14 and 20, and they were on *The Guardian*'s front page the next day. What mattered for the poet was to inject empathy into his public poetry, as opposed to producing mere journalistic reportage. Harrison believes in the cathartic function of the poetic form, and the first two poems from Bosnia attempt to create such a catharsis by blending private and public. The poet-reporter deliberately chooses to describe war through individual, and often trivial, anecdotes, a vision that contrasts with the epic rhetoric often used by governments and media. We are reminded of such clichés through the repetitions of terms such as "victory," "victor," or even "triumphal."[27] But rather than focusing on battles, conquests and retreats, fatalities and casualties, the poet prefers the daily routine of individuals trying to make the best of the conflict they are trapped in. This reality reveals ordinary lives in an extraordinary context. The emphasis on human dramas and passions brings war closer to the public and enables them to look at it with open eyes. Shocking images such as the one featured on the front cover of *A Cold Coming*, if unmediated by art, are likely to make the public close their eyes and mind in a reflex of psychic self-preservation. In "Poems from Bosnia," however, the apparent simplicity of the poetic language, the focus on private lives, and the possibly melodramatic temptation serve the public cause and the cause of the public: they help the readers apprehend the complexities, ambiguities, and horror of public events.

Only a few weeks before Harrison left for Bosnia, the film/poem *The Shadow of Hiroshima* was broadcast on Channel 4. As a meditation on memory and amnesia, and on the role of art in commemorating in the post–Holocaust period, *Shadow* strikes a similar balance between private and public. With this piece, Harrison illustrates the need to anchor the metaphysical in the concrete and the personal. The poet is looking for the right blend between proximity and distance to suffering, and he relies on the specific to give humanity to the historical event, to give meaning to suffering while making it bearable for the public.

In Tony Harrison's poetry, the return to psychic equilibrium is subject to the acceptance of past trauma. The film acknowledges the fictitious nature of the narrator, a persona produced by the mind of a poet obsessed with images of horror. It follows two inhabitants of modern Hiroshima. The first one, Hiroshi Hara, survived the bomb, unlike most of his schoolmates. His obsession with the A-bomb dome, which he keeps painting over and over again, provides one of the visual leitmotivs of the film. It is the only building left of the old Hiroshima, and it is a witness to the past and the focal point of the yearly ceremony of commemoration. The film/poem was broadcast on August 8, 1995, exactly fifty years after the bomb was dropped, and it is made to look as if it had been filmed on the fiftieth anniversary. The second main protagonist, Mitsufuji San, embodies the younger generation who are trying to ignore the past. The young man's participation in the ceremonies of commemoration is only due to his love of pigeons, not to any sense of historical duty. However, his beloved birds, symbols of peace released near the dome, are used as visual metaphors for the victims who died in the nuclear conflagration. The visual imagery is therefore a constant reminder of the history the young man is trying to ignore by indulging in the pleasures of his individual life.

The spectator is never allowed to separate the public story from the private tribulations of protagonist. When Mitsufuji takes a phone card out of his trouser pocket to phone his lover Sonoko, pigeon feathers fall out of it. Then, close-ups of a love scene between the young people alternate with images of a pigeon ablaze. The silk kimono that falls off Sonoko's body reminds us of a line pronounced at the beginning of the film/poem, a description of the physical effects of the nuclear fire: "skin slid off flesh like clothes."[28] Sonoko also symbolically recalls another young girl mentioned earlier in the poem, the narrator's lover, who was obliterated in August 1945. In *The Shadow of Hiroshima*, private and public are thus intimately woven together in the filmic fabric. They are clearly part of the same continuum between public and private, ironically sometimes in spite of the protagonists' pretending the contrary.

Throughout his career, private experience has fuelled Harrison's inspiration as a poet. His works are anchored in a recognizable realistic framework. Details and anecdotes are reinforced by a diction highly evocative of the north of England.[29] The poet's relatives and their problematic relations to language and culture feature in many sonnets and can also cross over the barriers of poetic genres. The intense emotion conjured up by the memory of the father in "Fire-eater" brings additional pathos to the tragicomedy of *The Trackers of Oxyrhynchus*. The latter, a play performed on the Olivier stage at the National Theatre (1990), contains the line: "We're not just the clowns sent in to clear the ring."[30] It is pronounced by the satyr Silenus in his powerful speech appealing for the acceptance of the continuum and complementarity between sexuality and politics, body and mind, comedy and tragedy as exemplified in the satyr plays that used to follow tragedies in Greek drama. An almost identical line,[31] though expressing acceptance rather than resistance, originally appeared in "Fire-eater," in which the poet pays a tribute to his tongue-tied ancestors and their influence on his passion for words and public expression. Harrison firmly believes in the power of representation to operate a catharsis.

By transferring private traumas into the public arena of theatre or television, events mediated by aesthetic form can be lived through collectively. Much of Harrison's concern for the private in the midst of history is derived from his fascination with Greek tragedy, especially its ability to imagine and represent the worst events and still have faith in the future. The catharsis is made possible by the feeling of community, the shared intimacy, of the members of the audience who experience the representation of historical trauma from a safe vantage point. Just as the highly stylized diction and movements of Greek drama were, for Harrison, evidence of the artificiality of the performed scenes, the strong rhymes and rhythms of Harrison's poetry help the public bear the traumas of working-class history and of twentieth-century wars. Whether at a poetry reading, in a theatre hall or gathered at an ephemeral open air theatrical venue, the modern public is allowed to experience something akin to the catharsis of Greek tragedy. Even television that gathers families to their sofas may be a modern equivalent of shared intimacy. If "a Greek theatrical mask is part of the existential survival gear"[32] for the Classics, for Harrison, the public dimension is part of the "survival gear" of poetry in contemporary society.

NOTES

1. Tony Harrison, "[Poetry is all I write]," *Tony Harrison: Critical Anthologies I*, ed. Neil Astley (Newcastle upon Tyne: Bloodaxe Books, 1991), 9.

2. John Haffenden, "Interview with Tony Harrison," *Tony Harrison: Critical Anthologies*, 231.

3. Luke Spencer, *The Poetry of Tony Harrison* (Hemel Hempstead: Harvester Wheatsheaf, 1994), 22.

4. Franck Despujol, "Corps et culture: l'apport de l'anthropologie," *Le Corps*, ed. Eugène Detape (1992, 13–26), 13 (my translation).

5. Ibid., 14.

6. Tony Harrison, *Selected Poems* (London: Penguin, 1987), 29–30.

7. Harrison, *Selected Poems*, 46 (repeated on 47 and 48).

8. Despujol, "Corps et culture," 25 (my translation).

9. Ibid., 13.

10. Haffenden, "Interview with Tony Harrison," *Tony Harrison: Critical Anthologies*, 231.

11. Ibid., 230.

12. The 1976 edition was a limited edition.

13. Haffenden, "Interview with Tony Harrison," *Tony Harrison: Critical Anthologies*, 232.

14. Cf. "Under the Clock," "Gaps" in *Under the Clock*.

15. Richard Hoggart, "In Conversation with Tony Harrison," *Tony Harrison: Critical Anthologies*, 42.

16. Harrison, *Selected Poems*, 127.

17. Ibid., 128.

18. Ibid., 140.

19. Ibid., 142.

20. Douglas Dunn, "'Importantly Live': Tony Harrison's Lyricism," *Tony Harrison: Critical Anthologies*, 254.

21. Haffenden, "Interview with Tony Harrison," *Tony Harrison: Critical Anthologies*, 233.

22. Harrison, conversation with Cécile Marshall at his home in Newcastle upon Tyne in February 2006.

23. Harrison, *Selected Poems*, 237.

24. "This House is appalled at plans by Channel 4 to screen with the approval of the Independent Broadcasting Authority the poem 'V.' by Tony Harrison; whilst recognizing that the poem may not be wholly devoid of literary merit, considers that the stream of obscenities contained in the poem is profoundly offensive and will serve to hasten the decline of broadcasting standards; and further calls on the Independent Broadcasting Authority to observe its own guidelines and instruct Channel 4 not to broadcast the poem." House of Commons, Early Day Motion, reprinted in Tony Harrison, *V. Second Edition with Press Articles* (Newcastle upon Tyne: Bloodaxe Books), 60.

25. Haffenden, "Interview with Tony Harrison," *Tony Harrison: Critical Anthologies*, 235.
26. His U.N. accreditation card hangs round the plaster bust of Milton standing on a trunk in the entrance hall of Tony Harrison's house in Newcastle upon Tyne.
27. Tony Harrison, *Laureate's Block* (London: Penguin), 20–21.
28. Tony Harrison, "The Shadow of Hiroshima," *The Shadow of Hiroshima and other film/poems* (London: Faber & Faber, 1995, 1–17), 7.
29. Cf. Claire Hélie's contribution to the present volume.

30. Tony Harrison, *The Trackers of Oxyrhynchus* (London: Faber & Faber, 1990), 60.
31. "I'm the clown sent in to clear the ring," Harrison, *Selected Poems*, 168.
32. Tony Harrison, *Tony Harrison: Plays 5*, 6. His vision of Greek tragedy and its relation to his quest for a public poetry is also discussed in "Facing Up to the Muses," Harrison's inaugural address as President of the Classical Association at the University of Bristol on 12 April 1988 (reprinted in *Tony Harrison: Critical Anthologies*, 429–454).

Works Cited

Aristophanes (1996). *Lysistrata*. Trans. A. Willems. Paris: Le Livre de Poche.
Astley, Neil (1991). *Tony Harrison. Critical Anthologies: 1*. Newcastle upon Tyne: Bloodaxe Books.
Baudrillard, Jean (1991). "The Reality Gulf." *Guardian*, 11 January 25.
Bernstein, Basil (1971). *Class, Codes, and Control*. London: Routledge.
Despujol, Franck (1992). "Corps et culture: l'apport de l'anthropologie." Ed. Eugène Detape. *Le Corps*. Roisny sous Bois: Bréal, 13–26.
Haffenden, John (1991). "Interview with Tony Harrison." *Tony Harrison: Bloodaxe Critical Anthologies 1*. Ed. Neil Astley. Newcastle upon Tyne: Bloodaxe, 227–246. (Interview held in Newcastle, 1983; reprinted from *Poetry Review* 73.4 [January 1984].)
Harrison, Tony (1970). *The Loiners*. London: London Magazine Editions.
_____ (1987). *Selected Poems*. London: Penguin.
_____ (1990). *The Trackers of Oxyrhynchus*. London: Faber & Faber.
_____ (1991). "[Poetry is all I write]." *Tony Harrison: Critical Anthologies 1*. Ed. Neil Astley. Newcastle upon Tyne: Bloodaxe Books, 9.

_____ (1991; first edition 1985). *V. Second Edition with Press Articles*. Newcastle upon Tyne: Bloodaxe Books.
_____ (1995). "The Shadow of Hiroshima." *The Shadow of Hiroshima and other film/poems*. London: Faber & Faber, 1–17.
_____ (2000). *Laureate's Block*. London: Penguin.
_____ (2004). *Tony Harrison: Plays 5*. London: Faber & Faber.
Hoggart, Richard (1991). "In Conversation with Tony Harrison." *Tony Harrison: Bloodaxe Critical Anthologies 1*. Ed. Neil Astley. Newcastle upon Tyne: Bloodaxe, 36–45. (The 1986 interview was recorded by TVS for the ITV network.)
Joyce, James (1992; first edition 1914). *Dubliners*. London: Penguin.
Marcuse, Herbert (1966). *Eros and Civilization*. Boston: Beacon Press.
Thompson, E. P. (1991; first edition 1963). *The Making of the English Working Class*. London: Penguin.
Spencer, Luke (1994). *The Poetry of Tony Harrison*. Hemel Hempstead: Harvester Wheatsheaf.

11. Private Voice and Public Discourse: A Poetics of Northern Dialect

Claire Hélie

Basil Bunting's *Briggflatts* (1965), Ted Hughes's *Remains of Elmet* (1979) and Tony Harrison's *From "The School of Eloquence"* (1987)[1] are three poetic auto-biographies in which the poets go back to the places where they spent their childhood to assess their heritage and search for the roots of their poetic voice. All three poets were born and bred in a different part of the North of England: Basil Bunting in Scotswood-on-Tyne near Durham, Ted Hughes in Mytholm-royd close to Brontë Country, and Tony Harrison in Leeds. Their respective poetries do not have much in common except for a deep love for their native North, which they claim is the source of their poetic imagination. Through publishing collections about their birthplaces, they bring the private act of creation into the public realm. None of these poets qualifies as a dialect poet, yet each one of them uses some kind of northern dialect or some idea of a northern dialect as spoken in their native area. Their use of poetic dialect artic-ulates their take on the public and the private. My aim is to shed light on their three different ways of dramatizing the divide between public and pri-vate through the use of dialect, on reasons to question a divide that sustains inequalities, and on ways to perform the negotiations between outside and inside, representation and self-representation, discourse and voice on the writ-ten page and in public readings. I begin with an overview of the problematic position of Northern England in contemporary poetry.

In *Looking North: Northern England and the National Imagination* (2004), Dave Russell contends that the North of England, roughly delineated as the region north of the Humber-Trent line, is no longer known through "personal experience" but via the "versions" people encounter "in the field of culture."[2] Indeed, the wars on the Scottish border during the Middle Ages, the War of the Roses, and the Pilgrimage of Grace gave rise to the image of a bellicose, separatist North, such as can be found in *The North of England: A History from Roman Times to the Present* (1990) by Frank Musgrove; William Wordsworth, the Brontë sisters, as well as J.M. Turner turned the bracing weather and the rich wildlife of the Lake District and Yorkshire into epitomes of the English sublime landscape; L.S. Lowry and David Hockney romanticized life in the industrial North, while the recent blockbusters *Brassed Off* (1996), *The Full Monty* (1997) and *Billy Elliot* (2000) have disseminated images of Northern pride in times of de-industrialization. Whether in the outsiders' or in the insiders' creative imagination, the North is a contested space.

Philip Dodd, in "Lowryscapes: Recent Writings about the North" (1990), argues that artistic work on the North is made "by acquiescing in or struggling with available representations,"[3] representations which can be contradictory. One could therefore argue that the literature on the North of England is nothing short of palimpsestual, meaning that writing the North is always rewriting a previous discourse on the North, erasing some of its characteristics, putting forward new ones, using old material to elaborate new conceptions of the North. Northern England seems to exist less as a geographical region one can stroll through or live in than as a mental space open to a multiplicity of public discourses.

Furthermore, critics in the field of cultural studies — such as Helen Jewell in *The North-South Divide: The Origins of Northern Consciousness in the North of England* (1994), Peter Davidson in *The Idea of North* (2005) or Katie Wales in *Northern English: A Social and Cultural History* (2006) — show how such discourses are usually disparaging towards the North. As a necessary correlative to this, they suggest that the South of England — or to be more precise, London, Oxbridge and the Home Counties — is where the sites of political, cultural and economic powers are located, where "Englishness" itself is traditionally searched for and found. Their respective attempts at retrieving the whys and wherefores of such opposition leads them to analyzing topography, climate, patterns of migration, agricultural transformation and other features, all in favor of the expansion of the pastoral South to the detriment of the hardships on the Northern borders. Public discourses on the North usually emanate from the South.

Consequently, post-colonial rhetoric offers useful language to speak of the condition of Northern England. Katie Wales, in "North-South: A Linguistic Divide?" (1999), coins the term "austro-centrism" to speak of the bias towards the South and "septentrionalism,"[4] a concept modeled on Edward Said's *Orientalism* (1978), to designate the historical and mental process that produces myths and fictions about the North. She lists a series of such stereotypes that work as "metonyms of the North and Northerners"—including poverty, factories, football — to which are opposed mental images of the South — the bowler hat, the thatched cottage, cricket, amongst others. Of course the reality is far more complex, but such clichés that construct the North as the radical Other, the idiotic brother, and even at times the Enemy Within are pervasive and seem to leave no room for a Northern point of view.

Yet David Gervais, in *Literary Englands: Versions of Englishness in Modern Writing* (1993), contends that since the Second World War Englishness has "moved northwards,"[5] after the North started spreading self-images. Such self-images aimed at "redressing"[6] the alleged cultural imbalance between North and South, to use Seamus Heaney's term about the powers of poetry. Indeed in the 1960s, when the post-war consensus started to fall apart, when Great Britain became "Little England," and when the disenchantment with national values gave way to the re-enchantment of regional places, private versions of the North emerged to correct public discourses on the region.

Nevertheless, one should beware of equating public and Southern on the one hand and private and Northern on the other hand. The public discourse on the North is shared nationally. For instance, Tony Harrison attacks John Nicholson in *Poetry or Bust* (1993) because by abandoning his dialectal voice and the industrial world he knew for London, the Airedale poet participated in rejecting the North from the field of High Arts. I understand public discourse on the North as a collective, shared, widespread discourse that gives in to general unquestioned conceptions of the region, and private versions of the North as individual responses that aim to show what is problematic about what is otherwise taken for granted. When imagined by Northerners, the private versions might even take on some extra vindictive dimension: the North writes back, to paraphrase the title of Bill Ashcroft, Gareth Griffiths and Helen Tiffin's 1989 work on post-colonial literatures.

Writing back means to undermine the rhetoric of the dominant discourse that is transmitted in political speeches, history books, and the media, to prove it wrong and harmful, to establish another truth, through the use of another vocabulary, voice, and syntax, in other words, through a language that comes closer to the experience of the previously subordinated individuals and their communities. Public and private languages are traditionally considered as antonymic, "public language" harking back to what Aristotle, in his *Politics*, called *koinon*, the common tongue, and "private language" to *oikos*, the mother tongue. In a time when there is broad consensus about the validity of a nation's values, there is no need to differentiate languages, the whole country is united under one language, the common denominator everybody participates in; but in times of crisis, when there are conflicts over national values, different languages re-emerge and clash, marginalized groups trying hard to make themselves heard literally, that is, through their own voice and language.

In England, to be from the North means to speak some kind of a dialect, a language which is spoken in a restricted part of a given country and which is mainly acquired within the private sphere of the family; therefore it is not the public language, which is Standard English, the codified language that the whole nation shares. Between the two, there are "phonological or lexical differences" which appeared as "a result of either geographical or social boundaries, both causing isolation and differentiation."[7] Although in linguistic terms Standard English is itself a dialect, it was promoted to the status of national language in the nineteenth century. The word "dialect," in reference to nonstandard linguistic variations, then became even more pejorative, because it was thereafter accompanied by the idea that this minor language lacked style and importance or that it was archaic. Its use was subsequently limited to the private world of the family and Standard English was imposed outside, in the public world, especially in school.

Before the 1960s the North was mainly recounted, but not heard, and northern dialects had no role to play on the national scene. For instance, the first radio broadcasts on the BBC tended to suppress non-southern accents. And if heard, it was mostly for comic relief; there is also a long tradition of mocking Northern dialects that ranges from Chaucer's "The Reeve's Tale" (fourteenth century) to Monty Python. In literature, up to the nineteenth century, dialect was confined to popular ballads or else used to denote a picturesque or eccentric character, or the low birth of a character, like Joseph in Emily Brontë's *Wuthering Heights* (1847). Dialect was descriptive, and even if the existence of different languages was thus recognized, in the end, the reader was left with a series of idiolects, a series of private utterances.

This hierarchy between regional and working-classes dialects and Standard English, which participates in the construction of a philistine North, is in fact far more complicated that that and deserves some critical attention. David Kennedy in *New Relations: The Refashioning of British Poetry 1980–1994* (1996) mentions that issues of voice constitute one of the fundamental subjects of British poetry since the Second World War.[8] Voice used to be coterminous with style only but is now understood in its physiological sense. Dialect is one aspect of voice in so far as they both share questions about accent, intonation, and rhythm, except that dialect also has specific lexical and syntactical features. Therefore the problems that arise are first and foremost linguistic: What definition of dialect do the poets give? How can it be differentiated from Standard English? How can they transcribe a spoken language onto the written page? How can they take up and extend the language of a man speaking to men advocated by Wordsworth and yet "make it new"? The poet has to find means to transcribe dialect using alphabetic but mostly poetic means, that is to say rhymes but more interestingly rhythm, the movement of the voice within discourse, the private within the public, the public through the private. What has to be established first is a *poetics* of dialect.

Given the implicit hierarchy of languages in England mentioned above, the problem of dialect and voice is particularly acute in the case of the North of England: how can the poet reconcile the private language he speaks and the public language he writes? How can he write in his own tongue, without sounding ridiculous? How can he use the language of a region or a class and yet be understood by those who do not belong to that region or class? How can he avoid the double pit of populism (using the language of a "prototypical reader"[9] to lash out against the establishment) and provincialism (writing for readers who share the same background and language)? Using dialect is paradoxical: on the one hand, dialect is a popular means of expression whereas Standard English is prestigious, if not elitist; on the other hand, dialect is exclusive in the sense that when using it the speaker chooses to be understood by those he shares his language with only, whereas Standard English is more democratic since it ensures general comprehension. This is one of the writer's main dilemmas, a dilemma that it is the poet's task to try and solve, as Ted Hughes argues in his seminal article "Myths, Metres, Rhymes" (1994). This leads to an *ethics* of dialect questioning the way the poet understands the social and historical dimension of the language he uses: the private voice criticizes a public discourse, and is questioned in its turn as a valid means to do so.

Since dialect takes the poem out of the solipsism of the printed page into the public arena of speech, the issue of poetry readings has to be tackled too. Frederick Stern in "The Formal Poetry Reading" (1991) makes an opposition between "performance poetry," an acting out of the poem via bodily gestures, and the "formal reading,"[10] when the poem is voiced. The latter focuses on the transmission of an emotion, a feel for sounds, the former on the meaning, the content of the poem, a feel for words. Dialect is at the junction between words and sounds. When reading out loud, the northern poet is indeed faced with a choice: shall he speak in his northern accent, or use Received Pronunciation? Is such a choice prompted by the text only or by the fact that the presence of an audience turns the poet into a speaker? How does listening to the poet's dialectal voice change the understanding of the poem? How does it affect the audience? These questions deal with a *praxis* of voicing dialect and the role of the poet in society: the private voice creates a new type of public discourse.

Writing poetry in dialect thus becomes a means to bridge the gap between the private voice and the public discourse, to play each one against the other. Consequently, using non-standard dialects is a political act at the same time as it is a filial tribute and an investigation into poetic possibilities. Such a claim is supported by a study of three poets born in the North of England before World War Two: Basil Bunting (Scotswood on Tyne 1900— Briggflatts 1985), Ted Hughes (Mytholmroyd 1930— Dartmoor 1998) and Tony Harrison (Leeds 1937–).

All three poets know their North first- and second-hand, privately and publicly, as northerners brought up "oop North" and as scholars interested in questions of regional identity. As a consequence, even if they have internalized the depreciative discourse held against their place in their childhood, they can offer, as mature poets, *private* versions of the North in order to respond to the *public* discourses: they can question the alleged naturalness of the divide, and they can assert the centrality of *their* North in the national imagination. By using dialect, they create a poetic space in which their voice stands for silenced voices and they carry these voices over in public readings, so these marginalized, indigenous voices can have a resonance in the public sphere.

Bunting's definition of dialect is not strictly a linguistic one, since it is dependent on his aesthetics, which consist in legitimizing Northumbria as a poetic center over London by selecting and annexing elements of northern culture for his own private version of the North. Therefore he claimed he spoke the language of a man speaking to men, rooted in the northern community he was at home with and not standardized by Oxbridge or the BBC. In the afterword to *Briggflatts* he states that there is a strong opposition between his native Northumberland and the "Saxon South of England,"[11] between the Northumbrian tongue and the *koiné* (i.e., Standard English) or American English. Yet, when one reads *Briggflatts*, one notices that the text sounds less dialectal than modernist: grammar is Standard English only packed to conform to Pound's principle of economy of words; there is no attempt at phonetic realism and most of the poem is written in free verse; the numerous references to local and international history and culture give the impression of a display of erudition. In a word, Bunting first reads as a modernist poet, not to say a poets' poet.

Therefore, despite his claim for a Northumbrian tongue that can be heard by anyone with an ear for poetry, one could argue that he gives his private version of the North in a voice which is standardized, or maybe even elitist, but in any case antonymous with the demotic and vernacular. Yet there is lexical evidence of a northern dialect, since some fifteen words are dialectal. For instance, the word "spuggy," a little sparrow, is introduced in an epigraph as a translation from *Il Libro de Alexandre* into the dialect of the poem. Two other dialectal words are explained in the endnotes: "Skillet: an American frying pan; and girdle, an English griddle."[12] The parallel construction of the definitions shows that the metathesis is enough for Southern English to be as foreign to Bunting's English as American English is. Bunting showed a keen interest in philology and also added many words derived from Old English and Old Norse to his northern lexicon. Historically, one dialect usually comes to dominate other dialects and becomes the standard language shared by all. To reinstate a dialect in danger of extinction is to make a public claim for the sovereignty of the region it was spoken in. As a consequence, if the pool of Northumbrian words is actually restricted, it is extended, as if by contamination, by quite a lot of words that sound northern.

And sound is what poetry is made of according to Bunting, who thought, just as John Cage did, that a composition is not completed until performed. He encouraged his readers to read out loud by constantly drawing comparisons between poetry and music. For instance, the line "their Baltic plainsong" refers to the chant of the Norse invaders in the ninth and tenth centuries. There is also a consonantal presence reminiscent of Welsh alliterative poetry in the sixth and seventh centuries, or "cynghanedd," which Bunting described as "all the things that hold poetry together by way of sound"[13]— rhymes, alliterations, assonances. Therefore the poem is a palimpsest of northern sounds that bear testimony to the various ways in which Northumbria was populated. The kingdom no longer exists, but Bunting claims the evidence is still there: in the afterword, he adds that "Southrons would maul the music of many lines in *Briggflatts*,"[14] thus asserting the superiority of his dialect over Standard English. The poet's voice presents itself as a synthesis of the history, culture, language and literature he chooses for Northumbria, regardless of what Northumberland was at the time of writing. Of course, such impressionism makes for a North that reflects his taste more than the reality of the place.

More than a regional dialect, his is a historical one, reaching back to old bardic times when the poet had a public role to play in the community. Osborn Bergin, in *Irish Bardic Poetry* (1970), describes the bard as a scholar who benefited from a high birth and was therefore entitled to hold an official position in society. His role was not only that of "a professor of literature and a man of letters" who was skilful enough in the handling of poetic device but also that of a historian, knowledgeable in the tradition and culture of his group.[15] Bunting was a bard in such terms and he took his role very seriously, most notably by giving lectures at the University of Durham when appointed Northern Fellow at the end of the 1970s.

This is also why he gave several public readings of his *Briggflatts*, especially in the poetry book room in the Modern Tower on the old walls of Newcastle where, some twenty-five years after his death, he is still considered as the "Grand Old Master of Northern Poetry." He is remembered by his voice in part because he had two main characteristic features of Northumbrian dialect — the flat As and the Northumbrian Burr, an uvular fricative, which, as well as being produced at the back of the mouth, involves lip-rounding (the <r> is elided in the South). Moreover, he promoted all weak syllables to the rank of strong syllables, which created a gripping resonance. Some said that his accent was a fake and that nobody would speak like that; his friend Denis Goacher even called it a "manufactured" accent.[16] Yet what is important is what he was trying to do with that dialectal accent: retrieve a lost language that would still be valuable in his contemporary Northern England and in the world at large.[17]

Indeed his audience, mostly young would-be poets from working-class Newcastle, was given the chance to hear poetry read in a voice they felt close to theirs, not in a standardized London voice. Moreover, the insistence on voicing out *Briggflatts* has to be re-contextualized in light of Bunting's American connections. A friend of many Black Mountain poets and of Allen Ginsberg, the Northumbrian poet revived public reading as a way for the individual to state his idea about society. A Quaker by faith, his Northern England prompts a return to a pacifist harmony with nature, far away from the turmoil of the capital. Dialect, for Bunting, is the embodiment of quiet dissidence, even if it means running the risk of marginalization and of the accusation of escapism: the private voice breaks away from the public discourse and suggests an alternative version — and a far better one according to his own standards — that can be shared in turn by an elected audience.

Ted Hughes's definition and use of dialect are radically different from Bunting's in that it is not so much historical as it is mythological, even ontological. It is dependent on his idea that his native region, the Calder Valley, is a healing center where mind and body can be reunited through the powers of poetry. In an interview in 1982, when asked about his West Yorkshire dialect, he said he did not speak it anymore but could still distinctly hear it when writing poetry. Then he differentiated it from the "language of culture,"[18] that is to say Standard English, implicitly arguing that Northern English is a natural language, a simple language connected to the body, a language that predates cultural accretions of significance. Dialect is not the language common to a place or a community, but the language of childhood, where Hughes thinks the real core of the self is. Dialect thus belongs to the most intimate, private self.

Yet, the dialect, just like the North and childhood, has "disappeared somewhere"[19] and only through ordinary language can the poet retrieve its primacy and its integrity, be it for just a second, as the prefatory poem to *Remains of Elmet* shows. The poet's language is dialectal in that it is a "last inheritance"[20] from his family: it is an archaeological treasure that reaches back to immemorial times, and it is in danger of disappearing when publicized. Such a conception of dialect as a language that runs the risk of falling apart when you try to grasp it is reminiscent of Seamus Heaney's in his bog poems in *North*

(1975): language is earthy and mysterious and loses its integrity when cut off from its natural element. Going downwards into language connects the two poets with wider concepts of the North, of England in Hughes's case, of Ireland in Heaney's. The concision of the expression "archaeology of the mouth"[21] shows the circulation of public and private imagery — the personal space of the mouth is also a site to be dug so that the history of a nation can be brought to light. The encounter with the fish that is told right after this passage is an allegory for the poetic act that consists in letting unseen things come to the fore, be it for just a second. The blanks between the two allegories can be read as a way to connect two apparently irreconcilable images: Hughes's poetry reveals what is hidden behind the surfaces of words and objects and is conscious that language can only offer a momentary stasis.

Despite the significance of this non-standard language in Hughes, it is difficult to trace any formal evidence, be it lexical or phonetic, of a specific northern dialect in his poetry. It could be said instead that his dialect is akin to "a song of the earth," a phrase borrowed from Gustav Mahler's 1911 masterpiece and taken up by Jonathan Bate to speak of ecopoetry in 2000, that is to say a language that dreams of a return to harmony with the region it describes. For instance, toponyms do contain some dialectal variations, such as "Crimworth Dean," in which "crim" is a local synonym for valley. Hughes makes one feel the regional context of the production of his poems — meaning that he uses a language that corresponds to the social reality of the valley; when the old men are "yarning" in "Crown Point Pensioners,"[22] they are both blabbering about and reasserting their link to the textile industry. More importantly, he uses a language in keeping with the matter of the North: his North is the Pennines, his North is rocky, and so are his words, as Heaney demonstrated in "Englands of the Mind" (1976). His words "crumble" in much the same was as the Pennines are subject to erosion.[23] His voice is the Northern landscape speaking.

Furthermore, the words the poet uses are mostly monosyllables derived from Old English, while Latinate words are reduced to a minimum. In an interview in 1971, Ted Hughes established that his "most intimate self"[24] as a West Yorkshire dialect speaker is directly connected to Middle English poetry. There again, the poet chooses not to use the iambic pentameter, but the alliterative tradition that harks back to *Sir Gawain and the Green Knight*. Although the origin of this text is a matter of dispute among scholars, it nonetheless seems to inspire Northern poets; Simon Armitage, for instance, published in 2007 a widely acclaimed translation of the poem into an idiom that is close to contemporary Yorkshire dialect. In "Myths, Metres, Rhythms," Hughes also shows how the new orthodoxy brought in by continental models — that is to say the iambic pentameter — became a vehicle for the royal court's public discourse on Englishness and eventually turned into hostility to alliteration and common speech. As opposed to this, his own poetry restores the native tradition through the rhythms of dialect. In his case, the cross-fertilization of languages leads to the revival of older forms of speech which can be deemed part of regionalism. He uses the resources of his private version of the North to question the literary history of England.

Since there is little evidence for the actual phonetic or linguistic realization of this dialect in the vocabulary or syntax on the written page, one might think that it can be better heard in public readings. Yet I would tend to agree with Tom Paulin, who said that Hughes's reading voice on tape was not specifically northern but composite, with phonetic features from Yorkshire, American, Devon, and also "with some standard flattening"[25], as if his language stretched across the map. His voice is rather hypnotic, not that of a bard, but that of a shaman, designed to reach the audience's inner, private selves. For instance, in "Mayday on Holderness," his accent cannot easily be situated on a phonetic map and takes us from the shore of East Yorkshire to a non-place of savagery without a hiatus, just by the sheer flow of alliteration. Indeed Hughes's dialect is less a matter of word sounds than a way to connect inner selves through deeply-ingrained rhythms. It strikes a musical, primitive, animal chord that elicits an immediate response in the audience. It demands "a new kind of psychosomatic co-operation with the vitality of the dialect."[26] The poetic voice, energized by its dialectal accents, flows into the ears of individual readers who are unconsciously dragged into a collective experience. Dialect for Hughes is ontological: the private voice rings as a means of public healing.

The use of dialect in Tony Harrison's *From "The School of Eloquence"* suggests yet another way to bridge the apparent gap between the private and the public. In an interview in 1991, he said that for him "the psychological issues are as historical as the historical issues are psychological."[27] There is no divide between the private and the public — the private is a synecdoche for the public and the public a synecdoche for the private. Yet private and public are spoken in conflicting languages since Northerners and more particularly Northern working-class children who went to school speak both Northern English and Standard English, in private or in public, depending on the situation of communication.

From "The School of Eloquence" dramatizes the angst of one such scholarship boy, a figure of the poet himself, who, because he has acquired Standard English through education and lives off it, feels like a traitor to his class, which is still in the dark as to the historical process that keeps it oppressed, and in which the poet participates in spite of himself. Therefore, Harrison uses dialect not only as an antiquarian bent on preserving old forms of language but also as a dissident intent on questioning the structures of power. The poems are like forums in which different voices can be heard, a phenomenon made clear by the typography: the voice of the working-class is transcribed in italics and there are many attempts at linguistic realism; the voice of the middle-class is quoted between inverted commas; the rest of the poem is the poet's own voice, torn between the two other public voices.

The dilemma of the language the scholarship boy should use when with his family is deeply felt in the poem "Book Ends" which shows that now that the mother is dead, father and son have even more difficulties in finding a language to communicate.[28] It suggests both how cultural determinations penetrate the family sphere and how private voices can question collective representations. For instance, the phrase "hog the grate" means "keep silent" in the context of a working-class sociolect, but its association with fire and metal also connects it to the industrial world. On the other hand, the relevance of the label "scholar," to designate the son, and the endearing terms "beloved" and "wife" to designate the mother, are questioned in the context of a class struggle over language.

While the poet is left speechless, at loss for words to carve his sadness in an epitaph to his dead mother, his access to the world of classical literature ironically depriving him of simple means to express grief, the father, the supposedly "clumsy talker" speaks in perfect iambic pentameters: "*Come on, it's not as if we're wanting verse.*" The father's blindness as to his potential articulacy is ironically enhanced by the double meaning of the word "wanting," which means both to desire and to lack something. Yet, only the poet — and subsequently the reader, who thus becomes connected to the poet's private experience — are aware of that cruel fact.

The reader is made to feel the poet's predicament because of the rhyme "cut / put." If she rhymes the two words, she speaks in dialect but maintains one of the vehicles of bourgeois culture, that is to say rhymed poetry. If she does not rhyme them, then she speaks in Received Pronunciation, but fails to fulfill one requisite of traditional poetry. It could be added that if the reader does not even realize the choice she has to make, then no matter how she reads, she is deaf to the language of power, be it the language of the oppressors, /kʌt/, or the language of the oppressed, /kŭt/. The poet's voice wavers between dialect and Standard English and is therefore constantly problematized to avoid the double pit of a sentimental yet philistine use of dialect and an official yet impersonal use of Standard English. Each gains by being energized by the other. In one word Harrison demonstrates there is no such thing as private voice that would not point to a public discourse.

In the 1980s, Tony Harrison liked to test his poems on a working-class audience to make sure he was still in touch with them. Apparently, he could make people cry by reading, and I think it was mostly because he sided with the working-class when such rhymes came up. Even in October 2008, when he read his opus magnum, *v.* (1985) at the Maison de la Poésie in Paris, he performed all the switches from dialect to Received Pronunciation and back. Even the French audience could feel how the private voices of the poet and the skinhead were socially loaded. For Harrison, dialect is a means to keep the wounds open: the private voice does not speak, it is spoken by cultural determinations while public discourse is undermined by private voices.

Aristotle, in his *Poetics*, stated that in poetry, standard words are clear but mean because shared by all: they belong to the public realm. By contrast, dialect words are out of the ordinary but gibberish, because part of an idiolect, private. Consequently, he advocated an admixture of the two which would be both clear and out of the ordinary: standard terms would be used for intelligibility and non-standard terms for poeticity (in much the same way as metaphors for instance). Basil Bunting, Ted Hughes and Tony Harrison understand dialect poetry in such a way and extend such understanding: they consider it as a sign that something is rotten in the state of England. For them, dialect tells of divisions and inequalities today but it also reaches back to a community related by a common speech. Hence the importance for all of them of public readings as communal experience since they create a community of readers that transcends the private act of reading a page on one's own. Therefore dialect, the interface between public and private, is both one of the diseases English is plagued with and the remedy against the disease.

Basil Bunting, Ted Hughes and Tony Harrison use dialect, the linguistic and phonetic component of their private voice, in order to question and ultimately deflate stereotypical public discourses about the North: Bunting refuses to submit to the cliché of a philistine North and contends that Northern English, a language that has the same historical value as Standard English, is the most poetic form and needs to be heard by all; Ted Hughes reworks the image of a wasteland to unravel the dormant energies of a North in constant recycling and connected to other parts of the world, and even to other worlds; Tony Harrison shows that just behind the opposition between dialect and Standard English, there is a class war that needs to be faced and waged. By delivering their own private versions of the North in their own dialect, they participate in problematizing the public discourse on a putative Englishness.

NOTES

1. Compiled partly from the collection *Continuous: Fifty Sonnets from "The School of Eloquence"* (London: Rex Collings, 1981), with the addition of "History Classes" *From "The School of Eloquence" and Other Poems* (London: Rex Collings, 1978) and several previously uncollected poems.

2. Dave Russell, *Looking North: Northern England and the National Imagination* (Manchester: Manchester University Press, 2004), 4.

3. Philip Dodd, "Lowryscapes: Recent Writings about the North," *Encounter* 32:2 (Summer 1990, 17–28), 17.

4. Katie Wales, "'North and South: A Linguistic Divide?' Inaugural Lecture for the Chair of Modern English Language at the University of Leeds" (1999), <http://www.leeds.ac.uk/reporter/439/kwales.htm>.

5. David Gervais, *Literary Englands: Versions of Englishness in Modern Writing* (Cambridge: Cambridge University Press, 1993), 271.

6. Seamus Heaney, "The Redress of Poetry," *Finders Keepers: Selected Prose 1971–2001* (London: Faber and Faber, 2002), 257–261.

7. "Dialect Poetry," *The New Princeton Encyclopedia of Poetry and Poetics*, ed. Alex Preminger and T.V.F. Brogan (Princeton: Princeton University Press, 1993), 288–290.

8. David Kennedy, *New Relations: The Refashioning of British Poetry 1980–1994* (Bridgend: Seren, 1996), 25.

9. Paul Volsik, "'The Essential Nexus': Philip Larkin and the Reader," *Etudes anglaises* 46:4 (October/November 1993, 427–439), 430.

10. Frederick C. Stern, "The Formal Poetry Reading," *The Drama Review* 35:3 (Autumn 1991, 67–84), 73.

11. Basil Bunting, *Collected Poems* (New York: New Directions, 2000), 224.

12. Ibid.

13. Andrew McAllister and S. Figgis, "Basil Bunting: The Last Interview," *Bête Noire* 2:3 (1987, 22–50), 49.

14. Bunting, *Collected Poems*, 224.

15. Osborn Bergin, "Bardic Poetry: a Lecture Delivered in 1912," *Irish Bardic Poetry* (Dublin: Dublin Institute for Advanced Studies, 1970, 3–22), 3–4.

16. Denis Goacher, "Denis Goacher Talks About Bunting," ed. Diana Collecott in *Sharp Study and Long Toil: Basil Bunting Special Issue*, ed. Richard Caddell (Durham University Journal Supplement, 1995, 195–207) 204.

17. The June 2009 new Bloodaxe edition of *Briggflatts* includes a CD of Bunting reading the poem, as well as a biographical DVD.

18. Stan Correy and Robyn Ravlich, "Ted Hughes: Language and Culture," transcribed by Ann Skea from ABC (March 1982) <http://www.zeta.org.au/~annskea/ABC1.htm>.

19. Correy and Ravlich, "Ted Hughes: Language and Culture."

20. Ted Hughes, *Remains of Elmet* (London: Faber, 1979), 7.

21. Ibid.

22. Ibid., 89.

23. Ibid., 7.

24. Ekbert Faas, "Ted Hughes and Crow: Interview with Ted Hughes," *London Magazine* 10:10 (January 71, 5–20), 11–12.

25. Tom Paulin, "Laureate of the Free Market?" *Minotaur: Poetry and the Nation State* (London: Faber, 1992, 252–269), 268.

26. Ted Hughes, "Myths, Metres, Rhythms," *Winter Pollen: Occasional Prose*, ed. William Scammell (London: Faber, 1994, 310–372), 334.

27. John Haffenden, "Interview with Tony Harrison," *Tony Harrison: Bloodaxe Critical Anthologies 1* (Newcastle upon Tyne: Bloodaxe, 1991, 229–257), 230.

28. Tony Harrison, "Book Ends," *Selected Poems* (London: Penguin, 1987), 126–127.

WORKS CITED

Aristotle (1981). *The Politics*. Penguin: London.
_____ (1996). *Poetics*. Penguin: London.

Armitage, Simon (2007). *Sir Gawain and the Green Knight*. London: Faber and Faber.

Ashcroft, Bill, Gareth Griffins and Helen Tiffins (eds.) (1989). *The Empire Writes Back: Theory and Practice in Post-Colonial Literature*. New York: Routledge.

Bate, Jonathan (2000). *The Song of the Earth*. Cambridge: Harvard University Press.

Bergin, Osborn (1970). "Bardic Poetry: a Lecture Delivered in 1912." *Irish Bardic Poetry*. Dublin: Dublin Institute for Advanced Studies, 3–22.

Brontë, Emily (1995; first edition 1847). *Wuthering Heights*. London: Penguin.

Bunting, Basil (2000). *Collected Poems*. New York: New Directions.

Chaucer (2005). *The Canterbury Tales*. London: Penguin.

Correy, Stan, and Robyn Ravlich (March 1982). "Ted Hughes: Language and Culture." Transcribed by Ann Skea from ABC. <http://www.zeta.org.au/~annskea/ABC1.htm>.

Davidson, Peter (2005). *The Idea of North*. London: Reaktion Books.

Dodd, Philip (summer 1990). "Lowryscapes: Recent Writings about the North." *Encounter* 32:2, 17–28.

Faas, Ekbert (January 1971). "Ted Hughes and Crow: Interview with Ted Hughes." *London Magazine* 10:10, 5–20.

Gervais, David (1993). *Literary Englands: Versions of Englishness in Modern Writing*. Cambridge: Cambridge University Press.

Goacher, Denis (1995). "Denis Goacher Talks About Bunting." Ed. Diana Collecott in *Sharp Study and Long Toil: Basil Bunting Special Issue.* Ed. Richard Caddell. Durham University Journal Supplement, 195–207.

Haffenden, John (1991). "Interview with Tony Harrison." *Tony Harrison: Bloodaxe Critical Anthologies I.* Ed. Neil Astley. Newcastle upon Tyne: Bloodaxe, 229–257.

Harrison, Tony (1978). *From "The School of Eloquence" and Other Poems.* London: Rex Collings.

_____ (1981). *Continuous: Fifty Sonnets from "The School of Eloquence."* London: Rex Collings.

_____ (1987). *From "The School of Eloquence." Selected Poems.* London: Penguin.

_____ (1996). *Plays Three: Poetry or Bust, The Kaisers of Carnuntum, The Labourers of Herakles.* London: Faber and Faber.

Heaney, Seamus (1975). *North.* London: Faber and Faber.

_____ (2002). *Finders Keepers: Selected Prose 1971–2001.* London: Faber and Faber.

Hughes, Ted Hughes (1979). *Remains of Elmet.* London: Faber.

_____ (1994). "Myths, Metres, Rhythms." *Winter Pollen: Occasional Prose.* Ed. William Scammell. London: Faber, 310–372.

Jewell, Helen (1994). *The North-South Divide: The Origins of Northern Consciousness in the North of England.* Manchester: Manchester University Press.

Kennedy, David (1996). *New Relations: The Re-fashioning of British Poetry 1980–1994.* Bridgend: Seren.

McAllister, Andrew, and S. Figgis (1987). "Basil Bunting: The Last Interview." *Bête Noire* 2:3, 22–50.

Musgrove, Frank (1990). *The North of England: A History from Roman Times to the Present.* Cambridge: Oxford: Blackwell.

The New Princeton Encyclopedia of Poetry and Poetics (1993). Eds. Alex Preminger and T.V.F Brogan. Princeton: Princeton University Press.

Paulin, Tom (1992). "Laureate of the Free Market?" *Minotaur: Poetry and the Nation State.* London: Faber, 252–269.

Russell, Dave (2004). *Looking North: Northern England and the National Imagination.* Manchester: Manchester University Press.

Said, Edward W. (1978). *Orientalism.* New York: Pantheon Books.

Stern, Frederick C. (Autumn 1991). "The Formal Poetry Reading." *The Drama Review,* 35:3, 67–84.

Volsik, Paul (1993). "'The Essential Nexus': Philip Larkin and the Reader." *Etudes anglaises* 46:4, 427–439.

Wales, Katie (1999). "'North and South: A Linguistic Divide?' Inaugural Lecture for the Chair of Modern English Language at the University of Leeds." <http://www.leeds.ac.uk/reporter/439/kwales.htm>.

_____ (2006). *Northern English: A Social and Cultural History.* Cambridge: Cambridge University Press.

12. Public or Private Nation: Poetic Form and National Consciousness in the Poetry of Tony Harrison and Geoffrey Hill

Carole Birkan-Berz

between / private and public, purpose, desire, hope— Geoffrey Hill, *Scenes from Comus*[1]

The social and cultural landscapes through which Tony Harrison and Geoffrey Hill journey have been similar, as John Lyon and others have suggested.[2] Their poetic landscapes and mappings of national consciousness, however, have been markedly different. This difference is not merely a matter of political positioning, but a radically different approach to poetic form. After analyzing the main tenets of the public-private dialectic with respect to the poets themselves, to poetic form, and to nationhood, this chapter will present close readings revealing the divergent approaches of these two poets.

Born within five years of each other in the 1930s, both of working-class backgrounds and from regions with a strong industrial past (namely Yorkshire and the Midlands), Tony Harrison and Geoffrey Hill both benefited from the 1944 Butler Education Act and were awarded scholarships to local grammar schools before going on to earn university degrees. Their paths then crossed briefly but significantly at Leeds University, where they both taught. As has been documented by Romana Huk, the two poets were part of the same atmosphere of engaged political thought and artistic creation, which led to their inclusion in Jon Silkin's anthology of *Poetry of the Committed Individual*.[3] After moving away from their native places, they both taught briefly in Nigeria and went on to have careers in the highest institutions of art and education: Harrison became resident dramatist at the National Theatre and Hill taught at Emmanuel College, Cambridge. They also share the experience of having lived and worked in the United States of America and have now both come back to England.[4]

Theirs is also the success story of two poets rising from marginal positions to central ones. Harrison's first sonnets, which he says "sold about five copies," now feature on English A-Level syllabi.[5] Though Hill's poems were already being included in anthologies in the early 1960s, his dense and obscure output put him in a difficult position in comparison to some of his peers.[6] Today, with Hill being at once more productive and more eager to speak out in interviews or give readings, and with the British poetry landscape having lost more of its living monuments, it seems less of a surprise to find him featured in the new canon of Penguin poets alongside Carol Ann Duffy or James Fenton, a move recalling his inclusion in a volume of the first Penguin Modern Poets series of 1966, alongside Edwin Brock and Stevie Smith.[7]

Being part of a newly-refashioned canon, both poets were unofficially named for the position of Poet Laureate after Ted Hughes died.[8] As their poetry suggests, however, neither of them would have accepted the offer. In "Laureate's Block — for Queen Elizabeth," an "occasional" poem originally published in *The Guardian* in 1999, Harrison tells the addressee in no uncertain terms that he will reject any such nomination, as "[he'd] sooner be a free man with no butts."[9] The "butts," which the poet refuses (together, presumably, with the "ifs" of political power) hark back to the cask of wine traditionally given to the Poet Laureate upon his nomination. In a similar passage in *Scenes from Comus*, first published in *Stand* in 2003, Hill muses on grudgingly receiving such a gift in a hypothetical future: "Say, thirty years until H. M. commands / a small obstruction for the mantelpiece / and senna's called on more than single malt."[10] Though both poets would indeed frown at the idea of writing verse to endorse a single national position, both do write and sometimes perform a kind of public poetry: that is to say, a poetry that "relat[es] to the people as a whole" or that "belongs to, affects, or concerns the community or the nation."[11]

Harrison could also be said to define public poetry as "open or available to all members of a community" or even "serving the public in a professional capacity."[12] In a recent interview, Harrison recounts his gradual adoption of this mode of writing:

> I think that the move for me towards public poetry came from some of the dilemmas I had, when having left a working-class background and started learning Latin and Greek at grammar school, I wanted to write a poetry which did some kind of honour to what I was learning, but also would reach people like my parents, and use what I think of as a common language.[13]

Harrison appears as not quite the nation's poetic civil servant, which would entail enforcing the dictates of the State, but rather as an individual poet whose singular condition has prompted a self-imposed mission to reach out to the people. His poetry, which he describes as "feeling-driven," starts out as private and ends up public.[14]

With Hill, it is the opposite. His first published poetry starts off as public, since it confronts the lyrical impulse with the shock of the last century's horrors. That Hill sees poetry as "public" has since then become obvious. In a recent talk at Warwick University, he described himself as a "condition-of-England poet," though he was quick to extend his domain to other parts of the Western world, be they the United States or Europe.[15] Despite viewing poetry as "civic action"[16] or "civic duty,"[17] however, he frequently derides the contemporary idea of poetic accessibility. In contrast to Tony Harrison, who supplies the reader with footnotes to poems, Hill links accessibility with simplification and thus to political tyranny, an idea first expressed in his *Paris Review* interview in 2000 and repeated many times since.[18] In *The Orchards of Syon* (2002), this distaste for accessibility comes out as a satire of the Welfare State or of an "all-shall-have-prizes" ideology: "Hand out the book prizes, my acceptance / speech is postponed."[19] One might read these lines either as an undeserved rejection of a system from which the poet benefited in his youth, or as a swipe at a poetic establishment still failing to award him the T.S. Eliot Prize. Yet Hill's indictment of "tyrannical simplicity" is nonetheless underpinned by the idea that a citizen is not made at the moment his material needs are met. In the lines appearing next in the poem, "Accessible / traded as democratic," *traded* can be seen as the key word.[20] In this poet's perspective, access to poetry is not equivalent to access to health care or education; neither do the alleged quick fixes of national poetic grants and prizes develop a civic conscience in the nation. For Hill, who writes of "our covenants with language / contra tyrannos,"[21] one of the favored routes to civil power is aesthetics, an awareness of how form interacts with meaning.[22]

Perhaps it is precisely because Hill starts off from such an abrupt public standpoint that his poetry can become more personal without losing its political edge. On the other hand, after its initial accessibility, Harrison's poetry runs the risk of being reduced to one individual's social history: in other words, it threatens to remain private.[23]

One way in which this public-private dialectic may be usefully highlighted is through the exploration of poetic form. Both Hill and Harrison experiment with certain traditional or so-called "fixed" forms, including the sonnet and the elegy, in radically different ways. A poetic form may be said to be public in the sense that it potentially belongs, if not to everyone, then at least to anyone well-versed in the language and literary tradition of a country or continent. By appropriating a given form (a creative activity done in private), poets create the singular poem. The particular approach is apt to balance, as T.S. Eliot wrote, "tradition" and "the individual talent."[24] It manages to be striking in its novelty while providing moments of recognition, even as it may subvert its template. Then, if the poet appropriates the form to a high enough degree, he can create a model that may become public. In Eliot's words, a literary tradition forms a whole that is "altered" by the new poet while still remaining "coher[ent]."[25]

For poets as deeply rooted in their social and political environment as Hill and Harrison, the use of certain poetic forms is also implicitly tied up with aspects of nationhood. The nation can be theorized both as a public realm and a site of personal belonging (the word "nation" comes from the Latin *nasci*, to be born). But whether one conceives of nationhood as primarily grounded in shared values and citizenship or in the personal experience of identity, the public and private strands of national identity are necessarily bound up together. In Hill's work, the two realms often intersect. National standards are seen to be embedded in self-construction, especially in representations of childhood. In *The Triumph of Love*, a recollection of school days prompts the phrase "Fairfield repels my imperium" (section LXXXII), and the child-speaker in *Mercian Hymns* recounts "his private derelict sandlorry named Albion" (section VII). Conversely, Hill's political models also show how civic values must be deep-seated in an individual to have any national impact, hence Milton's "vehement private ambition for the people's / greater good."[26]

The legal terms of nationality and citizenship also point to a permeable divide. Indeed, some countries are widely known to define "nation" as ethnic (basing nationality on *jus sanguinis* or right of blood), others as civic (basing it on *jus soli*, the right of soil), but all states continually modify their laws, especially when issues linked with certain migrant groups arise.[27] Since British identity, as famously defined by Edmund Burke, consists of various levels of loyalty to family, community, region, country, and finally to the State in the guise of Monarch and Parliament, it embodies the public-private dialectic on multiple levels and may reveal potential conflicts of loyalties.[28] These are outlined in Harrison's *v.* as "all the versuses of life":

> From LEEDS v. DERBY, Black/White
> and (as I've known to my cost) man v. wife,
> Communist v. Fascist, Left v. Right,
> Class v. class as bitter as before,
> the unending violence of US and THEM[29]

Harrison's *v.* uses the form of the pastoral elegy in a momentary bid to overcome all these struggles and turn an atheist's "prayer" for his deceased parents into one for a defunct national unity, "a call to Britain and to all nations."[30]

Whether one sides with the modernist or the perennialist theorists of nationhood, poetry and its established forms constitute powerful vehicles for national narratives.[31] These narratives attempt to bridge the gap between the ethnic and the civic, or the private and the public. Most famously, the iambic pentameter and the use of rhyme became national poetic staples from the Renaissance, when a national British literary canon distinct from European neighbors' and on par with the Greek and Roman models was constituted. In the same period, the sonnet became powerful in conveying a sense of national consciousness. Reliant on classical models, the Italian form was imported into England by Wyatt and nationalized by Surrey, Sidney, and Spenser through the development of a complex rhyme scheme particular to the English language.[32] The sonnet sequence can thus be seen as an instance of national writing beginning with Sidney's *Astrophil and Stella*, where courtly love for a lady is likened to a subject's awe of a monarch.

Both the pastoral elegy and the eclogue also partake of the public-private dialectic inherent in national consciousness; they traditionally combine mourning for a singular person with mourning for a certain era, paradoxically filling the nation with a renewed sense of identity. Indeed, as Peter Sacks reminds us, the right to inheritance was classically tied to the duty to mourn.[33] This phenomenon is especially fit to describe a nation's sense of itself. In order to claim a poetic or national sense of identity for the people, poets must mourn the past on behalf of all. Hence the prevalence of elegies in the Victorian era, when the nation mourned its past rural landscapes in order to embrace its industrial future — a dichotomy played out well in Hill's "An Apology for the Revival of Christian Architecture in England."[34] Established poetic forms carry national narratives with them and may fit or resist the poet's private narrative of nationhood.

Interweaving the personal and national strands of the elegy presents a special challenge when a poet stages the elegy in the space of the sonnet. Not only are the literary histories of both forms intertwined, but their formal constraints also constantly jostle and potentially jar each other. Space may be seen as the main constraint. Indeed, an elegy traditionally requires a drawn-out narrative that allows the speaker to carry out the various stages of mourning, as well as address a potential crowd of mourners who provide an antiphonal response.[35] Both the narrative and the antiphonal aspects of the elegy are potentially jeopardized when the elegy is set in sonnet form. When poets are alert to the resistance of the medium, the public-private dialectic is played out in a thought-provoking way; however, even if the poetry seems to denounce national ills, nationhood itself is ultimately not questioned when form and content cohere too closely.

Both Harrison and Hill use the sonnet with an elegiac purpose and a national connotation. The sonnet has already been used in this manner, especially by Gray and the Romantics,[36] but Harrison and Hill manage the constraints of both forms in their own modern way by setting the sonnets in elegiac sequences of various lengths — one of the strategies for coping with the restricted space of the sonnet itself. As close readings reveal, however, this often isn't enough. The other techniques they use also differ, as does their scope, resulting in varying degrees of success.

Harrison's sonnet "The Queen's English" from the *School of Eloquence* is part of a protean sequence appearing in various installments over the years; the sequence makes up the bulk of Harrison's *Selected Poems* with 63 of its sonnets.[37] The first section, plainly entitled "1," deals with the poet's youth and his gradual acquisition of eloquence. Flashing back and forth to various parts of the poet's life, the second section is largely an elegy for his parents, while the third depicts a bleak future that takes the poet out of his native Leeds. "The Queen's English" is from the second section, alongside poems usually bearing the names of objects ("Dividers," "Jumper," etc.), whose unearthing frequently prompts an elegiac recollection of his father and of a lost age. In "The Queen's English," the object is a particular one: a poetry book entitled *Poems from the Yorkshire Dales*[38]: "*'ere tek this un wi' yer to New York / to remind yer 'ow us gaffers used to talk*" (italics in original). Like *The School of Eloquence*, this volume manages to encapsulate the spoken and written dimensions of language, both private and public. It embodies the threatened disappearance of the Yorkshire dialect along with its poetry, as well as its impending supersession by RP (Received Pronunciation), Standard English, or perhaps the "Queen's English," a language analogically compared to the "Queen's Hotel" in City Square: "a grandish pile of swank," polished but with no real substance.

In the entire sequence, Harrison relies on the sonnet as a distant template and employs the Meredithian sonnet, which is at one remove from the sonnet proper. Designed by George Meredith to picture the sad tale of "Modern Love," this modernized form uses two extra lines to add another point of view (often in the third person), while the rest of the poem uses the traditional "lyric I." Harrison further modernizes the sonnet by using many types of stanza breaks, though his experiments may sometimes be disappointing, as when he turns the sonnet into a series of metronomic four quatrains. In "The Queen's English," however, the break in 4/6/3/3 mirrors the harmonious imbalance of the Italian sonnet. The lengthier, sixteen-line poem enables him to create two points of view — pitting, as well as pitching, two "I"s against each other. The rhyme scheme suggests that the two embedded miniature sonnets are mirror images, as the first series of alternate lines closes with a rhyming couplet ("sales"/"Dales," l. 9–10) and the last series begins with another

("York"/talk," l. 11–12). The space of the two adjacent couplets is also the space of two turns in the text: a minor one occurring with the logical "but" on line 9, closing a repetition of "nots," and a major volta as the father's voice intervenes and is given a full tercet. The space of poetic confrontation between the two sonnets is also the space in which the father's "*us gaffers*" becomes separated from the family-based "*we*" on line 9. These lines also resist the iambic pentameter, the meter Harrison favors as being closely connected to natural speech.[39] Line 11 remains a "broken line," as it contains fewer syllables than most. In contrast, the poem's lines in Standard English often feature more syllables than natural speech would require (for example, line 5 reads: "I knew that he'd decided that he'd die," whereas more standard phrasing might have been "I knew that he'd decided to die"; line 8 adds an extra stressed syllable with the initial "nor").

The conflict between two types of English is also perceptible in the rhyme scheme, as the final cross-lines would probably not rhyme if spoken in a broad Yorkshire accent (with *mahth* pronounced for "mouth"), while lines 5 to 8 might all have the same end-sound. This conflict also enables creative interpretations, since the "*wuds*" (italics in original) put in the mouth of the speaker at the end create an echo of the "woods" above, thus recalling Harrison's line about the "branks of condescension": sharp objects of wood or metal put in people's mouths as a means of punishment.[40] The last lines of the poem carry more gravity as a result of this formal variation. They also take the poem and the private nation out of itself. As the poet reads from this new source, his private nation — focused on his class-fraught relationship with his parents and city of Leeds — now incorporates the country and is able to spread south. Gaining momentum after starting from the restricted space of the sonnet, the poem espouses another point of view and enriches the nation.

A comparison of "The Queen's English" with "Pain-Killers I,"[41] situated later in the same part of the sequence, shows that formal variation can be less successful when not stretched to its limits. In this poem, the poet comes face to face with his dead father's American counterpart while standing in a post office queue. Here, the volta ("or learning to shop so late in his old age") merely draws the poem back into itself, rehashing a similar memory rather than delving further into the experience of old age across continents. The *status quo ante* of the first line, "My father haunts me," returns in line 14 with "my dad's ghost," and the last two lines only provide a skilful evasion of further haunting questions. Since its point of view never shifts, the poem remains solipsistic, private.

Harrison's other *opus magnum*, the 1985 long poem *v.* (and subsequent 1987 film directed by Richard Eyre), serves as another point of reference for the intersection of public and private, form and narrative. By Harrison's own standards, the poem has now aged and lost some of its shock value.[42] Reading it now, some twenty years after its publication, gives it an air of a respectable piece of work whose documentary aspect is almost quaint. Furthermore, though some have argued to the contrary,[43] its parodic reliance on Gray's "Elegy Written in a Country Churchyard" as a template is such that Gray's original viewpoint sometimes seems conveyed in total contradiction to Harrison's aesthetics and politics.[44]

Written in the same stanza form, both Harrison and Gray's poems begin with an early-evening graveyard setting, feature a meeting with a local youth, and end with the poet's epitaph. Gray's poem starts with an acknowledgement of pastoral conventions. Likewise, Harrison does not leave out his poetic predecessors, Byron and Wordsworth. Although Gray's churchyard is a peaceful place situated "far from the madding crowd," Harrison's is already crowded with delinquent youths. As Gray looks at the holy inscriptions and "uncouth rhymes" "strewn" by the Muse, Harrison also looks endearingly at the feeble engravings on the tombs. The "strew[ing]" is then taken literally as the poet begins to depict the four-letter inscriptions. In both poems, this is followed by an encounter with a young man, who in Harrison's text becomes a conflation of Gray's "hoary-headed swain" and his "little tyrant," with Gray's minimal antiphony being famously inflated in Harrison's work. Both poems end on the poets' planned epitaphs in italics. In Gray's work, a private moment of introspection leads to a sense of communal or national solidarity, which helps the poet privately come to terms with death. In Harrison's, however, this cannot occur. Though the poem's form invites a sense of national consciousness, the speaker's voice constantly defeats it. Accepting none of the consolations of the elegy, the poet nevertheless employs all its tricks.

In persisting with the elegiac form, Harrison appropriates it in support of lengthy descriptions of the town's dereliction and of his own sense of guilt. Because Harrison's elegy relies on the mirror figure of the skinhead as Gray's relies on the swain, it also excludes any other voices from the poem. With the final, self-deprecating vatic claims about the power of poetry ("Poetry Supporter!" l. 446) — or perhaps despite them — what prevails in the speaker's voice is a lack of faith in the word tantamount to a failure of trust in any communal or national structures. The poet's "meaning" is but "an accident" that contrasts with the explosive, compound-creating language in which the skinhead revels. In the final analysis, the paradox of a speaker-poet renouncing the word and a nihilistic skinhead espousing it puts the poem at a dead end. Far from having the dynamic quality of Harrison's best verse, this poem turns in on itself and stagnates, stuck in a dimension that is neither public nor private.

From Hill's earliest writings, readers have sensed his awareness of the perils of writing as either a private individual or a poet addressing the public. In an interview with Blake Morrison, Hill identified the first danger as "extreme naivety or else a reckless confessional mode," an excess he associates with much contemporary poetry.[45] Conversely, the early line "No manner of address will do" points to "the fear" of vanity in speaking to all.[46] From the 1950s to the present day, Hill's strategy has been to emphasize form. Although his poems repeatedly touch on public themes such as national history, warfare, Empire, and religious tolerance, any questions of importance boil down to issues of form.[47] Answering an interviewer's question on the religious nature of a sequence, Hill replied, "Each sequence has its own set of problems, which, as always in my case, are predominantly technical questions."[48] Arguably, the answer to a political question would have been the same one.

Predominantly relying on dramatic monologues set in the distant past or in foreign lands, Hill's first volumes contain poems that centralize public themes as they minimize the use of the lyric "I." In the poet's more recent volumes, however, the autobiographical lyric "I" returns to the fore, and the poems make more blatant use of the contemporary world as a point of reference. Hill's commitment to the formal demands of poetry has been consistent over the decades, and the technical mastery that he has painstakingly acquired has been the key to his poetry remaining political and civic, while still being able to incorporate the element of the singular self.

Much has been written about Hill's "September Song" on this issue. Jon Harris was among the first to argue that the poem fails as an elegy for a child murdered in the Shoah, but remains an effective elegy for the art of poetry itself. Regarding poetry as a public art form, Kelly Grovier's work on "post-temporalism," which may be read as a philosophical approach to Eliot's views on a nation's canon, has shown how "September Song" both comments on and informs readings of Keats's ode "To Autumn."[49] Finally, and of more interest here, Phyllis Levin and Jon Lennard have shown that this poem also follows the pattern of the sonnet.[50]

As a sonnet, "September Song" had precedent in Hill's œuvre with "Two Formal Elegies."[51] Subtitled "for the Jews in Europe," the short sequence was one of the first British poems to be written about the Shoah by a non–Jewish poet. Calling these sonnets "formal" elegies is problematic, however. If one reads the title literally, "Two Formal Elegies" can be understood as compressing all the thematic markers of the elegy into the sonnet form. In compacting all these elements, Hill restricts the time necessary for mourning and makes national contradictions appear in stark relief. The use of antiphony as a reflection of the wartime British mindset and in the accumulated images of water and vegetation, which point to a sense of national indifference, makes these contrasts especially apparent. No strict antiphony is actually heard in the poems, since there is only one speaker expressing himself with the public "we," but three points of view are potentially considered: the victims in sonnet 1, the witnesses in sonnet 2, and an introspective position placed between parentheses. More precisely situated than the first poem's, the second elegy's "we" opens a rift in the nation. The time and place is "here, yearly," and the protagonists are "the pushing midlanders," a word morphologically echoing "bystanders." Whereas the "we" in the first poem is linked to a preoccupation with good and evil, neither "we" nor "they" in the second poem question what they have seen on a "brief screen." The reader might have expected "stand/ trial," "stand/ fast," or "stand/ witness" in the run-on line ending in "stand," but instead it merely yields "stand/ to warm themselves." This condensed antiphony, instead of helping the speaker to mourn, only highlights how removed he is from the rest of the nation.

The piling up of natural images makes the idea of regeneration all but obscene. In the first poems, the "young roots" flourish directly from the ashes. The sonnet compresses these images to suppress any idea of just regeneration and replaces it with images of rape ("bedded in their blood," "abused bodies"). These images of nature and sexuality are associated with certain stock metaphors of the sonnet ("fires but play"/ "iced brain"), while showing "sufficient men" governing the nation and identifying the people as "brawny," a term that might mean "muscular," but also "grown fat" or "callous." Moreover, the omnipresent sea images remind us of Britain's naval power, which prevented the Jews' access to Mandatory Palestine during World War II. In these associations, Hill points to a national hardening of the heart, an indifference to the plight of the Jews.[52] For this hardening, aesthetics also bear part of the guilt: to quote a saying of Coleridge's often cited by Hill, "Poetry — excites us to artificial feelings — makes us callous to real ones."[53] These "Two Formal Elegies" compacted into sonnets show a speaker-poet, being at once complicit and at odds with his fellow countrymen, pushed to retreat privately into a parenthetical meditative utterance ("At whose door does the sacrifice stand or start" [2]).

Having established the centrality of formal concerns in the national divide as highlighted in "Two Formal Elegies," to read "September Song" as a sonnet may now throw light on Hill's struggle with the public-private dialectic. The poem indeed consists of fourteen lines, most of which are in iambic-anapaestic rhythm and five of which have four stressed beats (ll. 2, 4, 7, 11 and 13). These lines are arranged in a pattern resembling the Italian sonnet, with blanks marking one tercet (or amputated quatrain), followed by a full quatrain, then two tercets and finally a single line. Rhyming is reduced to internal rhymes ("leather"/"terror" ll. 6–7) or chiming ("time"/ "cries," ll. 3, 7). The sonnet form combines with a biographical element here, since the epigraph "born 19.6.32 — deported 24.9.42" identifies a child born one day after Hill himself.[54] These point to this "Song" as a sort of posthumous love poem for a child he has never known, where some common elements of courtly love are overturned beginning with the first two lines ("Undesirable, you may have been, untouchable / you were not"). The poem as an elegy for a victim of the Shoah presents a double bind: mourning an unknown person, one of six million victims, cannot be done, yet must be. As a sonnet, it presents another dilemma: this child can be spoken about from neither a fully private nor a fully public perspective. Indeed, the first two stanzas introduce a private "I-you" relationship, then bring the relationship into the public sphere by means of impersonal expressions such as passive forms ("forgotten," "passed over," "estimated," "patented"), vague terms ("Things"), and a nominal phrase (ll. 6–7). These passive and impersonal phrases only highlight the passivity and shame of individuals and nations. When the poet tries to retreat back into the "I-you" relationship that enables him to empathize with the victim, he is thrown back into a solipsistic world, exposing the earlier relationship as a fallacy:

> (I have made
> an elegy for myself it
> is true)

The second tercet blends the "roses" of the sonnet with the autumnal consolations of a Keatsian elegy. These canonical poetic images are public images: available to all, and therefore, in this context, of use to nobody. Acknowledging the impossibility of a private relationship with the dead and of a public relationship with the nation, Hill finally foregrounds the poem ("This") as the locus of this struggle, manifested by the mutual defeat of the sonnet and the elegy: "This is more than enough." The repeated and capitalized "This" also foregrounds the Shoah as an indelible, unexplainable moment, the responsibility for which must be borne by all nations.

At the opposite end of the spectrum, Hill's later elegiac treatment of his father in the 1996 volume *Canaan* points to a formal resolution of the problematics of the public-private divide in poetry. The poem "Pisgah" is a dramatization of a fleeting encounter with the ghost of the poet's father.[55] ("Pisgah" was the name given to a mountain near Hill's childhood home in Bromsgrove, Worcestershire, which was the last place on his father's beat.[56]) The poem is made up of fourteen lines of loose iambic-anapaestic tetrameter and pentameter. Two of these lines are actually broken or half-lines, which, being placed at the beginning and end of the poem, interrupt the flow of the recollection and respectively constitute an early volta and a makeshift closing couplet. Once again an elegy set in a broken sonnet form, "Pisgah" first acknowledges death and loss ("I am ashamed and grieve, having seen you then/ those many times"), then moves on to a long recollection of the father tending his garden and its many flowers before ending with half-believed consolation and mourning of the self ("Perhaps I too am a shade," l. 14). The shortening of the elegiac space here makes the "I-you" relationship appear with epiphanic strength. Indeed, the placing of pronouns in run-on lines highlights the dual temporality of the poem, as the first "you" ("having seen you then") is set in the past and the second in the poet's imaginary present ("as now/ you turn to speak"). Furthermore, lines 11 and 12 dramatize the shock of these two temporalities with the near juxtaposition of "yours" and "you": "This half-puzzled, awkward surprise is yours; / you cannot hear me or quite make me out." Indeed, the first refers to the living "you" of the past and the second to the present's deceased "you." This ultimate private moment remains striking in its modesty, the father's face remaining hidden until line 11. Yet, in line 4, the father is speaking "with someone standing deeper in the shade": another person is present on the scene. This might be a reference to somebody else's private life; "Pisgah" was the location of Christopher Morcom's house, where his lover Alan Turing visited him regularly, and this second reference is taken up in the later poem "A Cloud in Aquila," from *A Treatise of Civil Power*.[57]

Beyond the private aspect, the "other" person, who is not quite an outsider, enables the communal, public aspect of the poem to appear. Indeed, this location was the place where the poet A.E. Housman "gazed into Shropshire."[58] It also refers to the biblical Mount Pisgah, the place from which Moses was allowed to see the Promised Land before dying (Deut. 34.1). In the context of the volume *Canaan*, where other broken or irregular sonnets deal with English history, past and present political leaders, and the loss of political integrity in the 1990s, this poem enacts not only how removed the poet is from his departed father, but also how removed England is from her own mythical representation as a Promised Land. What remains is the receding image of a father or a guiding figure, acutely needed by the nation in an age of transition. The shadow of Housman (and, it may be argued, of Turing) here makes all the more poignant the desire for a public poetry, as well as for values stemming from (but also addressing) particular individual feelings. As *Scenes from Comus* has it: "between / private and public, purpose, desire, hope."[59] Even in its most intimate moment, Hill's poetry manages to have a public strain.

In conclusion, Harrison's poetic project has been one of inwardness expanding outward, while Hill's trajectory has been the reverse. Hill only arrives at inwardness after devoting most of his career to finding the right forms of public address. In both writers, poetic form has had a key impact. Both Harrison and Hill, in using the sonnet as a vehicle for the elegy, manage to open up the restricted room of the sonnet and to make the space a public one, even as they are engaged in private mourning. In doing so, they make national consciousness more complex and open to new dimensions, whether domestic or foreign. If they are not attentive enough to the resistance of the forms (Harrison's "Pain-Killers I" or *v.*)— or perhaps too attentive (Hill's "September Song")— their poetry risks having neither private nor public address.

Beyond national consciousness itself, atoning for the sins of the nation is a concern at the heart of Hill's poetry, a project that he shares with Harrison to some extent. This concern is tied to a Romantic desire to renew poetic forms. Analyzing their respective appropriations of these forms confirms how deeply these two poets are rooted in different traditions. In Greek fashion, Harrison favors a form of dramatic poetry easily adapted to theatre and with cathartic effect; it depends on constant action and formal movement. Hill, on the other hand, is steeped in a Judeo-Christian tradition whereby introspection is a crucial step in the rituals of atonement. In this respect, Harrison's poetry is outward-looking, whereas Hill's poetry looks inwards. Though Hill's poetry begins from a very public standpoint, it makes the individual reader attentive to the formal aspects of the poem, thus eliciting a form of political thought. This may constitute a move inward, into the text though never letting go of the context, and towards the individual conscience — perhaps re-enacting the late Romantic "shift to a spiritual and moral revolution" identified by M.H. Abrams.[60] This strain of Romanticism persists in modernist writing such as Hill's, and perhaps that it is its strength.[61]

NOTES

1. Geoffrey Hill, section 3.15, *Scenes from Comus* (London: Penguin, 2005), 64.

2. John Lyon, "'Que voulez-vous incinérer'? Geoffrey Hill et la culture populaire," *La Poésie de Geoffrey Hill et la modernité*, ed. Jennifer Kilgore-Caradec and René Gallet (Paris: L'Harmattan, 2007), 119. [French version of John Lyon, "'What are you incinerating?': Geoffrey Hill and popular culture," *English* 54:209 (2005, 85–98)]. See also Raphaël Ingelbien, *Misreading England: Poetry and Nationhood since the Second World War* (Amsterdam & New York: Rodopi, 2002).

3. Jon Silkin, *Poetry of the Committed Individual: A Stand Anthology of Poetry* (London: Gollancz, 1973); Romana Huk, "Poetry of the Committed Individual: Jon Silkin, Tony Harrison, Geoffrey Hill, and the Poets of Postwar Leeds," *Contemporary British Poetry: Essays in Theory and Criticism*, ed. James Acheson and R. Huk (New York: SUNY Press, 1996), 175–219. See also, by the same author, "Tony Harrison, *The Loiners* and the 'Leeds Renaissance,'" *Bloodaxe Critical An-*thologies I: Tony Harrison, ed. (Newcastle: Bloodaxe, 1991) 75–83.

4. For recent biographical information on Harrison, see Nicholas Wroe, "Tony Harrison: Man of Mysteries," *The Guardian*, 1 Apr. 2000, <http://books.guardian.co.uk/departments/poetry/story/0,,154405,00>. On Hill, see Carl Phillips, "The Art of Poetry LXXX: Geoffrey Hill," *The Paris Review* 42:154 (2000, 272–299). See also John Haffenden, *Viewpoints: Poets in Conversation* (London: Faber, 1981), 76–99 for an older, yet authoritative interview.

5. Wroe, "Tony Harrison."

6. A notable example of Hill's early inclusion in the canon is the second edition of Kenneth Allott's *The Penguin Book of Contemporary Verse* (Harmondsworth: Penguin, 1962; first edition 1950), which also features an explanatory essay by the poet on "Annunciations" (391–393). An example of his instability in the British canon is his exclusion from Andrew Motion and Blake Morrison (eds.), *The Penguin Book of Contemporary British Poetry* (London: Penguin, 1982).

7. Edwin Brock, Geoffrey Hill, Stevie Smith, *Penguin Modern Poets 8* (Harmondsworth: Penguin, 1966).

8. See John Morrish, "Much rhyme, little reason: The jury is out: there is no agreement on who would make a fitting poet laureate, even less on what they should spend their time doing," *The Independent* 18 Apr. 1999 (London), 17, and Sophie Harrison, "Monitor: Picking poets — what the world's newspapers say about the next Laureate," *The Independent on Sunday,* 8 Nov. 1998 (London), 14.

9. The poem is reprinted in Tony Harrison, *Laureate's Block and Other Poems* (London: Penguin, 2000), 12–17. See also "A Celebratory Ode on the Abdication of Charles III" (Harrison, *Laureate's Block,* 1–11).

10. Geoffrey Hill, section 1.3, *Scenes from Comus,* 4. First published in *Stand* 172, 6. References to Hill's poetic sequences are given by section number, in Roman or Arabic numerals, as in the original work.

11. "public, adj," *The Oxford English Dictionary,* 2d ed. 1989. OED Online. Oxford University Press. <http://dictionary.oed.com/cgi/entry/5019180>.

12. "public, adj," *The Oxford English Dictionary.*

13. John Tusa, "The John Tusa Interviews: Transcript of the John Tusa Interview with Tony Harrison" (2001) <http://www.bbc.co.uk/radio3/johntusainterview/harrison_transcript.shtml>

14. Ibid.

15. Geoffrey Hill, Untitled contribution, Poets and Philosophy panel, *Poetry and Philosophy Conference,* University of Warwick, Coventry, 26 Oct. 2007.

16. Geoffrey Hill, section LXX, *The Triumph of Love* (Boston: Houghton Mifflin, 1998), 36.

17. "The cultivation of depths of memory I see as a civic duty as well as a private burden and consolation" G. Hill, "A Matter of Timing," *The Guardian,* 21 Sept. 2001, <http://www.guardian.co.uk/books/2002/sep/21/featuresreviews.guardianreview28>.

18. Phillips, "The Art of Poetry LXXX," 276, 280.

19. Geoffrey Hill, *The Orchards of Syon* (Harmondsworth: Penguin, 2002), section XXXIX.

20. Geoffrey Hill, section 118, *Speech! Speech!* (Washington, D.C.: Counterpoint, 2000), 59.

21. Hill, section 1.1, *Scenes from Comus,* 3.

22. He also points to another source of "civil power," namely financial power, which he discusses in relation to issues of trust, in poems highlighting the etymology of the Latin word "*fiducia.*" See for example Geoffrey Hill, "Concerning Inheritance," *Canaan* (Harmondsworth: Penguin, 1996), 70 and section 19 of *Speech! Speech!,* 10.

23. This hypothesis is echoed by Ken Worpole, "Scholarship Boy," in *Bloodaxe Critical Anthologies I: Tony Harrison,* ed. Neil Astley, 61–74: "The whole *School of Eloquence* is about his own class and cultural predicament, obsessively worked over again and again" (71). "Against [social and political] disintegration, [Harrison's *v.*] can only offer [...] the possessive family circle" or an alternative between "betrayal and guilt" or "embracing a new class" (73).

24. T.S. Eliot, "Tradition and the Individual Talent (1919)," *Selected Essays* (London: Faber, 1999, first edition 1932), 13–22.

25. Ibid., 15.

26. Hill, *The Triumph of Love,* section XXVI, 14.

27. For an authoritative presentation of these models, see Rogers Brubaker, *Citizenship and Nationhood in France and Germany* (Cambridge: Harvard University Press, 1992).

28. Edmund Burke and J.G.A. Pocock (eds.), *Reflections on the Revolution in France* (Indianapolis: Hackett, 1987), 173.

29. Tony Harrison, "*v.,*" *Selected Poems* (London: Penguin, 2007, 1987, first edition 1984), 235–249, ll. 66–70.

30. Harrison, "*v.,*" ll. 175–176.

31. For modernist histories, such as Eric J. Hobsbawm's *Nations and Nationalism since 1780: Programme, Myth, Reality* (Cambridge, New York: Cambridge University Press, 1990), nation is a construct made up of artifacts chosen at will; for perennialist accounts, such as Antony D. Smith's *The Ethnic Origin of Nations* (Oxford: Blackwell, 1986), it must have an ethnic core to continue to exist.

32. On the pentameter and other forms of poetry as "national discourse," see Antony Easthope, *Poetry as Discourse* (London: Routledge, 1990, first edition 1983).

33. Peter Sacks, *The English Elegy: Studies in the Genre from Spenser to Yeats* (Baltimore and New York: John Hopkins University Press, 1985), 37.

34. The sense of a renewed identity is such that in W.C. Sellar's and R.J. Yeatman's famous satirical history of Britain *1066 and All That* (London: Methuen, 1999, first edition 1930), Gray's "Elegy in a Country Church-Yard" becomes the rather more invigorating "Gray's *Energy* in the Country Church-Yard" (26). See also Krishan Kumar, *The Making of English National Identity* (Cambridge: Cambridge University Press, 2003) for a discussion of tradition and modernity in the Victorian period.

35. Sacks, *The English Elegy,* 34–37.

36. Thomas Gray, "Sonnet [On the Death of Richard West]" (1775) can be found on the Internet: Alexander Huber (ed.), *The Thomas Gray Archive* (University of Oxford), <http://www.thomasgray.org/cgi-bin/display.cgi?text=sorw>.

Charlotte Smith's *Elegiac Sonnets and Other Poems* in *The Poems of Charlotte Smith*, ed. C. Smith and Stuart Curran (New York, Oxford: Oxford University Press, 1993), 2–126. See also the chapter on the sonnet in Stuart Curran, *Poetic Form and British Romanticism* (New York, Oxford: Oxford University Press), 29–55.

37. Harrison, *Selected Poems*, 112–171. "The Queen's English" is on p. 136.

38. Gordon Jefferson, *Poems from the Yorkshire Dales* (Clapham, North Yorkshire: Dalesman Publishing Co., 1979).

39. See Tusa, "The John Tusa Interviews": "[...] if you scan it properly and not like academics tend to scan poetry [...] you find iambic pentameter on the lips of people the whole time. And I love listening on trains to people speaking unconsciously in the meter that's natural to English speech."

40. Harrison, "On Not Being Milton," *Selected Poems*, 112.

41. Harrison, *Selected Poems*, 169.

42. Worpole makes a similar point about the documentary value of *The School of Eloquence* poems, but to deplore their late publication: "Yet had they been more widely published as they were being written, they would have had a quite different relationship to contemporary critical debate" (73).

43. Sandie Byrne finds little in common between the two elegies. See "On Not Being Milton, Marvell or Gray," *Tony Harrison: Loiner*, ed. S. Byrne (Oxford: Clarenden Press, 1997), 57–84.

44. Thomas Gray, "Elegy Written in a Country Churchyard" (1768) and all its versions and commentaries are available at <http://www.thomasgray.org/cgi-bin/display.cgi?text=elcc>.

45. Blake Morrison, "Under Judgement," *The New Statesman*, 8 Feb. 1980 (212–214), 212.

46. "The Fear," from the sequence "Metamorphoses" in *For the Unfallen, Collected Poems* (Harmondsworth: Penguin, 1985), 32.

47. For an account of religious toleration in Hill's sonnets, see part one of C. Birkan-Berz, *A Fa-*

bled England: Formes poétiques et valeurs nationales dans l'œuvre de Geoffrey Hill (Doctoral Thesis, Université Paris Diderot, 2007).

48. Morrison, "Under Judgement," 212.

49. Kelly Grovier, "Keats and the Holocaust: Notes Towards A Post-Temporalism," *Literature & Theology* 17:4 (2003), 361–373.

50. Phyllis Levin, *The Penguin Book of the Sonnet: 500 Years of a Classic Tradition in English* (London: Penguin, 2002), lxvii. John Lennard, *The Poetry Handbook, Second Edition* (Oxford and New York: Oxford University Press, 2006), 72–74.

51. Hill, *Collected Poems*, 30–31.

52. On "hardening the heart," see Peter McDonald, "Geoffrey Hill's Patience," *Metre* (Spring 2004), 97–108.

53. Hill, *Collected Critical Writings*, 5.

54. In a recent interview, Hill recounted encountering this child's dates of birth and death in an exhibition on Terezin. Anne Mounic, "Le poème, 'moulin mystique': entretien avec Geoffrey Hill," *Temporel* 6 (2008), <http://www.temporel.fr/Le-poeme-moulin-mystique-Entretien>.

55. Hill, *Canaan*, 52.

56. Hill has explained this in the course of many readings, such as the one he gave at Manchester Metropolitan University on February 12, 2006, and in the recording on audio CD *Poetry Reading, Oxford 1st February 2006* (Thame: Clutag Press, 2006).

57. Hill, *A Treatise of Civil Power* (Thame: Clutag Press, 2005), unnumbered page.

58. Ibid.

59. Hill, section 3.15, *Scenes from Comus*, 64.

60. M.H. Abrams, *Natural Supernaturalism: Tradition and Revolution in Romantic Literature* (New York: W.N. Norton, 1971), 12; quoted in Richard Eldridge, *The Persistence of Romanticism: Essays in Philosophy and Literature* (Cambridge: Cambridge University Press, 2001), 4.

61. See Eldridge, *The Persistence of Romanticism*, 11.

WORKS CITED

Abrams, M.H. (1971). *Natural Supernaturalism: Tradition and Revolution in Romantic Literature*. New York: W.W. Norton.

Allott, Kenneth (1962, first edition 1950). *The Penguin Book of Contemporary Verse*. Harmondsworth: Penguin.

Astley, Neil (ed.) (1991). *Bloodaxe Critical Anthologies I: Tony Harrison*. Newcastle: Bloodaxe.

Birkan-Berz, Carole (2007). *A Fabled England: Formes poétiques et valeurs nationales dans l'œuvre de Geoffrey Hill*. Doctoral Thesis. Université Paris Diderot.

Brock, Edwin, Geoffrey Hill, and Stevie Smith (1966). *Penguin Modern Poets 8*. Harmondsworth: Penguin.

Brubaker, Rogers (1992). *Citizenship and Nationhood in France and Germany*. Cambridge: Harvard University Press.

Burke, Edmund, Pocock J.G.A. (ed.) (1987). *Reflections on the Revolution in France*. Indianapolis: Hackett.

Byrne, Sandie (1997). "On Not Being Milton, Marvell or Gray." *Tony Harrison: Loiner*. Ed. S. Byrne. Oxford: Clarenden Press, 57–84.

Curran, Stuart (1986). *Poetic Form and British Romanticism.* New York and Oxford: Oxford University Press.

Easthope, Antony (1990; first edition 1983). *Poetry as Discourse.* London: Routledge.

Eldridge, Richard (2001). *The Persistence of Romanticism: Essays in Philosophy and Literature.* Cambridge: Cambridge University Press.

Eliot, T.S. (1999; first edition 1932). "Tradition and the Individual Talent (1919)." *Selected Essays* (London: Faber), 13–22.

Gray, Thomas (1768). "Elegy Written in a Country Churchyard." *The Thomas Gray Archive.* University of Oxford. <http://www.thomasgray.org/cgi-bin/display.cgi?text=elcc>.

_____ (1775). "Sonnet [On the Death of Richard West]." *The Thomas Gray Archive.* University of Oxford. <http://www.thomasgray.org/cgi-bin/display.cgi?text=sorw>.

Grovier, Kelly (2003). "Keats and the Holocaust: Notes Towards A Post-Temporalism." *Literature & Theology* 17: 4, 361–373.

Haffenden, John (1981). *Viewpoints: Poets in Conversation.* London: Faber, 76–99.

Harrison, Sophie (1998). "Monitor: Picking poets — what the world's newspapers say about the next Laureate." *The Independent on Sunday* (8 Nov). London.

Harrison, Tony (1987; first edition 1984). "*v.*" *Selected Poems.* London: Penguin, 235–249.

_____ (2000). *Laureate's Block and Other Poems.* London: Penguin.

Hill, Geoffrey (1985). *For the Unfallen, Collected Poems.* Harmondsworth: Penguin.

_____ (1996). *Canaan.* Harmondsworth: Penguin.

_____ (1998). *The Triumph of Love.* Boston: Houghton Mifflin.

_____ (2000). *Speech! Speech!.* Washington, D.C.: Counterpoint.

_____ (2001). "A Matter of Timing." *The Guardian* (21 Sept.). <http://www.guardian.co.uk/books/2002/sep/21/featuresreviews.guardianreview28>.

_____ (2002). *The Orchards of Syon.* Harmondsworth: Penguin.

_____ (2005). *Scenes from Comus.* London: Penguin.

_____ (2005). *A Treatise of Civil Power.* Thame: Clutag Press.

_____ (2006). *Poetry Reading, Oxford 1st February 2006.* Audio CD. Thame: Clutag Press.

_____ (2007). Untitled contribution, Poets and Philosophy panel. *Poetry and Philosophy Conference.* University of Warwick, Coventry (26 October).

The Holy Bible, King James version, Electronic Text Center, University of Virginia Library <http://etext.virginia.edu/toc/modeng/public/KjvDeut.html>.

Hobsbawm, Eric J. (1990). *Nations and Nationalism since 1780: Programme, Myth, Reality.* Cambridge and New York: Cambridge University Press.

Huk, Romana (1991). "Tony Harrison, *The Loiners* and the 'Leeds Renaissance.'" *Bloodaxe Critical Anthologies I: Tony Harrison.* Ed. Neil Astley. Newcastle: Bloodaxe, 75–83.

_____ (1996). "Poetry of the Committed Individual: Jon Silkin, Tony Harrison, Geoffrey Hill, and the Poets of Postwar Leeds." *Contemporary British Poetry: Essays in Theory and Criticism.* Ed. James Acheson and Romana Huk. New York: SUNY Press.

Ingelbien, Raphaël (2002). *Misreading England: Poetry and Nationhood since the Second World War.* Amsterdam and New York: Rodopi.

Jefferson, Gordon (1979). *Poems from the Yorkshire Dales.* Clapham, North Yorkshire: Dalesman Publishing Co.

Kumar, Krishan (2003). *The Making of English National Identity.* Cambridge: Cambridge University Press.

Lennard, John (2005). *The Poetry Handbook.* Second Edition. Oxford and New York: Oxford University Press.

Levin, Phyllis (2002). *The Penguin Book of the Sonnet: 500 Years of a Classic Tradition in English.* London: Penguin.

Lyon, John (2007). "'Que voulez-vous incinérer'? Geoffrey Hill et la culture populaire." *La Poésie de Geoffrey Hill et la modernité.* Ed. Jennifer Kilgore–Caradec and René Gallet. Paris: L'Harmattan, 117–135. [French version of "'What are you incinerating?': Geoffrey Hill and popular culture." *English* 54:209 (2005, 85–98)].

McDonald, Peter (2004). "Geoffrey Hill's Patience." *Metre* (Spring), 97–108.

Morrish, John (1999). "Much rhyme, little reason." *The Independent* (18 Apr.), 17.

Morrison, Blake (1980). "Under Judgement." *The New Statesman* (8 Feb.), 212–214.

Motion, Andrew, and Morrison, Blake (eds.) (1982). *The Penguin Book of Contemporary British Poetry.* London: Penguin.

Mounic, Anne (2008). "Le poème, 'moulin mystique': entretien avec Geoffrey Hill." *Temporel,* 6. <http://www.temporel.fr/Le-poeme-moulin-mystique-Entretien>.

The Oxford English Dictionary. 2d ed. 1989. *OED* Online. Oxford University Press. Term cited: "public."

Phillips, Carl (2000). "The Art of Poetry LXXX: Geoffrey Hill." *The Paris Review,* 42:154, 272–299.

Sacks, Peter (1985). *The English Elegy: Studies in the Genre from Spenser to Yeats.* Baltimore and New York: John Hopkins University Press.

Sellar, W.C., and R.J. Yeatman (1999, first edition 1930). *1066 and All That.* London: Methuen.

Silkin, Jon (1973). *Poetry of the Committed Individual: A Stand Anthology of Poetry.* London: Gollancz.

Smith, Antony D. (1986). *The Ethnic Origin of Nations.* Oxford: Blackwell.

Smith, Charlotte (1993). *The Poems of Charlotte Smith.* Ed. Stuart Curran. New York and Oxford: Oxford University Press.

Tusa, John (2001). "The John Tusa Interviews: Transcript of the John Tusa Interview with Tony Harrison" <http://www.bbc.co.uk/radio3/john tusainterview/harrison_transcript.shtml>.

Worpole, Ken (1991). "Scholarship Boy." *Bloodaxe Critical Anthologies I: Tony Harrison.* Ed. Neil Astley. Newcastle: Bloodaxe, 61–74.

Wroe, Nicholas (2000). "Tony Harrison: Man of Mysteries." *The Guardian* (1 Apr.) <http://www.guardian.co.uk/books/2000/apr/01/poetry.theatre>.

13. Geoffrey Hill: "A public nuisance"

Emily Taylor Merriman

The situation of a flawed individual, writing poetry for an imperfect society that does not read him much, has emotionally and intellectually possessed Geoffrey Hill. The mismatch between the poet's private ambitions and the public's unresponsiveness has long occupied his thought. One measure of the extent of this concern is the index to the *Collected Critical Writings* (2008), which gives fifteen cross-references to "public" and "private," as well as further individual references to each. Hill's writings abound with allusions to other authors' comments on the subject, and both his prose and poetry demonstrate the enmeshedness of the private and the public realms while resisting their conflation.

Although for the sake of self-preservation, a poet may understandably wish to retreat from a public sphere in which poetic value is not recognized, Hill maintains a tortuous commitment to public service in the area of a poet's expertise: language. As René Gallet has said, Hill has a "personal passion" for the "common good" that is language itself.[1] Kevin Hart has similarly declared, before introducing the topic of Hill's love for the English language, "he is deeply concerned with our common well being, in public and private life, to evoke a distinction that he would rightly deem to be divided and equivocal."[2] Early evidence of Hill's long commitment to public service can be found in what his headmaster, W.P. Baron, wrote in support of his English Exhibition at Keble College in 1950: "He is a public spirited boy of very good character and has done a great deal of good work for the School." The headmaster also noted, "He is a good worker and has a distinct flair for music and poetry."[3] Whatever one's commitment to public service, however, a contemporary worker in literature must participate in institutions (universities, publishers, bookstores) that often seek to generate private wealth. These institutions become part of the circumstances that exert control over poetry's form and audience.

Hill has taught in both public and private institutions, and his poems are produced for consumption and some, if perhaps little, profit by the private publishing houses of Western print-capitalism.

Especially from *Canaan* (1996) onwards, Hill contemplates intimate selfhood's complex interactions with the historical body politic from various angles, and he laments that the poet's voice is not more publicly heard and attended to. As in the excerpt from *The Orchards of Syon* section VII borrowed for my title — "at some / personal cost a public nuisance" — Hill mourns the sacrifices that the poet must make to be heard and received even by his tiny public. He implies that the result of all the poet's stubborn endeavors is to disturb only slightly the apparent peace of a society riddled with injustice. As he summarizes his own perspective in a 2008 piece on "Civil Polity and the Confessing State": "I have affirmed my belief that 'poetry is inextricably bound into the purpose and function of civil polity.' I have also conceded my incapacity to suggest how any real 'purchase' (a Burkean word) of poetry on polity might be achieved."[4]

The traffic across the public-private divide, as Hill sees it, moves both ways. Not only do "[o]ur private thoughts have public consequences and obligations," as he has declared in prose,[5] but human beings' thoughts and actions are constructed by public forces in ways that are mostly ignored. Writing of how commentators on John Ransom have demonstrated "understandable and proper reluctance to show the scars of the private man," Hill ponders, even isolating the word privacy in quotation marks: "But what is this 'privacy' of ours, whether of the intellect or of the passions?" In response to himself, he cites George Eliot's saying in *Felix Holt*: "'there is no private life that has not been determined by a wider public life.'"[6] Hill maintains a painful awareness that the individual life is not merely influenced by forces more powerful than the single human being, but that the "human being" is actually to some extent constituted by those forces. Nonetheless, human beings typically inhabit imagined enclaves of self-determination and individual autonomy that may — in the end — not be entirely illusory. Not given to submissive conformism, Hill is also invested in the notion that the self can assert its individuality by "Crying *What I do is me: for that I came*," like Hopkins's every being.[7]

Hill constitutes a striking exception to sociologist C. Wright Mills's assertion that "men do not usually define the troubles they endure in terms of historical change and institutional contradiction."[8] Hill's later poetry is an exemplary literary instance of what Mills calls "the sociological imagination," that is, "the capacity to range from the most impersonal and remote transformations to the most intimate features of the human self—and to see the relations between the two."[9] Hill does not rule out the influence of individual personality, psychological makeup, physical and chemical constitution, and the consequences of particular relationships, but he is painfully conscious that the private human being is an historical human being; even such intimate and personal matters as clothing, habitation, hygiene, and food — things that affect quality of life every day — are at stake in that historical formation. Highlighting one reason why the preoccupations of Hill's poetry make it outstanding as well as often difficult to understand, Mills's 1959 text (which is often excerpted in sociology textbooks) continues:

> Seldom aware of the intricate connection between the patterns of their own lives and the course of world history, ordinary men [a group label that begs further definition] do not usually know what this connection means for the kinds of men they are becoming and for the kinds of history-making in which they might take part. They do not possess the quality of mind essential to grasp the interplay of man and society, of biography and history, of self and world.[10]

Although Mills's argument could be heard as patronizing or elitist (as Hill's sometimes is also), his work has been influential in Marxist-inflected sociology. It is possible in Mills's view for people to develop the quality of mind that would enable them "to grasp the interplay of man and society, of biography and history, of self and world" (as in feminist consciousness-raising in the seventies; the argument that "the personal is political" is at the heart of Mills's text). There are many forces at work in this interplay, including politics, economics, social structures, law, media, health care, education, war, religion and even language itself. No single human being could grasp these complexities entirely, but Hill struggles consciously to grapple with them as fully as he can. In this struggle, he exempts himself from Mills's category of "ordinary men" and pressures his readers into similar exemption.

Mills's work has laid a broad and well-followed path in sociology, but I have no evidence that Hill ever read him. His thoughts on the topic of the public-private divide appear to arise from older sources and from his own emotional and intellectual struggles, which are sometimes laid bare in rhetorical questions. Pondering how human beings' class status (here marked by physical appearance) determines social roles and attitudes, the speaker of *The Mystery of the Charity of Charles Péguy* asks:

> But who are "we," since history is law,
> Clad in our skins of silver, steel and hide,
> Or in our rags, with rotten teeth askew,
> Heroes or knaves as Clio shall decide?[11]

Hill's simultaneous emphasis upon and questioning of "we" highlights the first person plural pronoun's capacity to include and to exclude. People find themselves part of, or apart from, specific communities, which may be communities of luxury, violence, or poverty. These communities remain inter-dependent, but their individual members are scarcely empowered to cross social divides, nor can they break down the structures that maintain wealth's violent complicity in poverty. The poem's attention to barriers to human self-determination places human beings very close to other animal beings. By describing human dress in animal terms ("skins" and "hide") and even in metallic ones ("steel" and "silver"), Hill suggests that the very nature of our humanity is at stake in the relationship between public and private. To have a sense of private self-determined individuality is a human characteristic, but Hill asks, to what degree is that sense an illusion?

Hill's grappling with this issue becomes more self-conscious and publicly acknowledged over time. Tom Clark, reviewing *The Triumph of Love*, hears a new tone in the 1998 volume: "Here the poet speaks of public life in a private voice, candid, personal and surprisingly self-revealing." Hill also speaks of private life — the self's feelings and experiences — in a public voice. His poetry is saturated with this awkward but productive sense of speaking both publicly and privately at once. In *The Triumph of Love*, he describes a classical rhetorical mode that the long poem itself adopts, *laus et vituperatio* (praise and blame): "public, forensic, / yet with a vehement / private ambition for the people's greater good."[12] One might legitimately ask: in what sense is this publicly announced ambition "private"? Also, what constitutes the "greater good" is a question of political contestation. Read simply, Hill's speaker is merely declaring one of his motivations to be a deep personal interest in the general well-being of the entire population. Although this is not on its own terms objectionable, it is neither sufficient nor necessary as a motivation for a potential reader to spend money on a book of poetry or even to borrow one from a public library.

Yet this text is full of heckling voices that interject and interrupt the harangue of the main speaker. Such disruptions ensure that the poem never feels entirely private, even though at moments the speaker dramatizes communing with himself: "Even now, I tell myself...."[13] Several instances of such interruptions insult the poet: "Shameless old man, bent on committing / more public nuisance."[14] This idea of the poet as a public nuisance lodged itself in Hill's imagination, to reappear later in *The Orchards of Syon*. Here, in *The Triumph of Love*, he combines intimations of impropriety, criminality, and even perversity with the virtue of stalwart, resolute determination. Morally speaking, the adjective "bent" inclines both down toward shame and up toward commitment. As he often does, Hill himself is bending his ethical and verbal pitch downwards — and, because words can do this although musical notes cannot, upwards at the same time. The use of the term "bent" here draws our attention unusually strongly toward this linguistic feat. The *OED* defines the term "bent" in a musical, specifically jazz, context as "To alter the pitch of (a note, etc.) upwards or downwards to create a deliberately distorted tone."[15] Such distortions, analogously speaking, are a trademark of Hill's middle poetic style. When such effects are brought to bear on many of the words and allusions of a poem, and on their mutual interactions, the poetry becomes difficult to follow semantically. For Hill such difficulty proffers resistance to the linguistic simplifications of tyranny, but for many readers it can make the poem seem to belong to a private club, from which they have been excluded.

Speech! Speech!, the volume between *The Triumph of Love* and *The Orchards of Syon*, concerns itself especially with the linguistic dimension of the public/private dialectic. The blurbs on the 2003 paperback Counterpoint edition, replacing those of the hardback from 2000, have been selected to reflect the book's interest in the relationship between the poet and the public.[16] *The Evening Standard* declares that Hill "assaults the emptiness of public discourse to which we have become accustomed." Rachel Polonsky in *The Daily Telegraph* states that the poem "enacts the 'death-struggle' in which poet and public are bound to engage."[17] An anonymous commentator demands, "With our minds and ears relentlessly fouled by degraded public speech — by media hype, insipid sermons, hollow political rhetoric, and the ritual misuse of words — how do we even begin to think and speak honestly?" David Bromwich from *The New York Times Book Review* similarly speaks of the poem's "horror and outrage," its "contempt of a public language that has become sheer detritus." Either Hill himself ("ritual misuse of words" sounds like Hill), or someone in Counterpoint's marketing department, is eager to underscore this long poem's attempt to reveal the supposedly dire state of public language, and to emphasize its keen effort to begin a vigorous cleansing of the words and even the grammar that now oil the operations of commodity capitalism. Yet language also constitutes the most comprehensive means of communication available in our relationships with loved ones, friends, colleagues, and enemies, and whatever the inaccessible features of Hill's work, it does not enact a withdrawal from community.

The feelings of disgust suggested by the terms of the preceding paragraph might imply a conservative, even authoritarian stance on the part of the poet (like Eliot's or Swift's), but the situation with Hill is not so straightforward. A desire for linguistic purification (especially when it is associated with "the tribe," as in *Four Quartets*) has its dangers: absolute purity requires absolute control, which is the essence of fascism. Hill's poetry, however, is aware of the risks and the ridiculousness of its rage for order. The verse is also not prudish; Hill associates his poetic creations with some of the most typically private activities of the physical body: urination, defecation, farting, picking scabs, childbirth, and sex. Such a dwelling upon bodily functions is a typical vein in the satirical tradition, part of how writers such as Pope, Swift, Smollett, Sterne and Hill deflate the pomposity of human beings by reminding us that we are full of shit. To cite just a few examples, after *The Triumph of Love's* "Shameless old man, bent on committing / more public nuisance," the poem identifies the nature of that nuisance: "Incontinent / fury wetting the air." In calmer but still caustic self-commentary, *Speech! Speech!* narrates the creation of the poem as if it were an evacuation of the bowels: "He voids each twelve-line block | a head / solemnly breaking water."[18] The same volume declares "Could keep this úp all night / rigid with *joie de vivre*"[19]; here, and elsewhere, there is particular insistence on sexual stamina. The opening section of *The Orchards of Syon* also refers to how long the speaker can "prolong the act."[20] Hill insists on these punning insertions of private physical activities into the public sphere of the published volume of poetry. By means of these bawdy displays, he makes the inappropriate singularly appropriate to his purposes. Like an exhibitionistic flasher, the poet seeks shock value from such indecent exposures, although less out of a desire for self-gratification than out of a yearning to be attended to and given time to make a worthwhile contribution. As the perceived line between sexual aggression and sexual generosity, or between pain and pleasure, may depend on the cognitions of the recipient, so Hill's poetic persistence and his male, rather British, raunchiness may be experienced by the reader as violations of propriety and morality, or as energetic gifts.

In the essay "Common Weal, Common Woe" (1989), Hill ascribes "protean energy" to the word "private" in the seventeenth century.[21] In his own writing, both that word and the word "public" manifest a similar energy. Hill deliberately worries away at the poet's divided consciousness and demonstrates how the private man becomes a "public nuisance." Echoing with a twist Hopkins's "O unteachably after evil, but uttering truth" ("The Wreck of the Deutschland"), section VII of *The Orchards of Syon* declares that the "human spirit" is "incorrigible" but also:

> cogent, unreadable, and at some
> personal cost a public nuisance:
> not ineradicable but not soon
> put down or uprooted.[22]

The notion of being "at some / personal cost a public nuisance" — like a resistant weed, as the trope elaborates — applies to the poet's unrewarded, expended effort to be heard and heeded, as well as to his own consequent deafness to his would-be audience, who are deaf to him.

The concept of "public nuisance" may have personal significance for Hill. As a village police constable, his father likely dealt with instances of public nuisance, which the *Oxford Dictionary of Law Enforcement* defines as "An activity or state of affairs that interferes [...] with the health, safety, or comfort of the public at large." It constitutes a crime that "includes such activities as raves, obstruction of the highway, carrying on an offensive trade, and selling food unfit for human consumption."[23] Much of Hill's poetry is more of a rant than a rave, and more of a tirade than a trade. While his work may be designed to interfere with the comfort of a complacent public, the poet is not likely to be prosecuted under these regulations. Nonetheless, a law textbook describes the statutes surrounding public nuisance as an "intellectual mess," "an amorphous and unsatisfactory area of the law covering an ill-assorted collection of wrongs."[24]

Perhaps because public nuisance is such a messy area of the law, since the 1930s there have been few cases of its use in practice in Great Britain. Michael R. Anderson argues that the situation was different in the colonies, however, where "convictions for public nuisance... [represent] the most frequent and systematic application of police power under colonial rule."[25] In a poetic usage that suggests awareness of this practice, Derek Walcott, a poet of Hill's generation, asks in *Omeros*: "When are our brood, like the sparrows, a public nuisance?"[26] In the context of this section of Walcott's poem, "our brood" suggests both people of color, especially immigrants to England, and also poets, who are often represented by birds in Walcott. Set in London, the section of *Omeros* that this line comes from repeatedly juxtaposes as well as blurs a private but unspecified and ambiguous "we" with violent public powers. For instance, the "red double-decker" that Londoners and tourists take is juxtaposed with the "Bloody Tower" of London, and the sugar in our cups of tea is associated with "our crystals of sweat."[27] Walcott thus underscores that even human beings' private moments of relaxation or refreshment are not divorced from the public realities of politics and the exploitative division of labor. As in the section from Hill's *The Mystery of the Charity of Charles Péguy* discussed above, Walcott draws attention to the problematic nature of "we": to which groups of exploiters and the exploited do "we" belong? Yet even though this epic of Walcott's has won the Nobel Prize, the most prestigious literary award in the world, can *Omeros* be said to be an active participant in global discourse, an agent for change in the direction of economic and social justice?

In the contemporary developed world, despite globalization, the directions and distances traveled by poetry's resonances are limited, at least in comparison to popular music, video games, or even literary fiction, and the poet himself chafes against those confines and their painful implications for his own sense of selfhood and purpose. Asked in an interview about how he sees his readership, Hill responded, "When I see my half-yearly royalties statements

I seem not to have a readership at all," but he also acknowledged a very well-attended poetry reading in Oxford in 2006 and the older people who sometimes bring him his entire oeuvre to sign at readings: "There are obviously devoted readers, but it's all rather subterranean, a bit like wartime resistance. When you ask about 'public role' you have to take into account this aspect also."[28] Given such a limited audience, poetry scarcely falls under the category of public nuisance, which, according to an oft-quoted legal ruling, must be "so widespread in its range or so indiscriminate in its effect that it would not be reasonable to expect one person to take proceedings on his own responsibility to put a stop to it, but that it should be taken on the responsibility of the community at large."[29] If the community at large is not attending to poetry, what is the poet's responsibility to his community — especially when he finds himself alienated by "communities of opinion," the phrase Hill borrows from Emerson in order to describe this phenomenon?[30]

Those responsibilities begin with his responsibility for himself—which, paradoxically, turns out to necessitate freedom from the bondage of self. The ironic modes and the atheistic religious intensity of J.V. Cunningham (1911–1985) withstand some worthwhile comparison with Hill. In the sentences preceding the prose material quoted below, Cunningham speaks philosophically in terms of "subjective" and "objective," a divide that bears some relation to, but is not co-equivalent with, "private" and "public." Both oppositions offer possible ways of describing the interaction between the sensing self and the wider world. Cunningham defines the poet's task:

> [To be successful in the enterprise of writing] is the conquest of solipsism, the dramatic conflict of self with, on the one hand, reality in all its objectivity and potentiality, and, on the other, with philology in its old and general sense: or, with private and with public history.[31]

This "conquest of solipsism"—or Cunningham's phrase in apposition, "the dramatic conflict of self" with reality and philology — aptly headlines much of what Hill's poetry performs. The poet's implicit hope is that out of this enacted conflict some change may occur. With a deeper understanding of how history and social structures mould our private lives (as Mills argues and Hill suggests that they do), partly through language, the individual's psyche can be changed, and the individual may then have greater power in the world at least to name and seek to confront these shaping forces. For example, as Stephen James asserts, "If one conceives of authority merely in terms of direct agency in the public sphere, then the poem is liable to be dismissed as irrelevant," but the commanding linguistic and rhetorical strengths of some poets enable them to write poetry that speaks "of and to the public realm in a persuasive, memorable manner."[32]

In overtly bringing to our attention such possible enablings, Hill sometimes speaks as if privately, even *sotto voce*, to the reader through the public
medium of the poem. The first two lines of the following excerpt from *The
Triumph of Love* sound like oratory, or lecture; the second two lines sound like
informal conversation:

> *Active virtue*: that which shall contain
> its own passion in the public weal —
> do you follow? — or can you at least take
> the drift of the thing?[33]

The same section announces a faith in poetry as means of social engagement,
perhaps even as an agent for change: "Still, I'm convinced that shaping, / Voicing, are types of civic action." *Without Title* (2006) similarly claims, adding
the necessity and reality of endurance: "Poetry's a public act by long engagement."[34] *A Treatise of Civil Power* (2007) is arguably the most public and the
most private of his works to date. Much of it ostensibly concerns the private
activity of reading to oneself, but the reading material discussed (as the reader
privately discovers) covers public matters and even the poet's role in those
public matters.[35]

In fact *power*— civil and personal — is what is most evidently at stake in
the semi-permeable divide between public and private in Hill's poetry. Hill
attempts to alter the power dynamics in the relationship between public and
private in two ways. First, he seeks to render the circumstances of the individual's life less unconsciously circumscribed by determining social forces. Second, he wants to equip the individual to participate actively in historical
change — but not in self- or family-interest, as is so often the case in politics.
In "Improvisations for Hart Crane," Hill describes an image (perhaps a photograph in the newspaper or a clip from the television news) that shows how
the spheres of public and private can be wrongfully reversed: the power to
make war has been hermetically sealed within a self-interested circle, while
the numinousness of governmental power is grandly displayed in a kind of
privates on parade:

> ...the National
> Guard at stand-to, half-tamed weaponry;
> the Chief's advisors, unsexed white and black,
> good with binoculars and shown to be so;
> their photo-faces lit with simple purpose,
> their public selves the sanctum, the arcane;
> their privacy the secrets of events;
> the keys of war bestowed like a small heirloom
> of sentimental value to the clan.[36]

The title announces that the main topic of this poem is an American poet, and in this section, the American government. But the United States polis now impinges on private lives across the globe. The binoculars signify, by way of synecdoche, the government's ability to intrude on people's privacy in the supposed interests of international public security.

It is not surprising that a poem in angry homage to Hart Crane stimulates Hill's consideration of the public and the private. In "Hart Crane's Poetics of Privacy," Tim Dean sees the closeted nature of homosexuality in a homophobic society as catalytic to the intensity of Crane's poetry. In Dean's analysis, Crane's poetic resistance to the social circumstances of enforced privacy for homosexuality leads to the alternative "hermeneutic privacy" of Crane's verse.[37] The reader's experience of privacy is informed by his or her encounter with Crane's commitment to an intensely liberating, ecstatic experience beyond that of sexual activity, in or out of the closet. Hence, perhaps, Hill's feeling of having been "screwed" by Crane and his "zany epic," which may at times break down "hegemonic constructions of sexuality and subjectivity," as Dean argues,[38] but which leaves his poetic inheritors without a public podium. In his own "Improvisations for Hart Crane," Hill also likely has in mind Robert Lowell's sonnet "Words for Hart Crane," which indicts an American culture whose public literary accolades rain upon the undeserving, not upon Crane, the failed prophet, "the Shelley of my age," as Lowell's poem has Crane call himself.[39]

The notion of the poet as a modern-day prophet or Socrates-like philosopher, condemned by the majority as a public nuisance, haunts Hill's work. Solitary but cognizant of his predecessors, such a poet stands at a crossroads between poetry, history, philosophy, and religion. The overarching title of a sequence of Hill's critical essays that address these issues at depth is "Alienated Majesty," a phrase borrowed from Ralph Waldo Emerson's essay on "Self-Reliance." Hill declares, "Emerson's genius, basically and substantially understood, is in the perception of this dislocation of public and private."[40] Hill expands on the theme by demonstrating how this dislocation brings about the exclusion of Emerson's God, the personal "Deity," from "places of civic power." In this social and theological analysis, Hill approaches more closely to where his own genius lies: for Hill, questions of religion are also inextricably linked to the public-private divide. Popular modern opinion holds religious belief to be simply a matter of personal choice, but this notion demonstrates the kind of sociological naïveté identified by C. Wright Mills. Brian Phillips negatively distinguishes Hill from John Donne and George Herbert, claiming that their work "does have religious aspirations, but the aspirations involve, at most, the hope of a merely private efficacy," while Hill errs in seeking the redemption of others too.[41] Whether or not Phillips is right about Donne and Herbert, Hill is writing at a time when the religious atmosphere of Great Britain is much altered from that of the early seventeenth century, and he is convinced that private beliefs and aspirations are not formed in a sphere free from dominant public ideas and common actions.

In demonstrating that Whitman's philosophy of poetic spontaneity comes from Ralph Waldo Emerson, Hill quotes Emerson on how the poet or orator finds that his inmost thoughts, recorded, speak for others: "the deeper he dives into his privatest, secretest presentiment, to his wonder he finds, this is the most acceptable, most public, and universally true."[42] *And yet, the poet is often not heard.* Even when poetry enters the political realm, as when the British government decides on a Poet Laureate, or when a poet is invited to read at a presidential inauguration, the public attitude, if there is one, is often either prurient or patronizing. When the President of the United States was spotted with a volume of Derek Walcott's *Collected Poems 1948–1984* under his arm, the *Telegraph*'s headline suggested that this was a matter of leisure not legislation: "Barack Obama still has time for a little poetry."[43]

Since the advent of high literary modernism, the forms of poetry have often proved off-putting to readers, and poets cannot be absolved of all responsibility for their own lack of an audience. Even if one goes further back in literary history, Blake's coded opacity does come across as rather mad; Dickinson's punctuation does seem unpublishably eccentric in the context of the poems of her peers; and the form of Hopkins's "The Wreck of the Deutschland," as public a poem as it undoubtedly is, would have proved profoundly and unpleasantly mystifying to the audience of the Jesuit journal *The Month*, which rejected it. To what extent should poets adapt their style in order to make their poetry accessible to more people? William Logan in a *New York Times* book review of *A Treatise of Civil Power* declares, "Hill has made brutally plain that the common reader is of no interest to him."[44] Later that same year, in a lecture in France, Hill hotly disputes this claim as libelous and quotes from his own prose to support his counterargument.[45] Yet if few people can grasp what his poetry is saying or doing, and he knows it but keeps writing in impenetrable ways, Hill's grounds for grievance in bemoaning his verses' lack of public significance can seem legitimate only from a strongly sympathetic perspective.

Other poets have argued that poetry can gain public power from the intensification and transformation of the poet's life. Hill's quotation of Emerson — "the deeper he dives into his privatest, secretest presentiment, to his wonder he finds, this is the most acceptable, most public, and universally true" — bears remarkable similarity to remarks by T.S. Eliot, at either side of whom Hill and Emerson form a line of reactive influence across two centuries. The final stanza of Eliot's "A Note on War Poetry" (1942) defines poetry as the sublimation of the "private" into the "universal."[46] This recaps in verse his earlier declaration in "Shakespeare and the Stoicism of Seneca" (1927) that the whole, difficult substance of a poet's life (with Shakespeare as an example, and borrowing Shakespeare's language in *The Tempest*) is nothing less than "to transmute his personal and private agonies into something rich and strange, something universal and impersonal."[47] The transmutation of the passions into artistic material is also at the heart of Eliot's earlier, highly influential essay, "Tradition and the Individual Talent."

Versions or revisions of Eliot's views on this topic frequently appear in twentieth-century poetics. The quotation from J.V. Cunningham about the conquest of solipsism discussed above provides one example. Derek Walcott has said, "the more particular you get, the more universal you become."[48] Another Caribbean poet, Jean "Binta" Breeze, has written of "a work so simple in its truth and in its details that it becomes as big as the universe."[49] To prove the impersonality, let alone the universality, of Eliot's, Hill's, Walcott's, Breeze's or anyone's poetry would require many pages of demonstration and argumentation, and even then the jury would be deadlocked. Nonetheless, these quotations reveal what a poet may think he or she is directly or indirectly aiming for in his or her practice.

Hill's poetry demands to be public, and rails against the fact that it is not more publicly noticed. As he says in "Alienated Majesty: Walt Whitman," "Desiring above all things to be understood, to be received, the great poet finds that he is not understood, not received."[50] In some of Hill's own poetry the effects of this perceived injustice are indecorous and sometimes downright unpleasant — like a child who refuses to stop using his outside voice indoors — and Hill knows it. He expresses resentment of other poets, criticizes his critics, and often swings away from modes of praise, or evocations of the beauty of nature, to condemnation of others or to the usually private obsession of self-excoriation. It can get ugly. These aesthetic sacrifices mirror in distorted form the sacrifices in ego satisfaction that result from writing poetry that meets so much passive, and occasionally active, rejection. Yet there is a power that comes from the anger, and it is not the only driving force of the poetry. Hill does not rail impotently, for in his persevering insistence on an intensely personal mode of public address, poetry asserts its own eccentric value, its own "alienated majesty" (to use Hillian terms). It pitches its private tent on the common if shifting ground of language, a ground that centralized public forces have no choice but to share, nuisance or not.

The poetry is conscious of sharing that ground with other poets whose compositions have found their way to the limelight. In *The Triumph of Love*, Hill writes of Eugenio Montale (for whom the later *Without Title* is written in homage). The speaker, briefly in the voice of the critic, notes that Montale's "private, marginal, uncommitted writing" has become famous (Montale won the Nobel Prize in 1975), and that the public life documented in Montale's journalism acts as "the anteroom to the presence-chamber / of self-containment." This figure of speech reverses the usual understanding of privacy as primary, something out of which the individual emerges to engage with the wider sphere of community (or impersonality or universality). In its stead stands a vision of the public life as a place that precedes an inviolate realm of personhood, one of equivalent importance. This supremely valuable psychological space is guarded by the hyphens of "presence-chamber" and "self-containment," while the line break after "presence-chamber" allows the purely private space to feel expansive, not claustrophobic. Yet the poem soon acknowledges that such experiences are not universal, and again, that "we" the public are most united by our shared subjection to forces greater than ourselves: "But one man's privacy is another's / crowded *at home*—we are that circumscribed."[51]

Few, if any, contemporary poets act as consciously concerned with the public-private divide as Geoffrey Hill. For him, it is the multi-dimensional field of human power and powerlessness in which literature wishes to play seriously. In the interests of fair play, and because it is so often excluded from the bigger games, his poetry sometimes even tries to referee, only to become angry that no-one heeds the poet's whistle when he calls a foul, including the fouls against himself, or even his own annoying fouls of fury. The poems are at their best, however, when they fit Hill's recently stated, and surprisingly Romantic poetics, playing defense for the human capacity to envision things as other than they are: "The public role of the poem is to be a stronghold of the imagination."[52]

Notes

1. René Gallet, "Les mots, le silence et la qualification de la poésie," *La Poésie de Geoffrey Hill et la modernité*, ed. Jennifer Kilgore-Caradec and René Gallet (Paris: L'Harmattan, 2007, 169–182), 169.

2. Kevin Hart, "Contra Tyrannos," Review of *A Treatise of Civil Power*, *Notre Dame Review* 26 (Summer/Fall 2008), 247.

3. W.P. Baron, Worcestershire Education Committee, 9 March 1950, Keble College, ref. KC/MEM 2 A1/43.

4. Geoffrey Hill, "Civil Polity and the Confessing State," *The Warwick Review* 2:2 (June 2008), 10.

5. Geoffrey Hill, "Alienated Majesty: Gerard M. Hopkins," *Collected Critical Writings* (Oxford: Oxford University Press, 2008, 518–531), 501.

6. Geoffrey Hill, "What Devil Has Got into John Ransom," *Collected Critical Writings* (Oxford: Oxford University Press, 2008, 127–145), 129, quoting Eliot, *Felix Holt the Radical*, 129. See also George Eliot at the end of *Middlemarch*: "For there is no creature whose inward being is so strong that it is not greatly determined by what lies outside it" (London: Penguin, 1994), 838.

7. G.M. Hopkins, "(As kingfishers catch fire)," *Gerard Manley Hopkins: The Major Works*, ed. Catherine Phillips (Oxford: Oxford University Press, 1986), 129.

8. C. Wright Mills, *The Sociological Imagination* (New York: Oxford University Press, 1959), 3.

9. Ibid., 7.

10. Ibid., 3–4.

11. Hill, Section 6, *The Mystery of the Charity of Charles Péguy, Selected Poems*, 129.

12. Hill, section XXVI, *The Triumph of Love* (Boston: Houghton Mifflin, 1998), 14.

13. Ibid., section XXXV, 18.

14. Ibid., section XXXVII, 19.

15. "Bent" ppl. a. *Oxford English Dictionary Online*.

16. Geoffrey Hill, *Speech! Speech!* (Washington, D.C.: Counterpoint, 2003), back matter.

17. Rachel Polonsky, "Puns, puzzles and dirty jokes," *Evening Standard* 12 November 2001 <http://www.thisislondon.co.uk/showbiz/article-368147-details/Puns%2C+puzzles+and+dirty+jokes/article.do>. In an unused portion of the review Polonsky also says: "Among the poem's public spectacles is the struggle within a scrupulous and demanding private conscience." "Scrupulosity," even "sick scrupulosity" is a recurring topic in Hill's verse. See, for example, *The Triumph of Love* LXXV, in which the speaker enumerates his supposed sins to an unnamed female interlocutor (perhaps an ironic Mary or Beatrice figure), from whom he colloquially asks forgiveness: "pardon, ma'am," 39.

18. Hill, section 86, *Speech! Speech!*, 43. Hill may be echoing Hopkins's poem "The Shepherd's Brow," which critics have termed "Swiftian." See "On rereading 'The Shepherd's brow'" by W. Bronzwaer (*Neophilologus*, 72:3, July 1988, 464–471).

19. Hill, section 100, *Speech! Speech!*, 50.

20. Geoffrey Hill, *The Orchards of Syon* (Washington, D.C.: Counterpoint, 2002), I, 1.

21. Hill, "Common Weal, Common Woe," *Collected Critical Writings* (Oxford: Oxford University Press, 2008, 265–279), 274.

22. Hill, section VII, *The Orchards of Syon*, 7.

23. "nuisance," *The Oxford Dictionary of Law Enforcement*, ed. Michael Kennedy (Oxford Reference Online, Oxford: Oxford University Press, 2007).

24. Simon Deakin, Angus Johnston and Basil Markesinis, *Markesinis and Deakin's Tort Law*, sixth edition (Oxford: Oxford University Press, 2007), 550.

25. "Public Nuisance and Private Purpose: Policed Environments in British India, 1860–1947," SOAS Law Department (London: School of Oriental and African Studies, 1992), 1–2.

26. Derek Walcott, *Omeros* (New York: Farrar, Straus, Giroux, 1990), 197.

27. Ibid.

28. Geoffrey Hill, "Strongholds of the Imagination," interview by Alexandra Bell, Rebecca Rosen and Edmund White, *Oxonian Review* (9:4; 18 May 2009), <http://www.oxonianreview.org/wp/geoffrey-hill/>.

29. *Markesinis and Deakin's Tort Law* 551, quoting L.J. Denning.

30. Geoffrey Hill, "Alienated Majesty: Gerard M. Hopkins," *Collected Critical Writings* (Oxford: Oxford University Press, 2008, 518–531) 530; quoting Ralph Waldo Emerson, "Self-Reliance," *Essays and Lectures*, ed. Joel Porte (New York: Viking, 1983), 264.

31. J.V. Cunningham, "The Journal of John Cardan," *The Collected Essays of J. V. Cunningham* (Chicago: Swallow, 1976), 427.

32. Stephen James, *Shades of Authority: The Poetry of Lowell, Hill and Heaney* (Liverpool: Liverpool University Press, 2007), 1–2.

33. Hill, section LXX, *The Triumph of Love*, 36.

34. Geoffrey Hill, *Without Title* (London: Penguin, 2006), 41.

35. See Emily Taylor Merriman, "Raging with the Truth: Condemnation and Concealment in the Poetry of Blake and Hill," *Journal of Religious Ethics* (37.1, 2009), 83–103.

36. Hill, *Without Title*, 71.

37. Tim Dean, "Hart Crane's Poetics of Privacy," *American Literary History* (8:1, 83–109), 84.

38. Ibid., 109.

39. Robert Lowell, "Words for Hart Crane," *Life Studies; For the Union Dead* (New York: Farrar, Straus, and Giroux, 2007); first edition of *Life Studies*, 1959, 61.

40. Geoffrey Hill, "Alienated Majesty: Ralph W. Emerson," *Collected Critical Writings* (Oxford: Oxford University Press, 493–505, 2008) 502.

41. Brian Phillips, "A Colder Spell to Come," *Poetry* (188:2, May 2006), <http://www.poetryfoundation.org/journal/article.html?id=178087>.

42. Geoffrey Hill, "Alienated Majesty: Walt Whitman," *Collected Critical Writings* (Oxford: Oxford University Press, 2008, 506–517), 507; quoting Ralph Waldo Emerson, "The American Scholar," *Essays and Lectures*, ed. Joel Porte (New York: Viking, 1983), 64–65.

43. Catherine Elsworth, "Barack Obama still has time for a little poetry," *The Telegraph* online <http://www.telegraph.co.uk/news/worldnews/northamerica/usa/barackobama/3401542/Barack-Obama-still-has-time-for-a-little-poetry.html> (7 November 2008).

44. William Logan, "Living with Ghosts," *The New York Times*. <http://www.nytimes.com/2008/01/20/books/review/Logan-t.html> (20 January 2008).

45. Geoffrey Hill, 8 Mar. 2008. Audio version: http://www.college-de-france.fr/default/EN/all/etu_cre/conferenciers.htm.

46. T.S. Eliot, "A Note on War Poetry," *Collected Poems 1909–1962* (New York: Harcourt Brace, 1963). 215–16.

47. T. S. Eliot, "Shakespeare and the Stoicism of Seneca," *Selected Essays*. 3d ed. (London: Faber and Faber, 1958; first edition 1932), 137.

48. Robert Hamner, "Conversations with Derek

Walcott," *World Literature Written in English* (16.2, 1977, 409–420), 412.

49. Jean "Binta" Breeze, "Can a Dub Poet Be a Woman?" *The Routledge Reader in Caribbean Literature*, ed. Alison Donnell and Sarah Lawson Welsh. London: Routledge (1996), 498.

50. Hill, "Alienated Majesty: Walt Whitman," 515.

51. Hill, section CXXXIV, *The Triumph of Love*, 72–73.

52. Hill, "Strongholds of the Imagination."

Works Cited

Anderson, M. R. (1992). "Public Nuisance and Private Purpose: Policed Environments in British India, 1860–1947." SOAS Law Department. London: School of Oriental and African Studies.

Baron, W.P. (1950). Letter of Reference from W.P. Baron, Headmaster of Bromsgrove Country High School, 9 March. Worcestershire Education Committee. Keble College, ref. KC/MEM 2 A1/43.

"Bent." *Oxford English Dictionary*. Online entry *bent*, ppl. a.

Breeze, Jean "Binta" (1996). "Can a Dub Poet Be a Woman?" *The Routledge Reader in Caribbean Literature*. Ed. Alison Donnell and Sarah Lawson Welsh. London: Routledge. 498–500.

Clark, Tom (1999). "Subversive Histories." *The American Poetry Review* (September/October), <http://findarticles.com/p/articles/mi_qa3692/is _199909/ai_n8858219>. [Expanded reprint of "British Poet Geoffrey Hill Casts a Cold Eye on History," *San Francisco Chronicle*, 11 Oct. 1998, <http://www.sfgate.com/cgi-bin/article.cgi?f= /c/a/1998/10/11/RV245799.DTL>.]

Cunningham, J. V. (1976). *The Collected Essays of J. V. Cunningham*. Chicago: Swallow.

Deakin, Simon, Angus Johnston, and Basil Markesinis (2007). *Markesinis and Deakin's Tort Law*. Sixth edition. Oxford: Oxford University Press.

Dean, Tim (1996). "Hart Crane's Poetics of Privacy." *American Literary History*, 8:1, 83–109.

Denning, L.J. (1957). *Attorney General v PYA Quarries Ltd.* 2 QB 169.

Eliot, George (1972). *Felix Holt, the Radical*. Ed. Peter Coveney. Harmondsworth: Penguin.

_____ (1994). *Middlemarch*. Ed. Rosemary Ashton. London: Penguin.

Eliot, T.S. (1958). "Tradition and the Individual Talent." *Selected Essays*. Third edition. London: Faber and Faber. 13–22.

_____ (1958). "Shakespeare and the Stoicism of Seneca." *Selected Essays*. Third edition. London: Faber and Faber. 126–140.

_____ (1963). "A Note on War Poetry." *Collected Poems 1909–1962*. New York: Harcourt Brace, 1963.

Elsworth, Catherine (2008). "Barack Obama still has time for a little poetry." *The Telegraph* online. (7 November). <http://www.telegraph.co. uk/news/worldnews/northamerica/usa/barack obama/3401542/Barack-Obama-still-has-time-for-a-little-poetry.html>.

Emerson, Ralph Waldo (1983). *Essays and Lectures*. Ed. Joel Porte. New York: Viking.

Gallet, René (2007). "Les mots, le silence et la qualification de la poésie." *La Poésie de Geoffrey Hill et la modernité*, ed. Jennifer Kilgore-Caradec and René Gallet. Paris: L'Harmattan, 169–182.

Hamner, Robert (1977). "Conversations with Derek Walcott." *World Literature Written in English*, 16. 2, 409–420.

Hart, Kevin (2008). "Contra Tyrannos." Review of *A Treatise of Civil Power*. *Notre Dame Review* 26 (Summer/Fall), 246–251.

Hill, Geoffrey, (1983). *The Mystery of the Charity of Charles Péguy*. London: Agenda Editions and Andre Deutsch. Reprinted in *Selected Poems*. London: Penguin, 2006. 119–135.

_____ (1996). *Canaan*. London: Penguin.

_____ (1998). *The Triumph of Love*. Boston: Houghton Mifflin.

_____ (2000). *Speech! Speech!* Washington, D.C.: Counterpoint.

_____ (2002). *The Orchards of Syon*. Washington, D.C.: Counterpoint.

_____ (2003). *Speech! Speech!* New York: Counterpoint.

_____ (2006). *Selected Poems*. London: Penguin.

_____ (2006). *Without Title*. London: Penguin.

_____ (2008). "Alienated Majesty: Gerard M. Hopkins." *Collected Critical Writings*. Oxford: Oxford University Press, 518–531.

_____ (2008). "Alienated Majesty: Ralph W. Emerson." *Collected Critical Writings*. Oxford: Oxford University Press, 493–505.

_____ (2008). "Alienated Majesty: Walt Whitman." *Collected Critical Writings*. Oxford: Oxford University Press, 506–517.

_____ (2008). "Civil Polity and the Confessing State." *The Warwick Review* 2:2 (June), 7–20.

_____ (2008). *Collected Critical Writings*. Ed. Kenneth Haynes. Oxford: Oxford University Press.

_____ (2008). "Common Weal, Common Woe." *Collected Critical Writings*. Oxford: Oxford University Press, 265–279.

_____ (2008). "What Devil Has Got into John

Ransom?" *Collected Critical Writings*. Oxford: Oxford University Press, 127–145.

_____ (2009). "Strongholds of the Imagination." Interview by Alexandra Bell, Rebecca Rosen and Edmund White, *Oxonian Review* 9:4 (18 May 2009) <http://www.oxonianreview.org/wp/geoffrey-hill/>.

Hopkins, G.M. (1986). *Gerard Manley Hopkins: The Major Works*. Ed. Catherine Phillips. Oxford: Oxford University Press.

James, Stephen (2007). *Shades of Authority: The Poetry of Lowell, Hill and Heaney*. Liverpool: Liverpool University Press.

Logan, William. (2008). "Living with Ghosts." *The New York Times*. (20 January). <http://www.nytimes.com/2008/01/20/books/review/Logan-t.html>.

Merriman, Emily Taylor (2009). "Raging with the Truth: Condemnation and Concealment in the Poetry of Blake and Hill." *Journal of Religious Ethics*. 37.1 (2009) 83–103.

Mills, C. Wright (1959). *The Sociological Imagination*. New York: Oxford University Press.

"Nuisance" (2007). *The Oxford Dictionary of Law Enforcement*. Ed. Michael Kennedy. Oxford Reference Online. Oxford: Oxford University Press.

Phillips, Brian (2006). "A Colder Spell to Come." *Poetry*, 188:2 (May). <http://www.poetrymagazine.org/magazine/0506/comment_178087.html>.

Polonsky, Rachel (2001). "Puns, puzzles and dirty jokes." *Evening Standard*. (12 November). http://www.thisislondon.co.uk/showbiz/article-368147-details/Puns%2C+puzzles+and+dirty+jokes/article.do.

Walcott, Derek (1990). *Omeros*. New York: Farrar, Straus, Giroux.

PART V

Taking Stock:
From Personal Encounter
to Ritual

14. The Public Intimacy of the Poetry of Sorrow

Catherine Phillips

Experiencing the poetry of sorrow can be a matter not only of hearing, but of overhearing oblique messages that are more than simply what the words say. A limited exploration of this potentially vast enterprise might start with a poem of the sixteenth century such as "O happy dames." Written by Surrey, it is included in the Devonshire Manuscript in the hand of Surrey's sister, Mary Howard.[1] As was frequently the case in the period, poems circulated in manuscript form in copies penned by their authors or transcribed by others. The Devonshire Manuscript is fascinating because its ninety-two used folios were written in nineteen different hands, including those of three women at the center of court intrigue: first, Margaret Douglas, who was the daughter of Henry VIII's sister, aunt of Mary Queen of Scots and mother of Lord Darnley, Mary's second husband; then there was Surrey's sister Mary Howard, who was the wife of Henry VIII's illegitimate son, Henry Fitzroy, the Duke of Richmond; and third, Mary Shelton, who was a cousin of Anne Boleyn and whose parents were in charge of the household of the princesses Mary and Elizabeth; she was also related to the Howards.[2] The Manuscript's contents range from poems attributed to writers such as Wyatt and Surrey and Margaret Douglas to transcribed sections of Chaucer's *Troilus and Criseyde*, such as Troilus's lament when he learns that Criseyde is to be sent from Troy. These verses, it is thought, were copied in various places: at court, in the tower by Thomas Howard (Margaret Douglas's first husband), and at Kenninghall by two of the three women during times when they were expelled from the court.[3] The difficulty of understanding the Devonshire Manuscript comes not from the language itself, which in its original orthography is difficult enough, but from our ignorance of the context. How are we to understand quotations from *Troilus and Criseyde*, or poems written ventriloquially, from the point of view of the opposite sex?[4]

We know that the relationships between some of those involved were dangerous: for example, when it was discovered that they had married, Margaret Douglas and Thomas Howard were imprisoned in the Tower, where she became ill and he died.[5] Communication was indirect, made through encoding private messages in situations, conventions, and symbolic characters all of which were public, perhaps in poems sung as court entertainment. John Stevens mentions the elaborate code of courtly love conventions that notionally governed court etiquette and could be turned to account for indirect communication.[6] It is not just the messages of love that fit this coded doubly public-private "language," but poems of grief and poems of solidarity and comfort between women. Surrey's "O happy dames" was written when he was posted in France and, phrased as a lament in his wife's voice, may have been a request that she be allowed to join him. It opens:

> O happy dames, that may embrace
> The fruit of your delight,
> Help to bewail the woeful case
> And eke the heavy plight
> Of me, that wonted to rejoice
> The fortune of my pleasant choice [...]

But the version written out in the hand of Surrey's sister Mary has different significance. It may have been a gift expressing sympathy for one of her friends, whose husband or lover was in the English army in France in 1544; perhaps, as Elizabeth Heale suggests, it was written "as a gesture of commiseration with a wider group of women, of whom Surrey's own wife was one."[7] It is part of a web of communication between women, as well as between men and women, contained in the Devonshire Manuscript. We do not know how much of the poetry that had a public face also conveyed private messages.

Although the critical attempts of our own era to distance writers from their work and to recognize the inherent cultural attitudes carried by works of literature have been useful, they have deflected effort away from understanding writers' deliberate attempts to communicate and downplayed the subtlety with which writers have simultaneously addressed different audiences. I will here try to counterbalance such an approach by pointing to a secondary layer of private or personal significance revealed by the contexts of a range of public laments and dirges.

When a poem of grief is officially sanctioned and the lament is for an important public figure, the speaker is required to convey an official, representative message; anything personal is subsidiary, perhaps oblique. When President John F. Kennedy was assassinated in 1963, the English composer Herbert Howells was asked to compose a piece for the memorial service.[8] Howells chose for his text Helen Waddell's translation of the *Hymnus circa Exsequias Defuncti* by the fourth-century Roman Christian poet Aurelius Prudentius Clemens (348–c.405).[9] Of Prudentius himself, little is known other than that he was an Hispanic gentleman, probably from Saragossa, and that in his late fifties he abandoned a successful legal career to lead a simple, ascetic life. Waddell writes, "to translate him is impossible: and if these halting versions have been included, it is because any collection of medieval lyric is poor unless his shadow falls across it."[10] "Take him, earth, for cherishing," written centuries before Kennedy lived, has nothing that elicits specific connection with him. Earth is addressed as our mother in a request that she cherish her son: "to thy tender breast receive him." The conventional thought of humanity's corruption and mortality, the human soul dependent on God for its salvation, is simply though beautifully expressed:

> Once was this a spirit's dwelling,
>   By the breath of God created.
> High the heart that here was beating,
>   Christ the prince of all its living...
>
> Take, O take him, mighty leader,
>   Take again thy servant's soul.
> Grave his name, and pour the fragrant
>   Balm upon the icy stone.

In Freudian terms, the poem may be considered good in that it seeks to help mourners disengage from the dead and consign the lost to memory without racking feelings of guilt.[11] What the music conveys — the motet is for an unaccompanied choir — is ultimately consoling, ending in a traditional harmonic cadence. Most of its structure, however, suggests emptiness and loss through frequent use of open chords — octaves and fifths lacking the normality and richness of major or minor thirds. There are also jarring discords that suggest grief and perhaps violence. Howells chose to leave the words as they were, general and without specific application, and convey feeling through the music. Again, it is a work from which if we simply looked at the text, we would glean much less than the message it conveyed in its time. Critics have also suggested that Howells was infusing his sorrow at the loss of his own son in the lament[12]: he had originally used Prudentius' hymn in the first version of the requiem for his son (the *Hymnus Paradisis*) and finally appended the hymn's first verse — "*Nunc suscipe, terra, fovendum, gremioque hunc concipe molli*" (Take him, earth, for cherishing, To thy tender breast receive him) — to the final version of that requiem.[13]

The nineteenth-century poet most associated with official mourning is

Alfred Lord Tennyson. Hallam Tennyson's biography of his father gives us a circumstantial context for the writing of Tennyson's "Dedicatory Poem to the Princess Alice," which prefaced his "The Defence of Lucknow," an event of 1857. Each year between 1875 and 1882, the Tennysons rented a house in London near the India Office because Tennyson's son, Lionel, was working there.[14] At this time, Tennyson also had meetings with John Lord Russell and General Gordon to discuss the relationship of different parts of the British Empire to each other, as well as the establishing of military colleges in Britain open to men of all classes — meetings indicative of a much less professionally specialized age than our own. "The Defence of Lucknow" was written in March of 1879, presumably occurring to Tennyson at this time because of his family and social concerns. The critic George Marshall points out that the siege of Lucknow was not directly a racial conflict, but rather the center of the mutiny of the Bengal army, sparked by British attempts to rush a Westernizing of India.[15] The poem is blatantly nationalistic in tone, and its utterly unsympathetic attitude to Indians makes it politically offensive today.

It is not the "Defence of Lucknow" in itself that is relevant here, however, but its relation to Tennyson's prefatory poem that dedicates it to Princess Alice, one of Queen Victoria's eldest children and, by marriage, the grand duchess of Hesse-Darmstadt. Princess Alice had just died at the age of thirty-two of diphtheria, contracted by kissing her sick child. The dedicatory poem is one long sentence that winds through twenty-one lines.[16] Obedient to the discretion requested by Queen Victoria, Tennyson included little that particularizes Alice except through mention of "the fatal kiss, / Born of true life and love" (ll. 3–4) and the reference to her dying request that the English flag be placed upon her coffin. This passionate Englishness seems to have had a particular appeal to Tennyson, and he addresses her as "England's England-loving daughter" (l.15). It is the flag that is the link between the two poems, and the loss of Alice is almost completely subsumed in nationalism.[17] The result is an extreme example of a feature common to such lyrics: the individual cause of sorrow triggers much more general thought (this quality is also a formal feature of elegies such as *Lycidas*). But such thoughtfulness is more than a matter of form; it seems to rise out of a psychological readjustment of values, a stopping of their ordinary, rushed lives in order to take stock of the relative worth of the different things that exact time and effort. Often leading to various degrees of remorse and perhaps partially disguised hurt and blame (as in Hardy's *Poems of 1912–13*), such considerations can develop into the meditation beyond selfishness found in some tragedies (*Lear* in his new-found concern for justice, "You houseless poverty, ... show the heavens more just." [III.4. 26–36][18] and Hamlet in his generalized meditations on the cost of conquest or the value of human life, "Two thousand souls.... Why the man dies" [IV.4.

25–9]; "What is a man ... to hide the slain" [IV.4. 33–65][19] for example). At other times, as here, the wider issues seem to have been the starting point. The elegy on the Princess Alice and "The Defence of Lucknow" were both part of Tennyson's work as Poet Laureate. There was nothing of personal grief in them, though that was to be indirectly infused in 1886 when Lionel died while returning from an official visit to India. The visit had included Lucknow, where the siege flag referred to in the poem had been raised in honor of the Poet Laureate and his poem.[20]

Tennyson's Dedicatory Poem might be compared with "In Memoriam," his more private elegy for A. H. Hallam, who died in his early twenties. The latter poem had two working titles: "The Way of the Soul" and "Fragments of an Elegy."[21] The fact that there were two such different titles suggests Tennyson's difficulty in fixing the relationship between his personal grief and concern over much more general issues. The wider problems arise in part from the literal treatment of the Christian promises of life after death, questions of belief Tennyson had discussed with Hallam in life (XXXVII) and which were now sharpened by the awkwardness he imagined they could create after Hallam's death. Tennyson worried about whether Hallam would continue to grow in the afterlife with his youthful vigor while Tennyson, perhaps living until he was a bent old man, might arise with a decrepit body (LX–LXIV). Would they, he wondered, still have so much to share if their experiences for decades were to be so different (XL– XLII)? And what could the dead know of the thoughts of those still living, their doubts and minor disloyalties (LI)? Tennyson's worries spread further to a concern over the value of individuals in a world that seemed governed by mechanical laws that paid no heed to what was lost (III, LV, LVI) leading to his doubting his belief in a paternal God as a Father who cared for each and every person (LV).

The poem's almost instant popularity when it was published in 1850 probably reflects the widespread experience of losing loved ones and the pervasive unease over the place of human beings in a world shifting from a biblical to a scientific worldview. (That those biblical ideas were still so potent is suggested by the fact that when Robert Chambers published his *Vestiges of Creation,* a layman's summary of contemporary scientific theories of the earth's origins in 1844, he took elaborate care to preserve his anonymity.[22]) "In Memoriam" was very much a poem for its time and place. It was written when Tennyson was a private man, but his elevation to Poet Laureate followed so soon on its publication that it was largely received from this public platform; its poetic voice was consequently perceived as more representative. Tennyson asserted retrospectively: "'I' is not always the author speaking of himself, but the voice of the human race speaking through him.... It is a very impersonal poem as well as personal. There is more about myself in 'Ulysses,' which was written under the sense of loss."[23] "Ulysses," written from the first for publication, explored behind the public story of the Greek hero's later years, as recounted in the *Odyssey* xi and Dante's *Inferno* xxvi, more personal feelings of irritable restlessness as well as a fear that, with Hallam dead, life might no longer be worth living.

The Anglo-Irish writer W. B. Yeats did not have an official position as Poet Laureate — the Irish avoiding such an English honor — but he strove through elevated tones to speak for and to his nation. His poem "September 1913," in which he lamented the unpatriotic, unambitious mediocrity of contemporary Dublin society, was to be answered by his elegy "Easter 1916," on the cost of the rebellion he had desired. Friends and acquaintances he had known had lost their lives; he saw women's hearts hardened to stone and their musical voices of sheltered femininity reduced to shrillness. In his "Meditations in Time of Civil War" (1922), Yeats toyed with the active participation he had advocated, wondering what it would be to become a soldier whose relevance to his time was beyond dispute. Yet the realities of war — dead young soldiers and houses burnt during a time when he was experiencing the responsibilities of fatherhood — led him to retreat to his verse. "The Circus Animals' Desertion," in which the poet overestimates his influence in wondering whether he had encouraged his friends to their costly rebellion in 1916, transmutes into an anxiety expressed by a number of modern poets about the integrity of their profession. The absorption in fashioning material into works of poetry and the elevated position of poet can lead to objectifying the very people who comprise their subject matter. Thus in "Bog Queen" Seamus Heaney accuses himself of an unattractive voyeurism in his laments for the dead adulteress discovered in the bog and for the Irish girls tarred and chained to railings for consorting with British soldiers; more poignantly, Geoffrey Hill questions the morality of his elegy for the young Jewish girl gassed in the concentration camps in his sonnet "September Song," which inverts Shakespeare's satisfaction in providing poetic longevity for his friend through his own enduring reputation. Such modern poets fear that the real intention in writing an elegy is self-aggrandizement at the expense of callous publication of its subject's suffering.

The relation between public and private works rather differently in Douglas Dunn's "The Butterfly House" from his *Elegies*,[24] written in memory of his young wife and published in 1985. Dunn could have closed down the form to express the intensity of his grief and tied each topic to nostalgic recollection of the past. Yet just as Tennyson's loss led him to metaphysical questions, so Dunn's elegy is aware of social issues, specifically the difficulty of using money in an environmentally and socially responsible way. The observations are sensitive, appreciative: "fruit in the bowl is good abundance," and the objects are "implicated" in his life and the couple's life together. The couple had chosen wooden chairs because of a love of wood and an admiration for trees; they had bought a quirky bronze frog and a metronome in a "strangely Egyptian" shape, belongings purchased because they caught the eye and projected their taste, and because by buying them together, they were building a nest for their love. But as the speaker looks around his house, Dunn's persona sees the room's contents — composed of the natural world's minerals, chemistry, plants, and clays — as a "slave trade in its raw materials." With a joyless vision desiccated by his loss, he laments "the cruelties of comfort": the books leather-bound at the cost of animals' lives, the potted plants "stolen" from their habitats, the wood drawn from trees that "long for unfootprinted forests." The strange title, "The Butterfly House," emerges towards the poem's end as he calls out the life in each of the room's objects, imagining them and his own spirit "breathing together," flying "on dusty wings." Just as the material objects had or have a physical life, so his being has a chemical basis and he feels "the large percentage of me that is water ... conspiring" to return to a river or the sea, an oblique acknowledgement of tears and a feeling of disintegration.

Published in 1985, the poem expresses environmental concerns that reflect the awakening, or re-awakening, of Britain to ecological issues and to the morality of shopping, well-known as our most popular national pastime. The previous year had seen the establishment of the Environmentally Sensitive Area scheme (ESA). Brought into being as a result of European Community legislation, the project was set up to protect some of Britain's most beautiful areas of countryside from damage caused by agricultural exploitation. The areas protected included the Pennine Dales, the North Peak District, the Norfolk Broads, the South Downs, and the Somerset Levels and Moors. These concerns of their time would have brought Dunn into closer contact with his readers, who may not have experienced similar grief, but knew something about the voice speaking to them — not because he spoke in clear English, but because they recognized the issues of largely middle-class readers of daily newspapers; they could recognize something of the personality, the class, the type of man speaking.

And yet, how big was Dunn's audience? Adrian Grafe points out that only 0.06% of books sold at present are volumes of poetry. Books of recipes, diet advice, and even Sudoku puzzles outsell them by far. Poets who try to appeal to a large audience, such as the Liverpool poets, seem to run the risk of producing work that lacks a sustaining profundity. In some ways English literary history has been here before, in that the history of poetry is intertwined with the history of song. In his still-central study of *Music and Poetry in the Early Tudor Court*, John Stevens traces out a transition from the dominance of music, when words conveyed the rhythm for tunes lacking notated music, to the dominance of words in lyrics that, in the Reformation, were allowed musical notes to clarify meaning. In some cases, music was intended to express the ideas or emotion bound up in the words.[25] Stevens establishes the existence of what he calls a tradition of songs that were not folk songs, but were intended to be popular because they conveyed political or religious ideas and were paired with deliberately catchy tunes. This provided a genre, a tradition of accessible songs with apparently clear messages within which poems could appear.

While there were poems with thought so convoluted that they were neglected for nearly two hundred years (some of Donne's longer and more theological works fall into this category), at the other end of the spectrum there were poems (perhaps labeled as songs, or with evidently lyrical titles or allusions to music) that seemed far simpler. Critics looking at those poems of Sir Thomas Wyatt's with titles suggesting music, or with phrases suggesting that they were accompanied by lute music, thought that many were likely sung. The forms of the poems do not themselves confirm or negate this and, finding no external evidence that Thomas Wyatt was a musician, Stevens suggests that his many poems calling upon musical accompaniment are actually literary works that play upon courtly love traditions, in which the lover covertly communicated with his beloved through a well-established set of conventions.[26] Some of these are included in the Devonshire Manuscript.

The critic Mark Booth develops rather different criteria for distinguishing between poetry and song in the modern period. Although there are exceptions, he generalizes that poems are texts meant to be read and pondered, while songs need to be simpler to be comprehensible on first hearing.[27] A thought in a song cannot be longer than a two-line unit and, unlike a modern poem, a song tends to work in units of phrases rather than words.[28] The experience described in songs, Booth suggests, "accumulates rather than developing,"[29] evoking responses to life that are already familiar to its audience.[30] In the latter part of the twentieth century, popular culture turned perhaps as never before to song; it was marketed so effectively that two or three generations grew up hearing much of the same music, as the songs of the successful early groups continued to be played by radio stations and at discos and were re-recorded by new groups. These songs voice all aspects of love relationships (except, rarely, parent-child), and although they sometimes express the experience of their writers, they more importantly provide a vehicle through which countless others can channel their experience. Although in modern poetry, Booth suggests, the reader most wants to find "the poet's personal encounter with reality, fixed with subtle rightness in a unique construction of language,"[31] by contrast, the "ritual" of the pop concert allows the singing of "fantasies for but also with the audience," providing the attraction, or illusion, of establishing bonds. These songs are not intended to change attitudes or be particularly new, but instead tend toward the "mythic," embodying "common, rather than personal, images of the world and self."[32]

Large-scale audiences in our time are not reached through words alone, as in poetry, but by song writers, who can even be asked to speak officially to those audiences. When Princess Diana was killed in August 1997, she was given a state funeral that combined verse and music of many sorts, from hymns such as "I Vow to Thee My Country," "The King of Love my Shepherd Is," and "Guide me, O Thou Great Redeemer"; to sections from Verdi's *Requiem*; Mary Ann Hall's poem "Turn Again to Life," and "Candle in the Wind 1997."[33] The original version of the song by Elton John and Bernie Taupin had been a meditation on the life and death of Marilyn Monroe and an attempt to penetrate the publicity machine to recognize the pain that it had caused an individual. Beginning "Goodbye Norma Jean," Monroe's real name, it blamed Hollywood for turning an ordinary human being into "Marilyn Monroe," a superstar manipulated by powerful men (the Kennedy brothers) and big business, and so hounded by the press that when she died, the papers were only interested in the fact that she had been found naked.[34]

In the rewritten version, Elton John almost certainly had the largest audience he had ever experienced: it is estimated that 2.5 billion viewers watched the funeral on television.[35] The song makes nothing of the friendship between Elton John and the Princess; he is less apparent as an individual than in the original song, where he appeared as just another member of the audience, too young to have known the screen star. Instead, in the 1997 version, the voice is entirely the spokesman's, using images by which everyone knew the People's Princess and words that often have more relevant meanings than might initially appear. Addressing Diana, he calls her the "grace that placed itself" where, in various ways, "lives were torn apart." In the use of "itself" rather than "herself," John suggests the representative role she fulfilled, and in "grace," he alludes to her royal title as well as her graceful carriage. He summons up the many television news items and countless magazine photographs picturing Diana with those mutilated by land mines, lives literally torn apart, or in Africa with those orphaned by AIDS or war. Subsequent lines recall her speaking to the nation in the speeches she made around the UK or "whispering" to those in hospitals in the numerous television clips of her bending down to say a quiet word to patients in British hospital wards. The clichés are allusions that resonate: "England's rose" refers not just to the old royal houses of Tudor and Plantagenet, but the naming of a new species of rose after Diana; "England's greenest hills" recalls the hymn "Jerusalem" (with words from Blake's preface to *Milton*), once proposed as an alternative to "God Save the King" and sung at the nationalistic ending to the last night at the Proms, one of the annual events in London's entertainment calendar.

This imagery makes the later song richer than its earlier version. Its ambivalence characterized many people's response to Diana: she was both "England's golden child" and also someone who "burnt the candle" at both ends, living harder and faster and getting into common difficulties. For all her glamour, she was humanly fallible. The success of the song lies in capturing both the sense of an individual, "packaged" as her image was by the media, and the complex relationship between celebrities and the public. The song had the second largest number of sales of any single in the recording industry's history, some 33 million; only Bing Crosby's "White Christmas" has sold more.[36] "Candle in the Wind 1997" raises none of the awkward questions towards which Diana's brother gestured in his address about the paparazzi. There would be no paparazzi without mass interest in salacious gossip, but this is no *Mutter Courage*, reminding us that economic participation raises moral questions. There is no open criticism of the press, though the re-use of the title and music of the earlier version, which did condemn such exploitation, is a significant reference. The recalling of the earlier version is, more generally, part of the meaning of the later version; the concern with the exploitation of a beautiful woman by powerful men, suggested in the early version by the lines where Monroe's uncertainty as to whom she could trust "when the rain set in," is made more explicit through parallel structure. Now Diana is praised for not "fading" into moneyed seclusion "when the rain set in," a discreet allusion to her divorce and continued participation in public concerns. There is an irony, however, that the cult of celebrity from which Diana suffered was something that she also encouraged, and which in the contemporary age gave a rationale to the privileged life she led. There were moral choices to be made in becoming a celebrity, reflections that Elton John and Bernie Taupin, whatever their inclination, would have been constrained to omit given their audience and the occasion of the song's performance.

In conclusion, we have in "Candle in the Wind 1997" far more pieces of both the private and the public contexts than with the Devonshire Manuscript. Lines and images can more easily be seen to carry meaning beyond their literal sense. The need for individuals to express their experiences, especially the most traumatic ones of grief, and the needs of nations to muster an official voicing of loss remain. Additionally, there is the more common problem that the piper must find ways of feeding himself. Although reaching mass markets does lead to simplifying at least the literal message, a complexity in the relationship between private feeling and public expression still seems to be possible. While poems such as "The Butterfly House" and "In Memoriam" may have a delicacy of expression that begs for greater attention than the genre of song can afford, and poetry that prompts readers to deeper thought and understanding may be on the wane, there is more of a continuum between such poems and songs with a range of allusion than might at first appear. Poems like Tennyson's on Princess Alice may have roughly the same simplicity as Prudentius' hymn or Wyatt's laments, while the dirge for Princess Diana by Elton John and Bernie Taupin accretes greater significance through its intertextual allusions to the earlier version. In each case these public statements carry multiple meanings with a range of more private significance.

NOTES

1. British Library Additional 17492. Elizabeth Heale, "Women and the Courtly Love Lyric: The Devonshire MS (BL Additional 17492)," *Modern Language Review*, 90:2 (April 1995, 296–313), 309.

2. Heale, "Women and the Courtly Love Lyric," 297–300.

3. Ibid., 300.

4. Ibid., 305–8.

5. Ibid., 298.

6. John Stevens, *Music and Poetry in the Early Tudor Court* (Cambridge: Cambridge University Press, 1979, first printed 1961).

7. Heale, "Women and the Courtly Love Lyric," 309.

8. Paul Spicer, *Herbert Howells* (Bridgend: Seren, 1998), 173–4.

9. As translated by Helen Waddell, *Medieval Latin Lyrics* (London: Constable & Co, 1929), 44–47.

10. Ibid., 297.

11. See Jahan Ramazani's *Poetry of Mourning: The Modern Elegy from Hardy to Heaney* (Chicago: University of Chicago Press, 1994), 3–4.

12. Spicer, *Herbert Howells*, 169–70; Christopher Palmer, *Herbert Howells* (Borough Green: Novello, 1978), 76.

13. Palmer, *Herbert Howells*, 76.

14. Hallam Tennyson, *Alfred Lord Tennyson: a Memoir* (London: Macmillan and Co., Ltd., 1906, first edition 1897), 604, 606.

15. George O. Marshall, Jr., *A Tennyson Handbook* (New York: Twayne Publishers Inc., 1963), 191.

16. Christopher Ricks (ed.), *The Poems of Tennyson* (London: Longmans, 1969), 1250. Hereafter cited as Ricks, *Poems of Tennyson*.

17. Christopher Ricks records in his head-note to the poem that the cause of Princess Alice's death was "well known": "Lady Ely wrote: 'The Queen thinks it might be lightly mentioned but not dwelt upon. I hope you will forgive my having asked the question, as it is best to know exactly what the Queen thinks and wishes.'" Alice's deathbed request to have her coffin draped with the English flag "was reported to Tennyson from the Queen, with the warning, 'Of course the exact words must not be made public.'" Hallam Lord Tennyson, *Materials for a Life of A.T.* (privately printed, no date), iii, 384 cited in Ricks, *Poems of Tennyson*, 1250.

18. *King Lear*, edited by R. A. Foakes (Methuen-on-Thames: Arden, 1997).

19. *Hamlet*, edited by Harold Jenkins (Methuen-on-Thames: Arden, 1982).

20. Hallam Tennyson, *Memoir*, 688–89; Marshall, *A Tennyson Handbook*, 191.

21. Ricks, *Poems of Tennyson*, 857.

22. Robert Chambers moved from his home in Edinburgh to St. Andrews. The book was then transcribed by his wife and posted to Alexander Ireland, a friend living in Manchester who then posted it to the publisher. The proofs followed the same circuitous route between the press and author. Gavin de Beer, Introduction to Robert Chambers, *Vestiges of the Natural History of Creation* (Woking: Leicester University Press, 1969), 25–6.

23. Christopher Ricks records this sentence in his head note to "In Memoriam." It is what Tennyson told James Knowles "when reading the poem" (*Nineteenth Century*, xxxiii [1893], 182), in Ricks, *Poems of Tennyson*, 859.

24. Douglas Dunn, *Elegies* (London: Faber & Faber, 1985), 10–11.

25. Stevens, *Music and Poetry*, 33–4, 40–1, 54, 214–8, 235ff.

26. Ibid., 132–8.

27. Mark Booth, *The Experience of Songs* (New Haven and London: Yale University Press, 1981), 7.

28. Ibid., 23.

29. Ibid., 24–5.

30. Ibid., 13–14.

31. Ibid., 23.

32. Ibid., 20.

33. "Funeral of Princess of Wales: Order of Service." 6 and 9 Sept. 1997. <http://www.internet-esq.com/diana/funeral.htm>.

34. Elton John, Music. Bernie Taupin, Lyrics. "Candle in the Wind," Dick James Music Ltd, 1973. < http://www.eltonography.com/songs/candle_in_the_wind.html>.

35. Elton John, Music. Bernie Taupin, Lyrics.

"Candle in the Wind 1997," <http://www.eltono graphy.com/songs/candle_in_the_wind_1997. html>.

36. All royalties went to the Diana, Princess of Wales Trust for distribution to charities with which she had been particularly connected.

WORKS CITED

Booth, Mark (1981). *The Experience of Songs*. New Haven and London: Yale University Press.

Chambers, Robert (1844, 1969). *Vestiges of the Natural History of Creation*. Woking: Leicester University Press.

Dunn, Douglas (1985). *Elegies*. London: Faber & Faber.

Heale, Elizabeth (1995). "Women and the Courtly Love Lyric: The Devonshire MS (BL Additional 17492)." *Modern Language Review*, 90:2, 296–31.

Marshall Jr., George O. (1963). *A Tennyson Handbook*. New York: Twayne Publishers Inc.

Michie, James (trans.) (1963, 1965). *The Odes of Horace*. New York: Orion Press.

Palmer, Christopher (1978). *Herbert Howells*. Borough Green: Novello.

Ramazani, Jahan (1994). *Poetry of Mourning: The Modern Elegy from Hardy to Heaney*. Chicago: University of Chicago Press.

Ricks, Christopher (ed.) (1969). *The Poems of Tennyson*. London: Longmans.

Spicer, Paul (1998). *Herbert Howells*. Bridgend: Seren.

Stevens, John (1961, 1979). *Music and Poetry in the Early Tudor Court*. Cambridge: Cambridge University Press.

Tennyson, Hallam (1897, 1906). *Alfred Lord Tennyson: a Memoir*. London: Macmillan and Co., Ltd.

_____. (n.d.). *Materials for a Life of A. T.* Privately printed.

Waddell, Helen (1929). *Medieval Latin Lyrics*. London: Constable & Co.

About the Contributors

Robert Archambeau, professor of English at Lake Forest College, is a poet and a critic, with interests in contemporary poetry and aesthetic theory. His collections of poetry include *Home and Variations* and *Citation Suite*. He is the editor of *Word Play Place: Essays on the Poetry of John Matthias* and the author of a book on the poetry of Robert Hass, Robert Pinsky, and their generation — *Laureates and Heretics*. He is currently at work on a collection of poems called *The Kafka Sutra*, and on *The Aesthetic Anxiety*, a book on aesthetic autonomy as it was understood by poets of the past.

Carole Birkan-Berz teaches at Paris Descartes University. Her doctoral dissertation was entitled "Poetic Forms and National Values in Geoffrey Hill's work." She has also written several articles on poetry and nationhood. Her research focuses on the intersection of literary forms and genres with national or communal narratives.

Torsten Caeners studied at the University of Duisburg. He finished his studies in 2004 with an MA on the Augustan poet Dr. William King. Since then he has been teaching at the Department for Anglophone Studies at the University of Duisburg-Essen while working on his PhD dissertation investigating the application of poetic writing to psychoanalytical treatment. He holds the position of coordinator for cultural economics within the Department of Humanities. He has published on Heaney, contemporary British fiction and popular culture.

Adrian Grafe hails from Oxfordshire and lives in Paris. A poetry specialist, he holds degrees from the universities of Oxford, Paris and Caen. After teaching at the Sorbonne for ten years, he took up the chair of English literature at Artois University, Northern France, in 2008. He wrote *Hopkins: la profusion ténébreuse* (2003) and edited *Ecstasy and Understanding* (2008), essays on modern poetry and religious awareness. He has published articles on Hopkins, Edward Thomas, and Hill, among others, and has written reviews for the *Hopkins Quarterly*, *Notes & Queries* (OUP), *Etudes Anglaises* and *Etudes*. He recently published a book on Emily Dickinson.

Pascale Guibert is a senior lecturer at Caen University, where she teaches English-language poetry, visual representations and critical reading. Her field is the representations of landscape in British and Irish poetry and the visual arts, from High Romanticism to our days. She has organized international conferences and edited a number of volumes on these topics, including René Gallet and Pascale Guibert, *Le Sujet romantique et le monde: la voie anglaise* (2009). She is working on an edition of the proceedings of the conference "Landscapes & Reflections" at Caen University, 2007.

Claire Hélie is preparing her doctoral dissertation at the Sorbonne Nouvelle on North of England poetry since the 1960s (Basil Bunting, Ted Hughes, Tony Harrison, Simon Armitage) under the supervision of Professor Marc Porée. She has published two articles on Tony Harrison, has one forthcoming on Basil Bunting and another on Simon Armitage. She is also interested in the translation of poetry and in masculinities. She teaches literature and translation at Perpignan University.

Daniella Jancsó teaches English literature at Ludwig-Maximilians-Universität, Munich, and is a member of the Pluralization and Authority in the Early Modern Period research center. She has published a number of articles on Shakespeare, metaphysical poetry, and contemporary fiction and is the author of the monograph *Excitements of Reason: The Presentation of Thought in Shakespeare's Plays and Wittgenstein's Philosophy* (Heidelberg: 2007).

Cécile Marshall is a lecturer at the University of Nantes where she teaches English literature, English as an applied foreign language, and translation. She previously taught at Bordeaux University while working towards her doctorate on the poetry of Tony Harrison. She is a member of the organizing committee for the British Film Festival in Nantes. She has worked with the Maison de la Poésie in Paris, translating poems and interpreting for Tony Harrison.

Emily Taylor Merriman is a native of Ohio, a patriot of Australia, an Englishwoman, and a Francophile; she lives in San Francisco. An assistant professor of English at San Francisco State University, she teaches modern British, American and Caribbean poetry. She has degrees from Oxford and London universities and earned a PhD in religion and literature from Boston University in 2007. She has written essays on Gerard M. Hopkins, William Blake, Geoffrey Hill, and Adrienne Rich and is working on a book, *Poetry's God*, about theology in the verse of Geoffrey Hill, Derek Walcott, and Charles Wright.

Catherine Murphy is an MFA student in the creative writing program at San Francisco State University, and teaches composition and literature in after-school programs. She holds an MA in creative writing and literature from San Francisco State. She has bachelor's and master's degrees from the National University of Ireland. Her publications include "Environmental Policy in Ireland" (with George Taylor) in *Issues in Irish Public Policy*, ed. George Taylor (2002). Her creative writing has appeared in *Bombay Gin*, *Sidebrow*, and *Fourteen Hills*, and she won the spring 2008 Mark Linenthal Award for poetry. She is writing a collection of poetry and short fiction on deconstruction.

Laurel Peacock is a PhD candidate at the University of California, Santa Cruz. Her research is on affect in women's literature, especially feminist poetry of the 1970s. She has studied and taught modern poetry and has written on the role of poetry and poetics in the fields of animal studies and environmental studies.

Catherine Phillips (Downing College, University of Cambridge) has written a biography of Robert Bridges (1992), edited the manuscripts of W. B. Yeats's *The Hour-Glass* (1994) and in 1996 completed the late A. J. Smith's *John Donne*, vol.ii (Critical Heritage series). Holder of the International Hopkins Society Award and the O'Connor Cup, her contributions include the Oxford Authors *Hopkins* (1986), *Selected Poems* (1995), *Hopkins: The Major Works* (2003), *Selected Letters* (1990), *Gerard Manley Hopkins and the Victorian Visual World* (2007). She is co-editing Hopkins's letters and preparing an edition of his poems for the *Collected Works of Gerard Manley Hopkins*, 8 volumes.

Marc Porée is a professor of English literature at the University of Paris III (Sorbonne Nouvelle). He has translated works by Byron, Conrad and Thomas de Quincey, co-edits R.L. Stevenson's fiction with Gallimard, and is the author with Alexis Tadié of a critical study on *Salman Rushdie* (1995). A romanticist by calling, he co-authored an *Anthologie de la poésie britannique* (1993), edited an edition of Keats's poems, and wrote a preface to an updated translation into French of Robert Browning's *The Ring and the Book* (2009).

Daniel Szabo received his PhD in 2007 from the University of Paris 7 on the theme of *Paradise Lost* in the poetry of two Anglican poets, T.S. Eliot and R.S. Thomas. He taught literature and translation in Paris 7 University from 2003 till 2008 and completed his first novel, *Peter Morris*, in 2009.

Index